LINGUISTIC ETHNOGRAPHY

SAGE was founded in 1965 by Sara Miller McCune to support the dissemination of usable knowledge by publishing innovative and high-quality research and teaching content. Today, we publish more than 750 journals, including those of more than 300 learned societies, more than 800 new books per year, and a growing range of library products including archives, data, case studies, reports, conference highlights, and video. SAGE remains majority-owned by our founder, and after Sara's lifetime will become owned by a charitable trust that secures our continued independence.

Los Angeles | London | Washington DC | New Delhi | Singapore

COLLECTING, ANALYSING AND PRESENTING DATA

LINGUISTIC ETHNOGRAPHY

FIONA COPLAND

ANGELA CREESE

with **FRANCES ROCK** *and* **SARA SHAW**

Los Angeles | London | New Delhi
Singapore | Washington DC

Los Angeles | London | New Delhi
Singapore | Washington DC

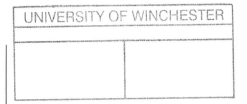

SAGE Publications Ltd
1 Oliver's Yard
55 City Road
London EC1Y 1SP

SAGE Publications Inc.
2455 Teller Road
Thousand Oaks, California 91320

SAGE Publications India Pvt Ltd
B 1/I 1 Mohan Cooperative Industrial Area
Mathura Road
New Delhi 110 044

SAGE Publications Asia-Pacific Pte Ltd
3 Church Street
#10-04 Samsung Hub
Singapore 049483

Editor: Jai Seaman
Assistant editor: Lily Mehrbod
Production editor: Ian Antcliff
Copyeditor: Rosemary Campbell
Indexer: Silvia Benvenuto
Marketing manager: Sally Ransom
Cover design: Shaun Mercier
Typeset by: C&M Digitals (P) Ltd, Chennai, India
Printed and bound by
CPI Group (UK) Ltd, Croydon, CR0 4YY

Library of Congress Control Number: Available

British Library Cataloguing in Publication data

A catalogue record for this book is available from
the British Library

MIX
Paper from
responsible sources
FSC® C013604

ISBN 978-1-4462-5737-1
ISBN 978-1-4462-5738-8 (pbk)

At SAGE we take sustainability seriously. Most of our products are printed in the UK using FSC papers and boards.
When we print overseas we ensure sustainable papers are used as measured by the Egmont grading system.
We undertake an annual audit to monitor our sustainability.

To our children, Rosie, Robert and Ida, sunshine through the window.

Contents

Figures

TABLE

Notes on Authors

PRINCIPAL AUTHORS

Fiona Copland is a Senior Lecturer at the School of Languages and Social Sciences at Aston University, Birmingham, where she is Director of the Centre for Language Education Research at Aston (CLERA). Before working in higher education, she was an English language teacher in Nigeria, Hong Kong, Japan and the UK, where she also taught on a range of teacher education programmes. This background has influenced her research interests, which include talk in pre-service teacher education conferences and teaching English to young learners, and she has published in these areas. Since attending a course in ethnography, language and communication jointly run by King's College London and the Institute of Education, University of London, she has been an active member of the Linguistic Ethnography Forum, co-organising three conferences. At Aston, Fiona is the Programmes Director of MSc TESOL courses and teaches a range of postgraduate modules. She also supervises PhD students in the field of TESOL.

Angela Creese is Professor of Educational Linguistics at the School of Education, University of Birmingham, and deputy director of the MOSAIC Centre for Research on Multilingualism. In the last ten years she has been funded to work in large multilingual research teams to research multilingualism. Her research interests are in linguistic ethnography, language ecologies, multilingualism in society and multilingual classroom pedagogy. Her publications include *Heteroglossia as Practice and Pedagogy* (with Adrian Blackledge, 2014, Springer); *The Routledge Handbook of Multilingualism* (with Marilyn Martin-Jones and Adrian Blackledge, 2012); *Multilingualism: A Critical Perspective* (with Adrian Blackledge, 2010, Continuum); *Encyclopedia of Language and Education, Volume 9: Ecology of Language* (with Peter Martin and Nancy Hornberger, eds, 2009, Springer); *Teacher Collaboration and Talk in Multilingual Classrooms* (2005, Multilingual Matters Ltd) and *Multilingual Classroom Ecologies* (with Peter Martin, eds, 2003, Multilingual Matters Ltd).

CONTRIBUTORS

Frances Rock is a Senior Lecturer at the Centre for Language and Communication Research at Cardiff University. Her work investigates the part that language plays in the mediation of experiences in the social world. This draws on close analysis of the written and spoken language which is created when people make meaning together. Frances's research examines language and policing, and recommendations following from her work have been taken up by police forces around England and Wales. Frances's publications in language and law include the monograph *Communicating Rights: The Language of Arrest and Detention* (2007 Palgrave Macmillan) and the edited collection *Legal-Lay Communication: Textual Travels in the Law* (with Chris Heffer and John Conley, eds, 2013, Oxford University Press). She also researches non-legal settings such as workplaces and has a growing interest in ecolinguistics. Frances teaches on a range of qualitative topics at undergraduate and MA level. She is one of the Editors of the *International Journal of Speech, Language and the Law*.

Sara Shaw is a Senior Lecturer in Health Policy Research at Queen Mary University of London. She has a background in medical sociology and policy studies. Her research interests lie in the social organisation of healthcare and health policy, and in using qualitative approaches to appreciate the interactions, power relations and decision-making processes that contribute to each. She has a particular interest in discourse and language and in exploring how political and organisational processes, routines and decision-making are created through language and social interaction and how this shapes healthcare. This has led her to publish widely on topics such as healthcare commissioning, health research policy, and interpretive approaches to policy analysis. Sara is committed to working across social, political and organisational boundaries. In addition to her position at Queen Mary University of London, she has undertaken work for a range of organisations, including the Department of Health, Royal College of General Practitioners and Faculty of Public Health.

Acknowledgements

We are in debt to Ben Rampton for leading the way in linguistic ethnography and for creating the impetus to start such useful, rich and rewarding discussion. We would like to thank our colleagues in the linguistic ethnography forum (LEF) who have inspired us to move forward with this project, providing a body of research to build on, challenging our thinking and offering safe spaces to develop our understandings, in particular Janet Maybin, Celia Roberts and Julia Snell. We are hugely grateful to the two additional case study authors in the book, Frances Rock and Sara Shaw, who worked with us collaboratively through major events in their lives, such as marriage and childbirth. The generosity of our recently graduated doctorate students must also be acknowledged. Elizabeth Chilton, Amanda Simon and Wei Lu kindly shared their original materials for inclusion in this book, as did Deborah Swinglehurst and Karin Tusting, LEF members and stimulating colleagues. Ida Willock-Creese contributed original and creative artwork. We are grateful to Sage Publications, particularly Jai Seaman and Lily Mehrbod, for their patience and guidance. We are indebted to Frances Giampapa and Keith Richards for their insightful reviews and encouragement, as well as to other anonymous reviewers as we journeyed from proposal writing to full first draft submission and finally to publication. Adrian Blackledge and Steve Mann have been critical and supportive throughout, as well as long suffering. Thank you both.

Introduction

It may be that you are a seasoned ethnographer with experience in the social sciences and humanities, assured of your rich contextual accounts of research participants' social practices in the routines and rituals of their daily lives. You may already be confident with the levels of reflexivity in your field notes and research diaries, which capture the ebbs and flows of participant beliefs, attitudes and practices. Nonetheless you might find yourself wondering if your data have more to offer in terms of understanding the social phenomena that interest you. Mulling over whether your analysis would benefit from a more discursive focus, you contemplate applying a linguistic analysis to the interactions in your data.

Alternatively, you may be a confident linguist working through your data and seeking ways to account for the different layers of context in your interpretations. You might find yourself wanting to report on the use of certain phrases used by people engaged in communication across a range of contexts but you are facing some anxiety about over-interpreting the linguistic forms available to you in your audio, video and textual files. You are aware that your interactional data is situated in social knowledge and mediated by cultural ideologies but you are unsure of how to make the link between your close analysis of linguistic data and the surrounding social context.

Then again, you could already be an experienced linguistic ethnographer, well versed in the literature of linguistic anthropology with several research projects under your belt. And yet, aware that each project throws up its own distinctive and unique set of challenges and rewards, you seek a community of scholars whose accounts resonate with your own in detailing some of the dilemmas faced and decisions reached by knowledgeable researchers such as yourself as you start out on another linguistic ethnographic research project with a new set of research questions.

On the other hand you might be new to it all. With some small experience of previous empirical work at undergraduate and Masters level, you see yourself beginning a new journey as a researcher, perhaps working on a doctorate, joining a research team, or looking for different approaches to answer the questions you want to ask. Your interest in, for example, communication, identities, cultures, translations, institutions, social power and ideology as they are expressed in the discourses of everyday interactions and literacies, have brought you to this book.

Whether, therefore, you are an ethnographer looking to hone your linguistic analyses, a linguist attempting to introduce richer contextual accounts to your data, a confident linguistic ethnographer persuaded by its combined focus on language and social practices, or new to doing interpretive research, we hope that there is something in this book for you. Maybin and Tusting (2011) argue that making ontological assumptions explicit in our research accounts, and working through the possibilities and limitations of our data can only strengthen the field of linguistic ethnography. This is good advice and the motivation for this book. We aim to uncover the processes of *doing* linguistic ethnography to show how we have grappled with and reconciled issues related to context, language, interpretation and ethics, amongst other things. It is accounts such as these that are often missing from books on research methodology but which have the potential to support researchers as they make their own ways through research projects.

As part of this process of uncovering we invite the reader to engage with four in-depth case study narratives written by experienced linguistic ethnographers working within the disciplines of health, law and education. The case study writers report on the different social settings of think-tank organisations, police stations, teacher education and community language classrooms. The case studies are organised in similar ways so that the ontological, epistemological and methodological assumptions behind their work can be identified and contemplated. However, these case study narratives are not sanitised accounts of unproblematic research designs, smooth data collection periods or seamless analytical processes. Rather they report on the dilemmas faced by researchers, the ensuing negotiations required and the decisions reached. Demystifying the research process is the shared agenda across the four case studies and each author directly confronts the often hidden-from-view engagement with data collection processes and analysis. We start this book with the four case study authors, Angela, Fiona, Frances and Sara, presenting short vignettes (throughout the book we use first names and order by first name alphabetically). A vignette is an ethnographic account providing 'a focused description of a series of events taken to be representative, typical, or emblematic' (Miles and Huberman, 1994: 81). Here the vignettes describe how each researcher came to linguistic ethnography.

ANGELA CREESE

In the early 1990s, I took a qualitative methodology module with Frederick Erickson, a leading linguist and ethnographer, while studying for a PhD at the Graduate School of Education (GSE), University of Pennsylvania. Erickson's module was required but I remember questioning its relevance before we started; issues like accessibility, feasibility, trust, relationships, ethics, design, all seemed like practical issues which required a common sense not best taught in the classroom. On the first day of class Erickson arrived in shorts, a Hawaiian shirt and a sombrero. Eminent scholars didn't usually arrive in class dressed like that and our first lesson in observation of routines and rituals had begun. By the end of the course he'd set us several assignments, one of which involved observing social practices in a local bar or restaurant, while another asked us to interview another student about family dinner routines. In the bar we described and counted drinking and eating practices, and interactions and movement, as customers sat alone, in pairs or in groups. Not a bad task! We wrote notes about the setting, objects, landscape, smells, appearances, people, and ourselves. In the interview with another student we asked for details on dinner preparation, eating and tidying-up arrangements. Through these two exercises I learned how to be interested in processes and interpretive practices. I thought about perspective and representation; about data – their complementarity and their incompleteness – and the tension between the ritualistic and exceptional, the habitual and unusual. I learned what Erickson meant by wiggle room in the construction of social categories in interaction, and developed an interest in performance and subjectivities. By the end of the course I also understood I was totally wrong about methodology classes. I needed more of them, not fewer.

Although I wasn't a student when Dell Hymes, one of the forefathers of linguistic anthropology, was Dean at GSE, his legacy was very much present in 1988 when I started my doctoral studies. The Hymesian tradition meant language and social life were always presented as being in conversation. In 1990, I was taking a sociolinguistics class with Nancy Hornberger and at the end of the semester was asked to answer the examination question 'What should educators know about the relationship between language and schooling?' Twenty years on, the question has no less relevance for me. Describing and explaining the role language plays alongside other social constructs in reproducing or unsettling social inequalities continues to be worthy of study in my opinion. This question drives my work in multilingualism and educational linguistics, and I have investigated language in schools but also in homes, staff rooms, playgrounds and offices.

When I returned to the UK in the mid-1990s to collect data in London for my doctoral research, I worked for several years as a contract researcher on two different projects at the Institute of Education. Working in interdisciplinary research teams gave me lots to think about, not least processes of theoretical and epistemological disagreement and reconciliation in teams, and how these shaped research outcomes. This has subsequently led me to an interest in knowledge construction in ethnographic teams and the representation of different voices in this process. It was during my time in London that Ben Rampton started the Linguistic Ethnography Forum. Ben was the founding member of the initial group, and I benefited hugely from his drive, generosity and vision in getting the Forum off the ground. At the 1999 British Association for Applied Linguistics (BAAL) annual meeting, Ben collected together a group of us whose presentations were broadly in the area of linguistic anthropology, and over the next couple of years organised us to convene a series of events, contribute to different writing projects and establish a special interest group (http://www.baal.org.uk/sig_ethnog.html). This provided an important network and community for those of us doing this kind of work, which had been missing in the UK until then.

But it is also through teaching that I came to this book. Between 2010 and 2013 I took part in an ESRC-funded teaching programme on multilingualism. This 'Researcher Development Initiative' (RDI), led by colleagues at the MOSAIC Centre for Research on Multilingualism (http://www.esrc.ac.uk/my-esrc/grants/RES-046-25-0004/read), University of Birmingham, created several intensive and very pleasurable teaching opportunities for me. We met doctoral researchers and early career scholars from around the world to discuss methodology and theory in research on multilingualism. What we hoped to achieve was to demystify the processes of doing linguistic ethnography by focusing on the doing. For me, this book presents an opportunity to extend these classroom discussions. In this book I hope we can present the reader with a range of challenges, questions, dilemmas, possibilities and contingencies. Including these ambiguities, tensions and decisions rather than deleting them is one of my aims for this book.

FIONA COPLAND

I came to linguistic ethnography while doing my PhD. In my original research proposal I stated that I wanted to record feedback conferences in pre-service English language teacher education and then analyse the talk, much as Janet Holmes and her team had done in her New Zealand project on talk in the workplace. In that project, the research participants had recorded their own interactions and submitted them to the researchers at various points in the project. My supervisor, Angela Creese, spent a long time outlining the benefits of observing the feedback conferences at the same time as recording them. She said that my data would be richer, my insights deeper and that I would in the end produce findings that were more nuanced if I also took an ethnographic approach.

I must admit, I took some while to be convinced, because I knew extra time would have to be spent in the field, time I felt I did not have as I was doing my PhD while working full time. I was also a bit wary of the 'field notes' aspect of this kind of research. What exactly was a field note? How would I know if I had written good field notes and how could my written-up observations be considered empirical data in the way that recorded talk clearly could?

In the end, I agreed to observe, not least because I knew that if I was present in the feedback conference, I could be sure the recording equipment would be switched on. Within minutes I knew I had done the right thing. My personal reaction to what I observed laid bare my understandings, biases and interpretations. I was part of the interactions as well as an observer of them. My eyes and ears were as an important part of the research process as the recordings were. My field notes became the expression of these understandings, biases and interpretations and a record of what I saw and heard.

My main area of interest at the time was feedback talk in post-observation conferences in teacher training. I had worked as a teacher trainer for many years on CELTA and DELTA programmes (Certificate and Diploma in English Language Teaching to Adults). These are the professional qualifications that British and, to some extent, Australian and New Zealand teachers, who want to teach English as a foreign or second language abroad or in private institutions, currently take. I had always found the feedback conference, which happened after the teachers had done a practice teaching session, challenging and fascinating. The CELTA was of particular interest as feedback happened with groups of trainee teachers and one trainer, and so issues of face and power were particularly apparent. I was also interested in how pedagogies of English language teaching were passed on in feedback and how trainees articulated their understandings of these pedagogies.

The fact is that much feedback on performance, in education, medicine, business and many other sectors, is 'hidden from view', an observation also made by Heritage and Sefi (1992) on health visitor/client meeting. Yet feedback can affect teachers' knowledge, beliefs and identities and plays an important role in how particular views on language learning and teaching are presented and disseminated. According to Brandt (2006) around 10,000 people a year take a CELTA course or equivalent, so the feedback conference is experienced by large numbers of people. However, the area was (and remains) under-researched.

In 2007–08, I attended a course called 'Key Concepts in Ethnography, Language and Communication'. This was a five-day programme focusing on linguistic ethnographic approaches to data collection and analysis run by a consortium of colleagues from King's College London and the Institute of Education, University of London, and funded by the ESRC through its Researcher Development Initiative. In research terms, this was a life changing course for me. Not only did I have the opportunity to develop my research skills within this new and exciting approach, I also met Julia Snell and Sara Shaw, with whom I started the Explorations in Ethnography, Language and Communication Conference, now in its fifth year. Working with these colleagues, attending conference sessions, and developing my own research under the guidance of my supervisor, I became aware that despite the fantastic work being produced under the auspices of linguistic ethnography, there was little support in the literature for those new to research or new to research in this field on how to 'do' linguistic ethnography. Hence the idea for this book was born.

FRANCES ROCK

Three rapid gunshots began my association with the study of language in legal settings and initiated my engagement with legal settings as sites of social life. Of course, I did not realise that these associations were beginning at the time. At the time, as a child witnessing an armed robbery in which two people were shot, my future research was understandably far from my mind. Yet that incident initiated a series of contacts for me with the legal system. The contact began with repetitive interviews and intense, confusing identity parades, and led into the courtroom's charged atmosphere of sometimes apparently motiveless questions.

Nearly ten years later, the person accused of the armed robbery appealed against his conviction. I then found myself back in the courtroom just as I was completing a degree in Language Studies. Many aspects of my undergraduate degree provided tantalising glimpses of ways to re-examine critically the legal world I had encountered. The experience of being an actor in the legal system combined with an undergraduate language degree presented me with many questions: about the linguistic practices of text production and textual travel; about talk and the multimodal experience of witnessing, particularly inference and performativity; and about how justice is accomplished through language.

As those gunshots rang out across a busy Saturday afternoon shopping centre and those interviews and court appearances ticked by, unbeknownst to that child, a focus on the language of the law was gathering pace in the academy. I encountered the sub-discipline of 'forensic linguistics', which was emerging as I began my PhD, and a focus on language in legal settings appealed to me. My research has given me opportunities to revisit some of the legal spaces that I encountered as a lay person, with different foci and from different perspectives, now with a voice that enables both scholarship and the practical application of linguistics.

My epistemological turn from language and communication to the ethnographic in my research practice began with an aside from a solicitor friend. Whilst we discussed the extensive, predominantly experimental-psychological research on the wording of the police caution, he gleefully critiqued that work, noting the difference between the words on the page and their use in context. In naturally occurring situations, the standardised wording takes a back seat as solicitors, police officers and even suspects explain such wordings to one another, in their own words, in pursuit of improved comprehension. I had been introduced to ethnographic research on an MA course at Lancaster University in the late 1990s, so rather than taking my friend's observations as back-to-the-drawing-board problems, I found that they provided a research motivation. He had introduced the clear need to move beyond attending only to lexico-grammatical features of decontextualised standardised wordings, the typical research focus until this time. Therefore, my point of departure was literacy practices and events which coalesce around the institutional requirements to collaboratively achieve such abstract accomplishments as 'comprehension'.

The noise of the blaring police sirens overhead, the dense smell of a busy custody unit at 6 a.m., the glaring strip-light of the interview room are not incidental to the language practices which emerge and develop alongside them. A focus on situated practices and events made it possible to consider the trajectories of texts through policing (Blommaert, 2005), the way in which officers draw on a range of resources, linguistic and otherwise, to do their work as part of a community of practice (Eckert and McConnell-Ginet, 1992), and the forms of engagement which suspects bring to an activity like the explanation of their rights (Gumperz et al., 1979). The ethnographic turn created, for me, a way to recognise and analyse the reality of contemporary policing.

It sometimes seems that particular researchers are strongly associated with a paradigm, such as systemic functional linguistics, or, conversely, with an analytic focus or topic, such as health communication or, more locally, GP consultations. Yet, of course, we all operate simultaneously within both; we use paradigms to inform and construct our scrutiny of social settings, or at least genres, so this distinction, and the resulting associations are perhaps bound to be illusory. I frequently find myself categorised as a 'forensic linguist' because much of my work focuses on legal settings. However the diversity denoted by that label is huge and the assumptions connoted by it can be problematic. Whilst I value and benefit from my engagement with the forensic linguistic community, it was refreshing to be invited to contribute to this book not as a 'forensic linguist' but as a linguistic ethnographer. It was particularly invigorating to be invited to construct a chapter, not on forensic matters exclusively, but on workplaces. Most of my research has approached policing settings as workplaces, not primarily as 'forensic' settings, so this seemed an insightful and productive invitation, more so because my orientation to policing settings as workplaces is a direct result of a broadly ethnographic stance. For me, legal settings are places where lives are lived, where situated talk and social action have consequences, where meanings are shaped and sustained through texts and practices amongst other resources and where institutions and their recognised and unofficial component sub-groups are shaped and controlled through discourse. The invitation to contribute to this volume also offered the opportunity for collaborative writing, in which I was keen to engage, with colleagues whom I was sure would broaden my view of work and of my own work. Indeed, by working on a chapter on work, an ethnographic circle becomes pleasingly apparent.

SARA SHAW

It was 1993, I was in the second year of my sociology degree and I'd signed up for Penri Griffiths's class on 'Sociology of Health and Illness'. His sessions were always engaging, guiding us to unpick taken-for-granted ideas about health, illness and medicine. In this particular session, we focused on the medicalisation of society and the way in which human conditions and problems come to be defined and treated as medical conditions. I was intrigued: not only might illness and social problems increase as a result of medical intervention, but government, professions and industry may well facilitate that process. I did not realise it at the time, but the seed was sown from which my longstanding interest in health policy would then grow.

In the early stages of my research career I was based in university medical schools and professional organisations, where policy was largely taken as given; the emphasis within policy analysis was on the tools of microeconomics and decision analysis and any qualitative analysis tended to focus on simply 'extracting' themes. My own interests – what is policy, how it is 'made', by and for whom – were simply not on the agenda. This changed when I began my doctoral work. Wondering how to take forward my work on the development of policy, I often browsed the aisles of the University of London library. I stumbled across a book by an American academic, Frank Fischer, called *Reframing Public Policy: Discursive Politics and Deliberative Practices* (2003). Whilst I was familiar with the concept of 'policy ethnography', this book opened my mind to a discursive approach to policy analysis that enabled a very different research journey and a radical overhaul of my doctoral project.

With hindsight, I was learning about 'interpretive policy analysis', an approach that has been influential in my work ever since. It is an approach that is sensitive to social meaning, historical context and the importance of human subjectivity; and one that recognises policy analysis as a moral activity. Knowledge is not disinterested or apolitical and interpretations are not constructed in isolation but in an environment of shared language, understandings and practices. All well and good. However, in the midst of my PhD, I struggled to make sense of how to bring such a set of principles to life in the context of my own work. A course on 'Key Concepts and Methods in Ethnography, Language and Communication' offered many answers and linked me with a community of like-minded scholars. I had not only found interpretative policy analysis, but I had also found linguistic ethnography.

Since completing my PhD in 2006 my interest in health policy has continued to grow, influenced by a range of scholars and coming from an increasingly interdisciplinary perspective. The focus of my work is on health policy and healthcare practices and on exploring how political and organisational processes, routines and decision-making are created through language/social interaction and shape healthcare. I have tried to build on my background in medical sociology and policy studies, by drawing on political sociology as well as critical approaches to health services research and healthcare administration. Whilst many researchers in medical schools have tended towards specialisation, I have been unashamedly broad; undertaking empirical work on topics ranging from care planning for people with long-term conditions to the development of national health research policy.

My most recent work focuses on the role of think tanks in shaping healthcare policy and planning. Despite their increasingly visible presence and concerns about the role they play in capturing debate, little is known about how think tanks operate in healthcare, by whom and to what ends. Existing literature on think tanks tends to define and categorise them as a disinterested source of 'policy expertise' that work alongside policymakers and other players to identify a range of healthcare policy options and select the 'optimal choice'. Following two years working within a think tank, I realised that I had an opportunity not only to challenge this view, but also to shed light on this mysterious and rarely accessed world.

The case study presented in the book attempts to do this by situating healthcare policy and planning as a drama, occupied by a range of institutions, actors and artefacts, involving a continual process of dialogue and exchange; and bringing a range of values, judgements and interests into play.

If truth be told, when the lead authors asked me to contribute to the book I was so taken with the idea of writing with like-minded colleagues that teasing out *why* I was involved rather passed me by. On reflection, I see my role as providing a 'health' perspective on the analysis of ethnography and language in the social sciences and one that, I hope, researchers from a range of disciplines and fields will find useful. Scholars in healthcare are increasingly turning to linguistic ethnography to answer some of the complex questions about how, for instance, communication shapes healthcare encounters. Such work has typically focused on the interactions between professionals and patients and in formal medical settings. Drawing in wider work on health policy affirms linguistic ethnography as a rich and interdisciplinary field, which I hope that my work both aligns with and adds to.

OVERVIEW

As you can see, the book sets out to provide a hands-on approach within particular theoretical, discursive and methodological frameworks informed by intellectual roots in ethnography and linguistics. But we have not written a 'how-to book'. Providing generalised answers to sets of contextualised problems does not sit easily with the epistemological orientation of ethnography and we do not attempt to set out a staged, normative process to conduct linguistic ethnography. Rather, the four case study accounts and the accompanying chapters surrounding them present the linguistic ethnographer as a decision-maker, agentive in shaping possibilities, relationships and outcomes.

In discussing these areas we resist accounts which speak of ethnography as messy and chaotic. Rather, the chapters discuss the thoughtful, careful, rigorous systems of data collection and analysis which researchers have deployed in their ethnographies. We do not wish to suggest that serendipity, changes of fortune, auspicious on-the-hoof decisions are not part of linguistic ethnography, indeed they are, but the case studies in the book show that the planning, conduct and analysis of research in linguistic ethnography is informed by judiciously informed decisions at every point in the journey. Linguistic ethnography involves being unusually thorough and reflective.

The four case study authors all claim linguistic ethnography as a primary influence to which they orientate. However, the range of approaches and interpretations is eclectic. A clear delineation of the boundaries of linguistic ethnography is thus avoided and the intellectual space in which we can ask the question 'what is linguistic ethnography?' left open. Rampton (2007b: 3) describes linguistic ethnography as an 'umbrella term, wide-ranging in its empirical scope'. Tusting and Maybin (2007: 578) refer to linguistic ethnography as a 'cluster of research'. If we extend Rampton's umbrella metaphor further – the golfing umbrella, with its wide canopy and generous coverage, provides room for a number of interpretive and discursive approaches to find shelter beneath.

Because there is as much to disagree about as there is to agree about among linguistic ethnographers, the book does not attempt a comprehensive review of the field. Rather, we have organised it to emphasise those aspects of theory, methods and practice most salient to the four case studies presented. Part One sets out the historical, theoretical and methodological underpinnings of linguistic ethnography (Chapter 1) and Chapter 2 examines common approaches to data collection and analysis. In Part Two, the four case studies are presented. Part Three engages with the practicalities of doing linguistic ethnographic research, focusing on: empiricism, ethics and impact (Chapter 7); technology, transcription and translation (Chapter 8); writing up: genres, writer voice, audience (Chapter 9) and, finally, ways forward in linguistic ethnography (Chapter 10).

I

Ethnography and Language

ONE

Linguistic Ethnography

INTRODUCTION

Linguistic ethnography is an interpretive approach which studies the local and immediate actions of actors from their point of view and considers how these interactions are embedded in wider social contexts and structures. According to Erickson (1990: 92), interpretive approaches are necessary because of the 'invisibility of everyday life' which when held at arms-length can empirically serve 'to make the familiar strange'. This contrasts with the approach which anthropology traditionally adopted which was 'to make the strange familiar'. Whereas the former requires we examine the institutions and social practices surrounding us in contemporary life, the latter looked to describe the exotic, unknown other to make sense of the daily existences of people in distant places. To make the familiar strange, we need the interpretive approaches of linguistic ethnographers because the institutions we know best, the routines we practice most, and the interactions we repeatedly engage in are so familiar that we no longer pay attention to them. Yet these contexts, very close to hand, contain fundamental questions about communication in a rapidly changing world which can benefit from a combined examination of language and cultural practices. Put simply, a shared interest in social and linguistic processes means a commitment to answering the questions, 'What is it about the way we use language that has an impact on social processes? What is it about social processes that influences linguistic ones?' (Heller, 1984: 54).

The necessity of looking in 'our own backyard to understand shifting cultural meanings, practices and variations' (Rampton, 2007a: 598) has been well made in ethnography. Heller (2008: 250) points out:

> Ethnographies allow us to get at things we would otherwise never be able to discover. They allow us to see how language practices are connected to the very real conditions of people's lives, to discover how and why language matters to people in their own terms, and to watch processes unfold over time. They allow us to see complexity and connections, to understand the history and geography of language. They allow us to tell a story; not someone else's story exactly, but our own story of some slice of experience, a story which illuminates social processes and generates explanations for why people do and think the things they do.

The imperative of uncovering the mundane, routine and everyday was described by leading linguistic anthropologist Dell Hymes in the 1960s when he spoke about bringing anthropological research 'back home' (in Rampton, 2007a: 598). Hymes was keen to argue that the skills and knowledge of the ethnographer were needed to study 'ourselves' rather than the 'other'. In particular, Hymes brought his authority as a leading scholar in linguistic anthropology to the social sciences where he set about investigating linguistic inequality as both a practical and theoretical problem.

In this chapter, we explore linguistic ethnography's historical antecedents and its current theoretical and academic movements. First though, we suggest why linguistics and ethnography should be combined.

LANGUAGE AND CULTURE: A SINGLE UNIT OF ANALYSIS

Linguistic ethnography, a mainly European phenomenon, has been greatly influenced by North American scholarship in linguistic anthropology. Because of this we share many of the same antecedents and some of these are summarised in this chapter. We set the scene by returning to the beginning of the last century. In 1921, Sapir suggested, 'Language does not exist apart from culture, that is, from the socially inherited assemblage of practices and beliefs that determines the textures of our lives' (Sapir, 1921: 207). According to Sapir, language and culture are inseparable. If we want to study language we have to consider its relationship to culture. If we want to investigate culture we must research language. Hand-in-hand, they are both socially inherited. Culture is not a fixed set of practices essential to ethnic or otherwise defined groups. Language is not an unchanging social structure unresponsive to the communicative needs of people. Rather, languages and cultures are practices and processes in flux, up for negotiation, but contingent on specific histories and social environments. This view of language and culture as processes rather than products finds long-term support in anthropology and ethnography. Goodenough explains further:

> I have found it theoretically helpful to think of both culture and language as rooted in human activities (rather than in societies) and as pertaining to groups. The cultural make-up of a society

is thus to be seen not as a monolithic entity determining the behaviour of its members, but as a melange of understanding and expectations regarding a variety of activities that serve as guides to their conduct and interpretation. (Goodenough, 1994: 266-7)

The interpretation of meaning is at the heart of Goodenough's definition here. We come to 'understand and expect' through the mundane routines we engage in regularly. We use language to practise and voice our communicative activities. According to Sapir (1921: 4), language is the 'product of long-continued social usage', a definition which points to the importance of shared conventions in inferring meaning. In other words, language can be understood as a socio-historical formation developed in particular cultural contexts of time and space.

A widely recognised definition of language is as a system of signs. In linguistics, the sign has attracted most attention through the work of Ferdinand de Saussure (1857–1913) who recognised two sides to the study of meaning, but emphasised that the relationship between the two is arbitrary. His labels for the two sides are 'signifier' (the thing that signifies, or sound image) and 'signified' (the object or concept referred to). The relationship between the signifier and the signified is known as the linguistic sign. The sign is the basic unit of communication.

Saussure provided two further key concepts to understand language and language use. The first, *langue*, is the system of language in the abstract. Saussure defined langue as a 'system of signs'. The second is *parole*, language as it is used in spoken or written form. Saussurean linguistics has typically focused on the study of linguistic signs within the grammatical system (*langue*). It has been less interested in the actual concrete act of speaking or using language – *parole* – which Crystal (1997: 411) summarises as 'dynamic, social activity in a particular time and place'.

Work in linguistic ethnography and anthropology has taken a different direction in its study of the sign. The scholarship of Charles Sanders Peirce (1839–1914) has been hugely influential in this regard. Peirce (1955) claimed that theory of signification consists of three not two inter-related parts: the signifier, the signified and an interpretant, or, in the more precise language of Peirce, the sign, the object and the interpretant.

To illustrate the process of signification, we can take the signifier /piːk/ (peak). The signified of /piːk/ is the object traditionally denoting 'summit' or 'pinnacle'.

However, the urban dictionary (http://www.urban dictionary.com/define.php?term=peak), a data source whose contemporariness and open-endedness can mean it is sometimes less than reliable, gives several other meanings, one of which describes it as an adjective used by teenagers to style something bad or not likeable, as in the following:

Alex: It seriously needs to stop raining.
Jess: I know, it's peak.

Clearly, there are two different dictionary definitions of 'peak' here. However, this isn't really the point; many words have a range of meanings. Rather it is the *process* of change and use in context which should attract our attention. Although peak has a range of referential meanings, it also indexes quite different social contexts, speakers and listeners. In the raining example above, we as readers start to make guesses about the kind of people who might say /pi:k/; we presuppose young rather than old, school kid rather than middle-aged rambler; hipster rather than fuddy-duddy. Within Peirce's theory of semiosis the 'interpretant' is the element which allows us to bring social and historical knowledge and experience into our interpretations. Interpretation, therefore, is a process of translation. Peirce understood the interpretant as providing a translation of the sign, allowing the development and construction of the object (Atkin, 2013). Interpretation is also a process of sedimentation as meanings settle and become conventionalised. In linguistic ethnography the role of interpretation is central to understanding the actions of people in their social contexts. The linguistic ethnographer attempts to describe and understand the relevance of signs in ongoing communicative activity and situated social action. Rather than the unitary object (signified) conceptualised by Saussure, Peirce also viewed the object as being of three types – the icon, the index and the symbol:

- The *iconic sign* reflects the qualitative features of its object. The object and sign are said to resemble one another. For example, paintings, portraits and onomatopoeia are all examples of iconic signs because they look like or sound like the objects they are representing.
- The *indexical sign* signposts its object and is contiguous with it. There is often said to be a physical or existential connection between the indexical sign and its object. Pronouns are examples of indexical signs. The personal pronoun 'I' does not mean much unless it is clear who 'I' is referring to. Other examples of indices include pointing fingers, proper names and regional accents.
- The *symbol* is a sign which is able to connect to its object through utilising convention. Symbols are words like table, cat and love. The sign and its object are connected through social practices in which people come to presuppose certain meanings because of conventions.

In the list above, it is the final sign type, the symbol, which has typically attracted the interest of linguists. Through examining how different linguistic constituents combine, linguists have long studied the functional ability of the symbol to create meaning beyond its context. It is the symbol which is closest to Saussure's signifier/signified type relationship. However, icons and indices are of increasing interest, particularly to linguistic ethnographers and anthropologists. This is because their research on interpretive processes has revealed how relatively small differences in icons and indices can function in large and consequential ways. For example, work on indexicality has shown how accents and linguistic styles become linked to social identities and institutionally recognised social standings, positions and statuses.

Recent work by US-based scholars Asif Agha and Michael Silverstein is relevant here. Agha (2003), for example, describes how British English became culturally valued through 'discursive chaining' as hearers of previous messages become the speakers of next messages. As part of this process, received pronunciation (RP) began to be held in high regard as it was associated with the circulation and transmission of social values, for example, respectability and economic security. Silverstein's (1976, 2003) 'indexical orders' show how the individual sign becomes linked to wider ideologies. He uses the example of wine talk to illustrate how a lexicon used regularly in the context of wine tasting comes to have wider institutionalised and ideological meaningfulness. In the case of wine consumption Silverstein shows how wine becomes an 'aesthetic object', consumed as an 'aesthetic experience' which manifests as a 'life-style emblematisation' (2003: 222). Silverstein presents evidence of wine being 'anthropomorphised' through reference to nature and breeding, connected to the 'prestige realms of traditional English gentlemanly horticulture and especially animal husbandry' (p. 225). Elites and would-be elites in contemporary society seek to use wine talk because it confers an aspect of elitism from which distinction emanates. Agha and Silverstein both argue that macrosocial processes always operate through microsociological encounters or interactions.

As this brief tour shows, the study of language has developed considerably in the last hundred years or so. In particular, the theoretical concept of signs has become central to the study of culture, context and meaning making and therefore to linguistic ethnography. In the next section, we shift our focus slightly to consider other key influences on our research approach.

ANTECEDENTS AND CURRENT RELEVANCE

In this section we move forward fifty years or so to the middle of the last century. We thread together four scholars who share an interest in language, culture, society and interaction:

- Dell Hymes
- John Gumperz
- Erving Goffman
- Frederick Erickson

Both Hymes and Gumperz have been described as 'metatheorists' by Bonny McElhinny et al. (2003: 316) in a paper about who gets referenced in linguistic anthropology. Their central role in establishing two major theoretical developments fundamental to the fields of sociolinguistics and linguistic anthropology is the reason for this. We add Frederick Erickson and Erving Goffman to the list of metatheorists because of their profound influence on the work of scholars in linguistic ethnography (for overviews, see Rampton et al., 2004; Rampton, 2007a;

Tusting and Maybin, 2007; Creese, 2008; Maybin and Tusting, 2011; Rampton et al., in press).

Dell Hymes (1927–2009)

A theory of language and social life is Dell Hymes's major contribution to the field. He saw multiple relations between language and society, and between linguistic means and social meaning. Back in the 1960s and the heyday of Chomskian grammatical competence, Hymes criticised linguistics for making its focus the structure of language (*langue*), rather than the cultural actions of communities in context (*parole*). In 1974 he wrote, 'Linguistics, the discipline central to the study of speech, has been occupied almost wholly with developing analysis of the structure of language as a referential code' (p. 32). He felt that such a focus on the part of linguistics was deliberate, and the failure to provide an explicit place for sociocultural features was not accidental (Hymes, 1972: 272). He accused linguistics of taking a 'Garden of Eden' view of language which consisted of an ideal speaker who was grammatically competent – existing as an 'unmotivated cognitive mechanism ... not a person in the social world' (p. 273). Hymes called for an analysis of speech (parole) over language (langue) to articulate how social action and speech interact in 'a systematic, ruled and principled way' (Hymes, 1968: 101). He developed and advocated the 'ethnography of communication' because linguistics was not utilising the 'multiple relations between linguistic means and social meaning' (1974: 31). Furthermore, he argued that humankind 'cannot be understood apart from the evolution and maintenance of its ethnographic diversity' (p. 33). He therefore proposed studying 'speaking' and 'communication' over 'language'. For Hymes, and others committed to a sociolinguistic perspective, the analysis of speech over language shifted the direction away from code to use. This point is taken up by Blommaert and Jie (2010) who similarly argue 'Speech is language in which people have made investments – social, cultural, political, individual – emotional ones' (p. 8). Blommaert and Jie make a distinction between a linguistic notion of language and an ethnographic notion of discourse. This battle for a more social orientation to the study of language rumbles on to this day, with linguistic anthropologists arguing that a continued focus on langue or code is restrictive, extractionist and exclusionary (see Agha, 2005, for overview).

Hymes's influence has been major in the field of language education. His riposte to Chomsky contributed significantly to a pedagogy based not solely on grammar but on social appropriateness. His concept of 'communicative competence' (1972) redirected language education and its professionals to think about setting, people, register, function and style. He was greatly influenced by the work of Edward Sapir and Roman Jacobson (1960) whose work focused on the components and functions of the speech situation. Hymes was committed to understanding how speech resources come to have uneven social value and saw the possibilities of applying a linguistic or discourse analysis across disciplines to 'build answers to new questions thrown up by social change' (Hymes,1974: 32). His orientation was interdisciplinary in nature.

Angela Creese (2005) used Hymes's framework to show how different teacher roles attracted varying degrees of institutional support and the implication of this support for emergent bilingual young people. Hymes's concept of the speech situation, event and act was used by Creese to record the diversity of speech, repertoires and ways of speaking in three linguistically diverse London secondary schools. Subject teachers and teachers of English as an additional language foregrounded different language functions in their interaction with emergent bilingual students, resulting in different relationships, identity constructions and learning opportunities for young people. Creese linked her micro recordings of classroom interactions to macro structures of educational power. Through an analysis of teacher pronouns, language functions and speech acts, she showed how classroom participants reproduced the transmission of subject content as more important and authoritative than processes of problem solving and facilitation. She found this had a significant negative affect on language learning opportunities and language enrichment possibilities in the secondary school classrooms.

John Gumperz (1922-2013)

A major contribution by John Gumperz was his development of a line of work usually referred to as 'interactional sociolingusitics' (IS) which focuses on everyday talk in social contexts (Gumperz, 1982). It considers how societal and interactive forces merge in the small and mundane conversations that people regularly have. The goal of interactional sociolinguistics is to analyse how people interpret and create meanings in interaction. An important concept is the 'contextualization cue', which Gumperz (1999) describes as the functioning of signs 'to construct the contextual ground for situated interpretation' (p. 461). Gumperz was interested in understanding how people read clues to construct meaning.

An interactional sociolinguistic approach focuses on meaning-in-action. It highlights the uniqueness of the moment and context while simultaneously acknowledging the social structures brought into play. That is, although the focus is on the here-and-now of the encounter at hand the 'there-and-then' of the world beyond is ever present. As Gumperz (1999) argues, even the most straightforward interaction depends on shared, tacit knowledge, both cultural and linguistic.

In the UK, Celia Roberts has pioneered an IS approach, usually combining the focus on interaction with social theory. For example, in '"Like you're living two lives in one go": negotiating different social conditions for classroom learning in a further education context in England' (with Srikant Sarangi, 2001) she shows how educational contexts create expectations about classroom interaction which can be upheld or subverted by participants, leading to different educational outcomes. Acknowledging the classroom as a particular cultural space, and the participants as actors belonging to social and cultural groups, means that IS can be used to examine interactions between participants living in the same country, speaking the same language. Indeed, Roberts has consistently and effectively used IS to draw attention to inequality suffered by minority ethnic groups and to show how these inequalities are achieved through talk.

Erving Goffman (1922–82)

Erving Goffman was a Canadian-born sociologist and cultural theorist who trained at the famous Chicago school of Anthropology. He carried out fieldwork in a number of countries, and developed a range of theoretical perspectives for examining how people behave in different social settings. Reading his work in the twenty-first century, it can seem odd that the theories he presents are not illustrated with copious examples of fine-grained data analysis and that he presents a method that cannot be replicated (Lemert, 1997). Nevertheless, his ideas are clearly based on hours of detailed ethnographic looking and the resurgence in interest in his work is testament to the longevity of his theoretical constructs and their relevance for developing understanding of talk in context.

Goffman observed that the social situation is the basic unit or scene in which everyday life takes place (Erickson, 2004a). Through painstaking attention to the details of interaction in social situations he noted the rituals, routines and performances of daily life. From this study, Goffman developed a huge number of theoretical constructs which can be used to interpret and explain everyday talk. Many of these draw on dramaturgical metaphors and draw attention to his view on the performance aspects of identity and talk.

Perhaps Goffman's most important theoretical contribution was on face. He described face as, 'the positive social value a person effectively claims for himself by the line others assume he has taken during a particular contact' (Goffman, 1967: 5). His conceptualisation launched a whole new area of pragmatics research, with Brown and Levinson (1987) arguing that interlocutors are aware of each other's face needs, leading to engagement in complex linguistic gymnastics as they aim to protect, or not, these needs. Others such as Arundale (2010) developed the concept of face to focus on its joint-constructedness (see too Copland, 2011).

Ben Rampton has been instrumental in championing Goffman in his teaching of ethnography, language and communication and has drawn extensively on Goffman in his own work. For example, in *Language in Late Modernity: Interaction in an Urban School* (2006), Rampton shows how teenagers use German, a language taught in school but to which students seem to have little or no out-of-school affiliation, to perform a range of in-class functions (such as apologising and commanding). He draws on Goffman's concept of 'interpersonal verbal rituals' (Goffman, 1981: 21) to suggest that students use German to do face work particularly when their independence, territory or good character is threatened (Rampton, 2006: 166). Using German in a ritualistic way allows the students to attend to both their own face needs and to those of their interlocutors.

Fredrick Erickson

Fredrick Erickson (1990, 2004b) describes his approach as a 'practical activity', using video recordings of 'naturally occurring interactions' to look 'closely and repeatedly at what people do in real time as they interact' (Erickson, 1996: 283). Erickson's approach is known as micro ethnography as he examines 'big social issues through careful examination of "small" communicative behaviours on the microlevel' (LeBaron, 2008: 763).

In the examination of 'small communicative behaviours', micro ethnography is concerned with the local ecology of speaker and listener relations and the micro politics of social relations between people rather than with the individual. The immediate ecology of relations between participants focuses on how people in inter-action 'constitute environments for each other's activities' (McDermott, 1976: 36, cited in Erickson, 2004b: 5). This requires paying attention to the nonverbal, partic-ularly gaze, gesture and posture, as well as the verbal. Speaking and listening have a mutual influence on one another and can be said to have a rhythmic organisation (Erickson, 1996: 288).

Regarding 'big social issues', Erickson uses micro ethnography in two ways. First, he identifies the relationships between interaction and societal processes. Second, he shows how interactions are situated in historical and societal contexts (Erickson, 2004b). For example, in 'Seventy-five dollars goes in a day' (2004b), Erickson's meticulous analysis of dinner table talk demonstrates that discussion focuses repeatedly on the spiralling cost of living for a lower-middle-class family in the USA in 1974. In terms of societal processes, the discussion is the opportunity for 'language and discourse socialisation' (p. 50) to take place as the family learns to talk not just about the economy in general but about the particular issue of their dwindling financial resources. The topic of cost and lim-ited income has clear relevance for this family given their material circumstances, and Erickson argues that the discussion is class-based as those on higher incomes would not be discussing the issue with the same level of anxiety. In terms of situating interactions in 'historical and societal contexts', Erickson links the resentment talk at the dinner table to a growing dissatisfaction in similar families about rising costs, which leads in time to the formation of a discourse. He suggests that this kind of talk 'acted in synergy with large-scale social processes' to 'sweep Reagan into the White House' (2004b: 51), drawing on evidence that families such as this switched allegiance and voted in their millions for a Republican.

Erickson's work has been seminal in illustrating that people do not unthinkingly follow cultural rules but can also actively and non-deterministically construct what they do and who they are. This is not to say that cultural expectations play no part. Erickson uses the term 'wiggle room' to describe people 'finding just a little bit of space for innovation within what's otherwise often experienced as the crushing weight of social expectation/social structure' (Rampton, 2011: 5). Indeed, Erickson (2004b: viii) suggests there is a paradox between local talk in social interaction being unique and locally constituted and the reality that this social talk is influenced by forces beyond the immediate context of the talk. He uses micro ethnography to illustrate this paradox.

THE LEGACY

These four scholars leave an important legacy which continues to have a major influence in the US and Europe on both linguistic anthropology and linguistic ethnography. Certainly the four case studies in this book can all be said to draw on this rich hinterland of theory. We can see traces of the ethnography of communication, interactional sociolinguistics, ethnographic micro-analysis and face in the linguistic ethnographies produced by Angela, Fiona, Frances and Sara. Angela draws across the four theorisits to consider voice and indexicality as theoretically and methodologically relevant for investigating multilingualism in multilingual teams. Fiona is interested in the dynamics of power as they play out in the micro interactions of trainers and trainees in feedback sessions and draws on Erickson and Goffman. The features of interactional sociolinguistics are relevant to Frances as she examines how communicating 'rights' to those in custody is accomplished by different police officers in different contexts. She scrutinises this event through the lens of different social and linguistic theory, making the interdisciplinary connections which Hymes suggested were not only possible but desired. Sara makes use of scholarship deriving from Goffman to describe how 'think tank' organisations shape the policy of a publicly funded body: the UK health service.

LINGUISTIC ETHNOGRAPHY TODAY

Given the illustrious past and vibrant scholarship of the present in linguistic anthropology, readers may well find themselves asking, why do we need linguistic ethnography? Shouldn't we accept that so much is shared and the line so thin between the two that introducing another term to the field is redundant and might be seen as empire building (Hammersley, 2007)? Rather than describe ourselves as linguistic ethnographers, what's wrong with linguistic anthropologists? Indeed, why have a label at all?

We have already established that linguistic ethnography has been greatly influenced by North American scholarship in linguistic anthropology and because of this we share many of the same influences. Indeed, as we have already suggested, a common bedrock of 'metatheorists' such as Gumperz and Hymes, Goffman and Erickson, Agha and Silverstein, highlights the theoretical and methodological backgrounds we share. We are keen, therefore, to emphasise the continuities with linguistic anthropology rather than make claims of distinction. Nevertheless, the appearance of linguistic ethnography in Europe has not happened by accident. In this section we seek to explain its emergence. Our contribution highlights particular arguments in relation to the four case studies appearing in this book.

A moment in time

According to Rampton (2007a: 594), there isn't any 'properly institutionalized linguistic anthropology in Britain'. This is one of the reasons anthropology has not been able to provide a home for British scholars pursuing an interest in language, culture and society, in contrast to the situation in North America, where linguistic anthropology has flourished. Instead these scholars have turned to the annual meetings of the British Association of Applied Linguistics (BAAL) to fine tune their analytical conversations. Over the last 10 years, BAAL meetings have created a context for contact and cross-fertilisation resulting in the coming together of scholars with a distinctive mix of traditions. Maybin and Tusting (2011) describe how linguistic ethnographers have been drawn to the disciplinary frameworks of linguistics and sociolinguistics through BAAL's remit. European scholars have also felt rudderless, as illustrated by a special issue of the journal *Text and Talk* (2010), which describes European perspectives on linguistic ethnography (see Flynn et al., 2010; Jacobs and Slembrouck, 2010).

A key moment for linguistic ethnography came in 2001 when the Linguistic Ethnography Forum (LEF: www.lingethnog.org) was established and a number of lines of enquiry were 'pushed together by circumstance, open to the recognition of new affinities, and sufficiently familiar with one another to treat differences with equanimity' (Rampton, 2007a: 585).

As indicated in the earlier case study vignettes, linguistic ethnography has clustered a community of scholars around its themes and heritages and brought together doctoral students, early and mid-career researchers and senior academics. Within these clusters of scholarship different conversations between academics have seen some traditions of discourse analysis become established, and robust and new kinds of conversation around language and ethnography develop. Although too early to speak of its legacy, linguistic ethnography has created a forum to develop researcher capacity at a key moment in time (for overviews, see Rampton et al., 2004; Rampton, 2007a; Tusting and Maybin, 2007; Creese, 2008, 2010b; Maybin and Tusting, 2011; Rampton et al., in press).

The interdisciplinary agenda

In UK higher education there has been a general shift away from the organisation of academic knowledge in terms of disciplines to one which is based on interdisciplinarity (Rampton, 2007a; Creese, 2010a). Many universities in the UK are undergoing a reorganisation in search of 'effective structures and mechanisms to encourage and foster inter-disciplinary activity' (University of Birmingham website, 2009). This is mirrored in the research funding bodies in the UK and Europe. In the UK, there is a new emphasis on interdisciplinary research and funding is made available to achieve 'beneficial societal impact'. Teams of academics from the social sciences, environmental sciences and the humanities might find themselves working together on a project and debating methodologies which can best respond to the questions being asked.

Rampton et al. (in press) describe two modalities of doing interdisciplinary research. The first approach brings different academic disciplines together to work on a problem. Cross-referencing to different paradigms can be made to investigate the phenomena at hand and researchers commonly move out of their comfort zone in discussion with colleagues as they learn about different ways to research the phenomenon. The second approach to interdisciplinarity sees collaborations between academics and non-academic institutions in the private, public and third sectors. Such partnerships see joint planning, question setting and a commitment to bring different expertises, experiences and knowledge to the challenge. Rampton et al. (in press) describe 'the multi-dimensional complexity of the problem that motivates the mixing'.

An example of a project which combines both modes described by Rampton et al. above can be found in a recently funded project by the one of the UK's research councils. The Arts and Humanities Research Council (AHRC) Translating Culture's theme has funded three large grants which are required to network across academic disciplines and with non-academic partners (http://www.ahrc.ac.uk/ Funding-Opportunities/Research-funding/Themes/Translating-Cultures/Pages/ Translating-Cultures.aspx). These partnerships have created mixes of people, both academic and professional, engaged in question setting, research design, data collection and analysis. Discussions of emergent themes and outcomes in such projects cannot make use of the strictly disciplinary and faculty driven research programmes of yesteryear. An openness to and curiosity about other ways of doing things is essential. Partnerships between universities and other organisations are also important in ensuring the visibility and impact of the research.

Ethnography with its democratic approach to participation and interpretation of local perspectives is often a good starting point around which interdisciplinary teams can cohere. Moreover, because language is at the heart of any exercise in social life, linguistic ethnographers have a key role to play. Agha (2005) speaks of the 'linguistic turn' in the humanities and social sciences which he defines as 'a vast number of intellectual projects that take up particular aspects of human affairs mediated by language, in a variety of modes of departmental, disciplinary, and inter-disciplinary organizations' (p. 228). Furthermore, he describes the dangers of staying too narrowly focused within the disciplinary boundaries of linguistics:

Linguists of a certain type might well say, 'That's not linguistics.' But no one cares. For the reciprocal fact is this: the 'linguistic turn' is an orientation to the linguistic aspect of human affairs not toward what happens in departments of linguistics. (Agha, 2005: 228)

Discourse analysis presents a set of methodological tools which are attractive to many in the social sciences. Linguistic ethnography in particular is open to a wide variety of discourse analytic traditions in its combination with ethnography. Through its focus on discourse and detailed interactional analysis, linguistic ethnography is already adopted in a variety of disciplines (see Snell et al., in press). However, there are productive tensions in engaging in interdisciplinary scholarship. What constitutes data may radically differ across disciplines, and the ontological and epistemological underpinnings of each discipline may fundamentally conflict. Furthermore, disciplines differ in what they constitute as their object of study or unit of analysis and this shapes the organisation of research activity.

For example, while the linguistic ethnographer after sustained participant observation may come to be interested in how a sports teacher uses a particular phoneme to develop a shared identity position with a group of students, the sport and exercise academic might be interested in which activities motivate students to do most exercise. A cross-disciplinary perspective would require both academic parties to discuss their interests and underlying rationale, perhaps considering alternative research foci before commencing. The methodology of collecting ongoing audio recordings while observing might surprise the sport and exercise academic; the linguistic ethnographer, on the other hand, might view the setting up of controlled tests for measuring motivation as limiting naturally occurring interactional data. There would need to be a good deal of negotiation about different research methodologies. However, the two parties might also find common ground. The role of language in motivation could be of shared interest while the success of particular ways of using language for improving health could be highlighted in addressing public health and policy issues. They two parties might also find methodological agreement in their use of observation and interview. There is, therefore, the potential risk of a loss of focus and rigour but also for research gains.

Post-modernity

Modernist ideas about language seek order and purity and are troubled by 'hybridity' (Blommaert et al., 2012). In structuralist linguistics various techniques were and still are employed to identify and classify features of sentence structures and to categorise these into constituent parts. Modernist ideologies of language 'centered on denotational functions' and sought to count, bound and structure strings of signs, particularly at the sentence level (Blommaert, 2010: 10). Such a view of language is often put to work for 'higher-scale institutional hegemonies' like national language policies and educational policies, resulting in the 'national language' constructed as one of the purest icons of the nation state.

As Blommaert et al. point out, if you are viewed as speaking a pure language you are authenticated as a real member of a particular culture, a common modernist view.

Post-modernist approaches to the study of language deconstruct these 'entitlements' or social constructions. Deconstruction involves processes of scrutiny which pull apart dichotomies such as 'order versus disorder; purity versus impurity; normality versus abnormality' (Blommaert et al., 2012: 5). Linguistic ethnography investigates the construction and robustness of social categories and categorisation processes; taken-for-granted assumptions about groups, categories and peoples are the objects of their research, as are the processes of diversity and change. Indeed to date, linguistic ethnographers have played their part in the rapid debunking of reifications and essentialisations about languages, dialects, ethnicities and cultures in the economic and social processes of globalisation (see for example, Blackledge and Creese, 2010, 2014; Lefstein and Snell, 2013).

Post-modernism also makes clear that assumptions are dangerous. In linguistic ethnography, assumptions about communicative practices in particular are challenged and must be empirically investigated, as the earlier review of Erickson made clear. However, as Maybin and Tusting (2011) point out, this is a 'formidable' task. Heller (2011: 400) explains why: 'The challenge is to capture the ways in which things unfold in real time, and the ways in which they sediment into constraints that go far beyond the time and place of specific interactions.' Linguistic ethnographers see attention to the 'sign' in discourse as a means to linking to wider historical, social, political and cultural structures, and as one way forward to responding to this challenge.

CONCLUDING COMMENTS

In this chapter, we have suggested that linguistic ethnography has developed at a particular moment in time in which the study of language, culture and identity resonate loudly. Its empirical nature and bottom-up orientation to data, require working from evidence towards theory. This means linguistic ethnography is well placed to produce critical, systematic and rigorous scholarship. Linguistic ethnography links the micro to the macro, the small to the large, the varied to the routine, the individual to the social, the creative to the constraining, and the historical to the present and to the future.

Hymes, Gumperz, Goffman and Erickson have been particularly influential in linguistic ethnography. Their theoretically informed ways of working provide springboards from which cultural practices and their links to wider social processes can be investigated. It is immediately obvious from the preceding discussion in this chapter that linguistic ethnography shares many connections to North American oriented research in linguistic anthropology. However, an argument has been put forward for its instantiation based on a particular set of European circumstances.

First, anthropology has developed in Europe without a strand in linguistics. With no local scholarship to turn to and American linguistic anthropology generally concerning itself with issues in and around its borders, researchers doing work combining linguistics and ethnography in the UK and Europe had no natural home. A new forum, linguistic ethnography, has provided one. Second, as interdisciplinary working gains momentum, scholars who can combine approaches to data collection and analysis and work collaboratively with differently-minded researchers are likely to be in demand. Linguistic ethnographers also have a tradition of working with professional groups (see Roberts, 2012; and Lefstein and Snell, 2013). Research 'with' rather than 'on' follows in the interdisciplinary orientation first advocated by Hymes. Third, linguistic ethnographers contribute to post-modernity and its deconstruction of social categories. This work has been particularly relevant in terms of new and emergent constructions of language, culture, ethnicity, race and diversity.

Linguistic ethnography views language as communicative action functioning in social contexts in ongoing routines of peoples' daily lives. It looks at how language is used by people and what this can tell us about wider social constraints, structures and ideologies. It achieves this by investigating the linguistic sign as a social phenomenon open to interpretation and translation but also predicated on convention, presupposition and previous patterns of social use. Because the sign is the basic unit of meaning, linguistic ethnographers are keen to understand how it is interpreted within its social context. Through rich description, the use of audio and video transcripts, a range of interview techniques and other textual documents, the researcher attempts to appreciate the relevance of signs in ongoing communicative activity and situated social action. In the next chapter we describe our orientation to collecting signs as data and describe the importance of discourse, fieldwork and interviewing in linguistic ethnography.

KEY READINGS

Agha, A. (2003) 'The social life of cultural value', *Language and Communication*, 23(3/4): 231–73.

Hammersley, M. (2007) 'Reflections on linguistic ethnography', *Journal of Sociolinguistics*, 11(5): 689–95.

Hymes, D. (1968) 'The ethnography of speaking', in J. Fishman (ed.) *Readings in the Sociology of Language*. The Hague: Moulton. pp 99–138.

Roberts, C. and Sarangi, S. (1991) '"Like you're living two lives in one go": negotiating different social conditions for classroom learning in a further education context in England', in M. Heller and M. Martin-Jones (eds) *Voices of Authority: Education and Linguistic Difference*. London: Ablex Publishing.

TWO

Data in Linguistic Ethnography

INTRODUCTION

Unlike some other research methodologies and approaches, linguistic ethnography does not prescribe a set of data collection and analysis tools. Researchers working from a linguistic ethnographic perspective have a range of research interests and investigate these interests in different and various ways. Nonetheless, data are collected and analysed and particular ways of doing data collection and analysis are particularly salient, given the joint focus on linguistics and ethnography.

In this chapter, we illustrate four approaches to data collection and analysis used by the case study writers: interviews, fieldwork, interactions and text. In each section, we describe each data collection tool, how the data can be collected and how it can be analysed. We also engage reflexively with each data collection method so that we discuss underlying theory as well as practical applications. We concur with Snell and Lefstein (2012) that linguistic ethnographers share a particular analytic disposition and that this involves a focus on data and close analysis of situated language in use. The aim of this chapter is to show how this analytic disposition can be achieved.

INTERVIEWS AS EVIDENCE IN LINGUISTIC ETHNOGRAPHY

Interviews are used to support researchers in gaining an *emic* perspective on research, that is, understanding from the participant's perspective. Research participants are invited to give their opinions on the issues and questions identified by the researcher, or are asked to give an account of their experiences, for example.

The data from interviews provide an alternative perspective to that recorded by the researcher, usually in field notes, and support interpretation of naturally occurring data, such as recordings of interactions. Taken together, these perspectives can generate new analytical angles and findings.

Types of interviews

Interviews can be divided into two types, formal and informal (Richards, 2003). The former denotes interviews which are scheduled in advance and organised in the canonic interviewer/interviewee format. These interviews are often comprehensive and used to elicit information on a range of topics. Informal interviews, on the other hand, are interviews that are 'held impromptu' (Gobo, 2008: 191) and generally focus on a specific area or topic. We discuss both in turn.

Traditionally, formal interviews have been less common in ethnographic research than informal interviews (Agar, 2008; Gobo, 2008). However, in linguistic ethnographic research they are pervasive and used by a large number of researchers (see for example, Maybin, 2006; Rampton, 2006; Tusting, in press). This may be because some of the contexts in which researchers work make conducting informal interviews difficult (for example, when researching children in classrooms it can be awkward to sidle up to a child after class to ask him/her about an incident that has just occurred). It may also be because a good deal of linguistic ethnographic research can be described as adopting 'an ethnographic perspective' (Green and Bloome, 1997: 6) rather than taking a traditional ethnographic approach, which means that limited time is spent in the field or in a range of contexts in the field. Answers to research questions that might have traditionally emerged through observation may not do so in this kind of research, making formal interviews valuable data sources. Furthermore, opportunities for informal interviewing may also be limited; researchers often have to rush off to their next site or back to their institutions and do not have time to chat to participants at their leisure. The formal interview, though not in all cases ideal (see Agar, 2008) enables time-pressed academics to attend to the perspectives of their participants as well as providing an efficient medium for getting answers to questions.

Formal interviews are commonly divided into structured, semi-structured and open (Richards, 2003), and in linguistic ethnography, a semi-structured approach is usually preferred. For the most part, interviews are conducted on a one-to-one basis, but pair, or group interviews (often called focus groups) are becoming increasingly popular, particularly when working with vulnerable groups such as children (see for example, Maybin, 2006, who interviewed children in pairs) or when time is short (see Wilkinson, 2004, for an insightful discussion of the affordances and issues of focus group research). In semi-structured interviews, a set of questions is designed which acts as a guide for the researcher. Figure 2.1 shows the list of interview questions that Fiona used to interview trainees in a group in her case study.

Questions for trainees post feedback

1. What is the purpose of the feedback session do you think?
2. What have you found most/least helpful?
3. What is the role of the trainer in feedback?
4. What is the role of other trainees?
5. Has your teaching improved do you think as the result of feedback?
6. Do you always agree with the feedback you are given?
7. Is the feedback always delivered with respect for your feelings?
8. Was the feedback generally positive or generally negative do you think?
9. Is it helpful do you think to be shown excerpts from the feedback?
10. Why did you not take notes in the feedback sessions?

Figure 2.1   Questions for semi-structured interview

As you can see, the questions, which were asked at the end of the course, and so at the completion of the observation phase, were designed to orient the discussion to topics that had attracted Fiona's analytic attention. For example, questions 3 and 4 focus on the roles of the participants in the group interview as Fiona had been fascinated by the expectation that trainees were expected to become 'mini trainers' in the feedback conference and she was interested to gain trainees' views on this experience. Question 7 oriented to a central theoretical concern with the negotiation of face in feedback, while question 10 aimed to draw out the purpose of feedback from the trainees' perspectives. Of course, in retrospect, Fiona wishes she had worded some of the questions differently and, in fact, in the interviews themselves, the questions were often delivered in different ways. Here is question 4 as posed in the second group interview and the response it generated:

Extract 1

```
1.  Fiona:   so what's the role of the other trainees then in the feedback because
2.           you have the feedback in a group, don't you?
3.  T1:      mm
4.  Fiona:   so what, what's the role of everybody else doing there? Why, why
5.           not just have it on a one-to-one basis?
6.  T2:      I suppose just to get other people's opinions as well, if they've seen
7.           The same as erm (.) the the m, the m, erm Trainer 1 or, or Trainer 2
8.           you know =
9.  T3:      = we can learn from their lessons as well showing you've done
10.          wrong or right
```

Fiona felt that the silence from three trainees and minimal response from T1 to her first question indicated that the trainees did not understand the question, perhaps being confused by the word 'role' (although, of course, there are other potential reasons for these responses). She rephrased her question and in doing so constructed group feedback in contrast to one-to-one feedback, the more usual mode (lines 4 and 5). This question elicited the fuller responses which helped Fiona to understand the value of group feedback from the trainees' perspectives.

Frequently, interview questions exist in order to orient to certain topics and some researchers prefer to prepare a list of areas for discussion rather than questions per se.

The researcher (and participant) are free in semi-structured interviews to divert from the questions and pursue topics that arise in the course of the talk (see Richards, 2003, for a full discussion).

As well as being prepared to move off topic, researchers may create 'probe' questions to follow up on responses to main questions. Probe questions will elicit details or examples that help the researcher to understand the interviewee's experience more clearly. In the extract below, Fiona uses a probe question to dig deeper into the responses to her planned question, 'Do you always agree with the feedback you are given?' The answers to the question were generally positive (that they agreed) but one trainee had said that sometimes she did not understand the feedback when it was delivered and had to go back to it 'later on', at which point the feedback made sense:

Extract 2

1.	Fiona:	Right (.) so sometimes there might be more the the problem isn't
2.		so much with what they're saying but maybe the that you're you
3.		know yeah tired
4.	T1:	Yeah I think it's just after you've done a lesson you're just
5.		like tired you can't always take it in
6.	T2:	Yeah
7.	T1:	Well that's me
8.		((laughter))
9.	T2:	I'm just like (.) a bit glazed and then afterwards the next day I
10.		think 'Oh yeah yes I can see it'
11.	T1:	It's not just you

Fiona's probe question uncovers two things: first, trainees can feel physical and emotional stress from teaching and being observed; second, trainees' understanding of feedback might be delayed because of 'tiredness'. The second point in particular contributed to the findings of the research. Taken with other data (field notes, the recorded feedback session and interviews with trainers) Fiona was able to demonstrate that there was a mismatch between what trainers expected from feedback and what (some) trainees were able to deliver.

It could be argued that Fiona's question in Extract 3 is what Gobo (2008) calls 'a leading question' (p. 197) that is, the question is designed to elicit a specific reply (that the trainees are tired). However, Agar (2008) maintains that all questions are to some extent leading (he calls leading questions 'baits' (p. 142)) and that it is sometimes sensible to lead (after all, the interviewee 'may not follow' (p. 142) or the interviewee might contradict the interviewer's interpretation). Furthermore, Spradley (1979) argues that the purpose of the ethnographic interview is for the researcher to know what the participants know in the way that they know it. When the researcher is focusing on learning from participants in this way, his/her questions will respond to the interview context and will not necessarily follow a schedule of carefully constructed questions. For these reasons, we tend not to be too concerned about leading questions. Indeed, if a discursive approach to interviews is taken, leading questions will draw the analytic eye of the researcher as a matter of course, as we show below.

There are a number of benefits of using semi-structured interviews in linguistic ethnographic research, not least gaining this emic perspective. However, there are downsides too. As Atkinson and Silverman (1997) have argued, we live in an 'interview society' and participants think they know what to expect from taking part in this interactional event. Awareness can lead to complacency on the part of interviewers, as they 'take for granted' what an interview is and what it produces (Briggs, 1986: 2), and to apprehension on the part of interviewees as they accommodate to the formality of the interview (as opposed to the informality of much observation) and to the realisation that what they say will be recorded and could have consequences, either directly or indirectly. It is of course true that the ethnographic interview is very different from other forms of interviewing, as Frances argues in her case study. It is expected that 'researchers have established respectful, ongoing relationships with their interviewees' (Sherman Heyl, 2001: 369) and that the aim of the interviewer is to understand the social world from the interviewee's perspective. Nevertheless, it is difficult for both the interviewer and interviewee to relinquish their knowledge and experiences of contemporary interviews. Another problem is that it can be difficult for the interviewee to recall experiences that interest the interviewer, particularly if those experiences seem unremarkable to them. In other contexts, where interviews are viewed as high status, high stakes genres (which is the case in Japan) interviewees might be very circumspect about what they say and so the data constructed in interviews can be vague or superficial.

Concerns such as these, as well as the desire to elicit an immediate response to what the researcher has observed, have heralded an interest in informal interviews in linguistic ethnographic research. It is to these that we now turn.

As described above, informal interviews have a long and sustained history in ethnographic work. Agar (2008) describes three features of the informal interview. First there is no list of written questions but rather 'a repertoire of question-asking strategies from which you draw as the moment seems appropriate' (p. 140). Second, in informal interviews the researcher does not take on the role of the interviewer, with the weight of knowledge and authority this brings. Instead, he/she positions him/herself as ignorant and the interviewee as the one taking the lead. Finally, informal interviews happen in many different contexts and situations, such as during a tea break or an activity, rather in an interview room. Gobo (2008) adds another feature to this list when he suggests that the researcher is 'less concerned to achieve his knowledge objective [than] with one single interview, because doubts, ambiguities and interpretative uncertainties can be resolved by subsequent interviews over the entire span of the research' (p. 191).

Collecting interview data

As discussed above, the opportunity to hold informal interviews in linguistic ethnography can be curtailed by the researcher having limited time on site or attending only to a particular event in or an aspect of the context where the research takes place. However, researchers also recognise the affordances of the approach, not least because of its informality and timeliness. The mismatch between opportunity and desire has been overcome by some researchers adopting the 'go-along' technique (Kusenbach, 2003). This approach is less pervasive than the informal interview as it tends to take place immediately before or after the researcher has observed the activity in which he/she is interested. It is an informal interview usually conducted 'on the hoof', that is, while the researcher and participant are moving from one space to another. During this often brief period, the researcher engages the participant in discussion about what he/she has just done/is about to do in order to gain a better understanding of the context and issues involved. In the case study presented in this book, Frances, for example, spent time in custody suites, shadowing police interviewers, and on targeted raids with officers. However, she did not generally go out 'on the beat' (see, too, Rock, 2007). Of note is that Frances did not replace the research interview with the go-along. Instead, she recognised that both the interview and the go-along afford opportunities not open to the other.

An issue with informal interviews, particularly go-alongs, is that they are difficult to record. It may not be appropriate to thrust a recording device in front of a participant as he/she races along a corridor, or there may not be time. This means that the interviewer has to rely on memory to record the interview in writing after the event. An argument could also be made that there are ethical issues with informal interviews as participants may not recognise that they are in a research context and may be more off-guard than in, for example, a formal interview setting. Likewise, the research participant might think the researcher is being aggressive or at least 'pushy' conducting informal interviews whenever there seems to be breathing space in his/her busy schedule. Gobo (2008) suggests that informal interviews are only conducted once a strong relationship has developed between the researcher and the researched.

Analysing interview data

Analysing interview data can be done in a number of ways. If the interview has been recorded it is common first of all to transcribe it as a written version so it is easier to work with. Then codes (or themes) can be generated through repeated reading of (and listening to) the interviews. Frances took this approach to her interview data. She makes the point that while some researchers analyse the data according to the questions' responses, she found it more productive to look for themes across the interview data. With small interview data sets, coding can be completed manually, using coloured pens or comments boxes/coloured fonts in *Word* (Fiona took this approach). Sometimes researchers cut up the interviews into sections and sort them into piles, each representing a code. The value of this approach is that when codes become unwieldy or too broad, the sections can be easily re-sorted (see Agar, 2008, for a description of coding using this approach).

There are also computer programs which can be used to code data, such as NVIVO. Tusting (in press) explains how she used Atlas.ti to code interview and other research data and how the programme helped her to organise the data and to keep track of codes (see Figure 2.2).

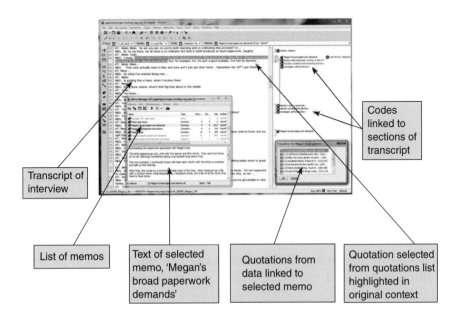

Figure 2.2 Using Atlas.ti to code data (Tusting, in press)

Developing reflexivity about interview data

So far, the discussion has suggested that qualitative research interviews are a pretty straightforward and useful research tool which can be used to provide a different perspective to that of the researcher on the research questions. Since Briggs's (1986) seminal work, however, researchers have been made increasingly aware of the requirement to 'theorize qualitative research interviews' (Talmy and Richards, 2011). Specifically, researchers have been minded to pay attention to their discursive nature. From this perspective, the interview is acknowledged to be 'a socially-situated "speech event"' (Mischler, 1986), in which interviewer(s) and interviewee(s) make meaning, co-construct knowledge and 'participate in social practices' (p. 2). The central point from this perspective is that data created in an interview must be taken as a joint construction so that both the content of the interview and also the process of the interview, that is, how the interview is interactionally accomplished, are analysed. As Holstein and Gubrium (2004) argue, 'Meaning is not merely elicited by apt questioning, nor simply transported through respondent replies; it is actively and communicatively assembled in the interview encounter' (p. 141). Researchers who theorise interviews as discursive practice tend to use linguistic analysis to deconstruct the interview event to show how meaning is constructed on a turn-by-turn basis (see, for example, Baker, 2002; Roulston, 2006; Garton and Copland, 2010).

In order to explain this discursive approach in more detail, we return to Extract 2 above. We have already argued that the content of this discussion was relevant to understanding why there was a mismatch in expectation between the trainers and trainees. However, if we look at the extract from a discursive perspective, we will also need to make the point that Fiona's interpretation of the trainees' answers contributed to this finding. In the interview, Fiona asked the question, 'Do you always agree with the feedback you've been given?' In response, one trainee answered:

Extract 3

T1: I think there's been occasions where like ... think, 'Oh, I don't really understand that, but then when you've thought about it afterwards you think oh yeah. i mean you know, I always know they're right, but sometimes you think, 'Oh, what do they mean?' And then ... later on when you read the notes and go over it you think, 'Oh yeah, of course'. That's what we're trying to learn about it'.

In response to this answer, Fiona then asked her probe question given at the beginning of Extract 2, 'So sometimes ... the, the problem isn't so much with what they're saying, but maybe the, that you're, you know, yeah, tired'. As can be seen from Extract 3, Trainee 1 suggests that she better understands feedback after the conference when she has had the opportunity to 'go over it'. It is Fiona who attributes this lack of initial understanding to being 'tired' in the feedback session. The trainees readily pick up on this adjective, as can be seen in Extract 3 when the adjective is repeated by Trainee 1 ('you're just like tired') and reiterated in the word 'glazed' by Trainee 2.

The point is not that the trainees do not feel tired after teaching. The talk suggests that at least two of the trainees do. Rather, the point is that the idea of feeling tired after teaching is co-constructed between the interviewer and interviewees from Trainee 1's admission that the feedback is sometimes difficult to understand when it is presented and Fiona's experiences of conducting feedback conferences. An approach which theorises interviews discursively would take this co-construction into account in presenting findings. In linguistic ethnography, analysis which focuses on the language of interviews in this way is common and researchers are as likely to attend to the way interviews unfold as they are to content (see Frances's case study and also Garton and Copland, 2010).

Given the focus on reflexivity in linguistic ethnography, it is not surprising that we encourage a discursive approach to interview data collection and analysis. Mann (2011) provides a number of suggestions about how we can work towards this goal taking such an approach, from ensuring interview questions form part of transcripts to making full interviews available where possible. We would add that the researcher needs to bring the same reflexivity to bear on collecting and analysing interview data as he/she would to collecting and analysing observational data. By this we mean that the researcher needs to 'develop awareness of the complex interplay of "self" and "other"' (Sherman Heyl, 2001: 377, drawing on Fine, 1994) so that he/she recognises how his/her questions, assumptions, attitudes and ideas affect both the construction of the interview and the findings.

Interviews are a valuable research tool which can provide a window onto the lived experiences of research participants and provide interpretation and opinion that might not be available from observation alone. On the other hand, interviewing, like observing, is a skill, and requires the interviewer to pay attention to a range of factors, from the interview venue to the interaction between the interviewer and interviewee. Advice about how to conduct interviews can be found in a number of publications (for example, McKinney et al., 2012) and should be heeded. Just as important, however, is the requirement as a researcher to reflect on the interview process. We should always ask how our questions, responses and demeanour affected how the interview unfolded and the data were generated, and be ready to account for these.

OBSERVATION AS EVIDENCE IN LINGUISTIC ETHNOGRAPHY

Types of observation

In ethnography there is only one kind of observation which can be broadly described as open ethnographic observation. It is open in the sense that a blank page and pen are the tools of the ethnographer, who writes down what he or she sees, hears, smells, feels and senses in the field. This differs from other kinds of more structured or 'closed' observations which use observation schedules sometimes organised by time or activity type.

All ethnographers engage in some kind of open observation. However, not all ethnographers participate in the field in same way. Ethnography creates different levels of participation and these are all negotiated in an ongoing fashion throughout the research process. Observation often involves some kind of shadowing of those we are researching (Kusenbach, 2003; Czarniawska, 2007), requiring movement between settings and opening up opportunities for informal interviews between researcher and participant while on the move. Observations are generally used to build rapport and develop trust in the field and so usually precede audio, video or interview recordings. But mostly observations are used to record the lived stuff. They are records of social complexity (Blommaert, 2007a).

Blommaert and Hymes highlight different but not oppositional perspectives on observation. For Blommaert (2007a), ethnography 'does not, unlike many other approaches, try to reduce the complexity of social events by focusing *a priori* on a selected range of relevant features, but it tries to describe and analyse the complexity of social events *comprehensively*' (Blommaert, 2007a: 682). Hymes argues, 'since partiality cannot be avoided, the only solution is to face up to it, to compensate for it as much as possible, to allow for it in interpretation' (Hymes, 1980: 99). While Blommaert reminds the ethnographer to remain open to what s/he observes in the field and avoid the use of imposed external categories, Hymes tells us we can't but help arrive in the field without some prior view of what's interesting and relevant. Miles and Huberman (1994: 27) point out that '[Any] researcher, no matter how unstructured or inductive, comes to fieldwork with some orienting ideas, foci and tools.' Erickson (2004a) describes how temperament, prior experience and all sorts of personal idiosyncrasies enter into the research process. In other words, we never start from a completely clean slate and will always bring ourselves into what we observe while simultaneously retaining an open orientation to what we see. Geertz (1988: 144) calls it an 'un-get-roundable fact'. This fundamental reality can make the researcher feel exposed to criticisms of bias, partiality and subjectivity. However, ethnographers refute these criticisms by suggesting that bias is not the most useful of terms in describing the interpretative process. Rather we might think about how we work into our accounts the partialities and subjectivities that are necessarily part of any interpretive process.

One way that ethnographic observation achieves this is through writing field notes. Field notes have a special place within ethnography because of their role in documenting complexity in participant observation and recording the ethnographers' partialities. In writing field notes, we keep observation open, choosing to describe what appears significant to our participants. But in field notes we also record our emotions, feelings, values and beliefs. In field note data the two perspectives put forward by Blommaert and Hymes are reconciled.

Emerson et al. describe field notes as an act of inscription rather than description; inscription because field notes are authored accounts from a particular perspective rather than neutral descriptive accounts:

> In writing a fieldnote then, the ethnographer does not simply put happenings into words. Rather such writing is an interpretive process: it is the very first act of textualizing. Indeed, this often 'invisible' work - *writing ethnographic fieldnotes* - is the primordial textualization that creates a world on the page and ultimately shapes the final ethnographic, published text. (Emerson et al., 1995: 10-16)

The reference to 'primordial textualizations' points to the need for the researcher to get things down on the page without too much reflection. Delamont (2002) refers to field notes as hurried private writing, which is unsuitable for outsiders to read. Jackson (1990: 64) suggests that field notes are 'betwixt and between a personal diary and a scientific document'. A similar point is made by Emerson et al. below:

> Many seem to regard fieldnotes as a kind of backstage scribbling - a little bit dirty, a little bit suspect, not something to talk about too openly and specifically. Fieldnotes seem too revealingly personal, too messy and unfinished to be shown to any audience. For this reason, scholars do not have ready access to original, unedited fieldnotes but only to completed ethnographies with the selected, recorded fieldnotes they contain. As a result, how ethnographers write fieldnotes remains largely hidden and mysterious. (Emerson et al., 1995: ix)

The hidden nature of field notes has come in for some criticism. Silverman (2001) points out that observational studies rarely provide readers with anything other than brief, persuasive data extracts. Bryman (1988) notes that, unfortunately, typical ethnography rarely gives full versions of original field notes. He argues that 'these would be very helpful in order to allow the reader to formulate his or her own hunches about the perspective of the people who have been studied' (p. 77).

We share a similar concern and argue in this book that original field notes, like other transcripts, should be made available for scrutiny and as evidence. We use the case study chapters to illustrate this. Chapter 9 on writing up also contains further examples of how original field notes can be incorporated directly as evidence in scholarly work. Field notes represent not only the 'being there' (Geertz, 1988) of ethnographic research but provide evidence of the social tensions and relations in the field. Making them available means the reader can judge the link between data and argument and can also see linkages and lines of argument developed across data sets.

We started this section with a claim that in ethnography there is only really only one kind of observation – open observation. However, this does not mean that there is no structure to field notes or that organisation is not required to conduct effective observation. In fact ethnographic observation requires detailed planning and negotiation and a keen understanding of how information can be marshalled on the page. In terms of organisation, it is a good idea to write a timetable of observations, including as much detail of who will be observed and when/if the study is to be structured in that way. At the very least, letting participants know how long observation will go on for is essential. Whether field notes will be shared or exemplified at different points in the data collection schedule can also be helpful in allaying fears about observations.

In the field the ethnographic observation often starts with the researcher taking a wide angled view. This might mean that the researcher visits and observes as much as possible, taking notes about the people, social spaces and social practices in the site under investigation (including virtual sites). However, as time goes on and participants' beliefs, values and actions become more apparent, the researcher will look more intensively and repetitively at an action, site, person, group, or routine and ritual, and these areas will become the focus of the field notes.

Conducting observations and writing field notes

Field notes differ in gaze, length, emotional voice, structure, grammatical coherence and level of description. They may be long and detailed on first entering the field and become more succinct and brief over time. Early field notes may be full of wonder while later field notes may describe the mundane and routine. This is entirely acceptable, and even expected. Little information is available on how to write field notes as explained by Hammersley and Atkinson:

> The compilation of fieldnotes may appear to be a straightforward matter. However, like most aspects of intellectual craftsmanship, some care and attention to detail are prerequisites, and satisfactory note taking needs to be worked at. It is a skill demanding continual reassessment of purposes and priorities and of the costs and benefits of different strategies. Thus, the standard injunction, 'write down what you see and hear', glosses over a number of important issues. (Hammersley and Atkinson, 1983: 146)

There are several good sources for responding to the questions raised in the above quote (see Sanjeck, 1990; Emerson et al., 1995). These sources set out some of the conventions of field note writing. They describe the process of scribbles on the page to first typed-up drafts to polished analytic vignettes. There is also a plethora of terms for writing about observations and emotions while in the field. Despite the overlap in terms such as 'observational notes', 'field notes', 'researcher diary/journal', 'headnotes' and 'autoethnography', all of which describe the ethnographer watching, listening, feeling and 'being there', there are distinctions too. The differences can be quite important to the researcher who might use more than one of the above to distinguish elements of data collection and data analysis.

For example, Fiona makes a distinction between 'observational notes' (rough notes taken in the field) and her typed up, more reflective and analytically engaged, 'field notes'. Sara makes a distinction between her 'autoethnographic accounts', which she kept before she joined a larger team and which she viewed as more reflexive and personal, and her research diary, which focused much more on 'research processes'. For others the distinction is between a private and personal diary and a public set of field notes. This distinction is often linked to place. Whereas a diary can be written up at any time and any place during the research process, field notes are temporal accounts of time in the field and are linked to a particular time and context. Others do not even make this distinction and view their field notes as both diary and observational notes, adding detail to them whenever they wish. Nevertheless, despite the differences, most field notes are iterative and go through a series of changes from 'headnotes' made while in the field, to coherent documents, rid of spelling errors and polished for publication. Angela provides an example of this metamorphosis in her case study in which she exemplifies different drafts of field notes and analyses how they change over several drafts for different audiences. She shows how original field notes can be basic, written for the researcher's eyes only in shorthand and full of spelling errors, but later developed into polished texts used to support an analytic account.

Because field notes involve perception and interpretation, different descriptions of the same situation and event are possible. This is particularly noticeable when researchers work together in teams and is evident in the three field notes extracts below. They come from three researchers who visited the same event in 2003 in a Leicester complementary school, teaching Gujarati during weekday evenings (Creese et al., 2008). Arvind Bhatt, Angela Creese and Peter Martin together attended a prize-giving evening. It is not possible to produce the full set of field notes for each researcher due to their length. For example, Arvind's entry was 1340 words and Angela's and Peter's were around 750 each. Rather, we have selected a point in the evening which all three researchers commented on. This was when the administrator, Deepa, first addressed the parents and young people in the audience.

Arvind Bhatt

Deepa begins a prayer in Gujarati using the microphone. Hush begins to spread in the hall. She then makes a welcome speech in Gujarati and uses both the mike and the computer to project PowerPoint slides on the screen. The slides are bilingual in Gujarati and English, some are only in English. She explains in Gujarati that it is the 15th anniversary of the school and projects a slide in Gujarati only which displays the motto of the school. An English translation of the slide is projected next (speak Gujarati with pride . . . etc.). Deepa continues to speak in Gujarati. She is using formal register and is very fluent. This is in contrast to her usual use of English at other times in the past. It surprises me (pleasantly).

Angela Creese

Deepa makes for a very accomplished MC. Her fluency in Gujarati was apparent and I found myself registering surprise at this and at how much Gujarati was used throughout the evening. It makes the assemblies and classes more interesting in terms of the amount of English used. Deepa and some of the teachers clearly have a rationale for their choice of language in particular domains.

Peter Martin

The Prize Evening started bang on time at 6.30 (no whistle!). Very polished presentation from Deepa using colourful (and noisy) PowerPoint presentation. Did not take details of the slides but thought we could get a copy of the presentation. Slides outlined the present structure and history of the school. The constitution of the school was signed on 4.10.1988. After the initial slides in Gujarati, there was a switch to English.

There is a considerable overlap in these researcher accounts. The three short extracts are connected around the theme of language proficiency, language function and linguistic ecology. These themes were inherent in the project's research question which sought to understand the practices of multilingualism in the setting of complementary schools. All three researchers were focused on the language use, choice and proficiency of Deepa. They shared the same agenda. This initial research question directed their ethnographic gaze and served to remind them of why they were there and what they were looking at. Research questions can assist in focusing the researcher. Because commencing fieldwork can be overwhelming in terms of settling on a focal point, it is helpful to keep research questions to hand in both doing the observation and writing the field notes.

However, despite shared interest in the theme of language, the extracts show different levels of emotional attachment and these are reflected in the writing style and content of the researcher accounts. As the only bilingual researcher in the setting, Arvind commented authoritatively on both Gujarati and English in Deepa's presentation. Arvind was very much involved in Gujarati complementary schooling in Leicester and had been a long-time advocate of complementary schools and bilingual education. Angela and Peter were also interested in language but were not bilingual in Gujarati and were not involved in the Gujarati-speaking communities. In the field notes above, it is possible to read Angela's 'surprised' as qualitatively different from Arvind's surprise. One is much less emotionally invested in the setting than the other.

Field notes cannot avoid being evaluative: a language of description does not allow us to be neutral. Whatever we write down positions us in relation to what we observe in one way or other. All three researchers evaluated and commented on Deepa and her linguistic proficiency and performance. Arvind describes being 'pleasantly surprised'. Peter assesses Deepa as 'very polished' and Angela evaluates her as 'accomplished'. Emerson et al. describe choosing what to write down as both intuitive and empathetic, reflecting the ethnographer's sense of what is interesting or important to the people s/he is observing. However, in teams, ethnographer researchers are also aligning and disaligning themselves with others in the team (Creese et al., 2006).

The extracts we have presented above show three researchers commenting on the same phenomenon, Deepa's language use. However, in each of the fuller set of researchers' field note entries for that evening there was a good deal of variation, with each pursuing different lines of enquiry and interest. As well as being data for analysis, field notes provide a distinctive resource for preserving experience close to the moment of occurrence and for also recording changes in focus. We can return to field notes to conjure up the experience again, reflect on it, and seek a deeper understanding of the actions and practices that occurred during that time and place.

Analysing field notes

Field notes describe 'the units, criteria, and patterning of a community' (Hornberger, 1995: 238). While in the field, these units and patterns may not be immediately obvious. We are working hard to get as much down as possible. As Emerson et al. suggest:

> In writing fieldnotes, ethnographers have as their primary goal description rather than analysis. But these contrasting terms - description and analysis - refer more to recognized kinds of writing than to separate cognitive activities. In that sense, writing fieldnotes is a process of 'analysis-in-description'. Indeed, all descriptions are selective, purposed, angled, voiced, because they are authored. (Emerson et al., 1995: 105-6)

On departure from the field and after an opportunity to prepare the data for analysis, these patterns need to be identified usually through coding. At this stage researchers get the opportunity to look at their own and sometimes others' field notes again, this time with a little distance and detachment. Several processes are going on at this point. The researcher will first need to organise the notes, usually by date but with other variations possible. Data are made ready by creating an inventory of data sources and tagged for essential information such as place, time, researcher and number of drafts. The different drafts, including scribbles, typed-up versions and analytical vignettes and memos may be collated together for ease of reference. Once the data have been collated the researcher is able to start reading through the complete set of notes. This reading provides an opportunity to reflect on whether the original research questions are in alignment with the researcher's observations or if there is evidence of new foci emerging. If this is the case, it may be that new research questions are required. Should this happen, the researcher needs to make a note of any shifts so they can be included in methodological accounts later in the process. At this reading-through stage there is also an opportunity for the researcher to consider his or her own positioning in the research.

After a first complete read-through, a second-read through begins in which the researcher starts to thematically code or categorise the data. Erickson (2004a) suggests being comprehensive in the kinds of questions we ask of our field notes at this stage, such as:

- What are the different kinds of things going on here?
- What are the biggest differences?
- What are the biggest shifts in activity within the interactional occasion?

Themes must emerge from the field note descriptions and not be imposed by existing frameworks. Erickson counsels against focusing too small and too early and suggests looking at the bigger units of meaning. For example, rather than looking at the utterance or grammatical constituents at the sentence level he suggests looking for routines and repeated practices. In linguistic anthropology, Wortham (2003: 18) reminds us: 'Instead of imposing outsider categories, linguistic anthropology induces analytic categories that participants either articulate or presuppose in their action, and it insists on evidence that participants themselves are presupposing categories central to the analysis'.

A third reading of the field notes reduces categories by collapsing data further into manageable units. At this point the researcher is looking for connections between categories. The researcher should be linking themes to field note quotes. When it comes to publication, finding an appropriate field note quote will add rich data to the line of argument and so a good referencing system is very helpful here. Researchers adopt different procedures for collecting the categories together such as spray diagrams, analytic vignettes or qualitative software. We provide specific examples of all stages of field note analysis in the case study chapters and in Chapter 9.

A thematic analysis of field notes and other data sets should mean you feel ready to begin tentatively talking about findings. At this point 'talking about' means engaging with a fairly limited audience – probably a research group, peers or a supervisor. But nonetheless, after trawling your data you should be settling on some ideas you wish to develop further. This is a significant stage of the research because it is time to address the connection between description and theory. While we believe analysis and theory go hand in hand throughout the whole process of conducting a linguistic ethnography (see 'Analysing interactional data' below), there is a point where data description must connect explicitly with theory. If this fails to happen, the research collapses into mere description and will not reach the standards of rigour required in research. While a descriptive analysis may be an important first move used to illustrate the connection between theme and data, a further and crucial stage is required.

Throughout the research you will have been reading theory, others' empirical investigations and methodological literature. You may also have been attending conferences, taking part in seminars, classes, research meetings and tutorials. All of this activity prepares you well to make the jump from descriptive accounts of your data to theoretical accounts of your data. This process doesn't usually happen in a one-off eureka moment but rather gradually through trying out different theoretical and empirical frameworks to explain your data. For example, you might be reading Blommaert's (2007b) work on scale, or Goffman's (1981) work on footing or frame analysis, or Hornberger's (2002) work on the continua of biliteracy. It may be that one of these resonates with your thematic analysis and encourages you to dig deeper. Importantly, your readings of the research literature should help you to better explain and explicate your data. A theoretically informed analysis moves you from a descriptive analysis of a context you know well to an engagement with other theoretical frameworks used by a wider community of scholars. In other words, theory lifts description to explanation through evaluating data through the lens of existing frameworks.

Such analytical frameworks may vary from well-established theoretical paradigms to specific empirical studies. The important thing is to make the connection between the literature and your own work through trying out and finally settling on a range of published resources which connect your study to the larger academic community and help to explain your data more robustly. In linguistic ethnography, an interest in discourse often drives the kind of theoretical resources we end up drawing on. Discourse analytic (DA) frameworks themselves draw on a wide range of cultural (e.g. Stuart Hall), social (e.g. Pierre Bourdieu), linguistic (e.g. Monica Heller) and literary theory (e.g. Mikhail Bakhtin), with each DA framework itself connecting to theory and bringing sets of tools for discursive analysis.

INTERACTIONAL DATA AS EVIDENCE IN LINGUISTIC ETHNOGRAPHY

Types of interactional data

Interactional data comprise recordings of research participants as they go about their daily practices. The recordings can be both audio and video. We refer to both in this section but draw mostly on our experiences of working with audio.

There are as many types of interactional data types as there are contexts. However, we would like to distinguish between interactional data which is private and interactional data which is in some way public, what Goffman (1981) calls a platform event. For platform events, there is some kind of audience. Fiona's interactional data could be classified as coming from a platform event. She recorded the interactions of trainees and trainers in the feedback conference, an activity in which participants had particular roles and in which talk was 'performed' for the overhearers as well as the interlocutor. Much classroom data which is of interest to many researchers in linguistic ethnography could be classified as coming from

a platform event. So too does much professional discourse, such as business meetings (indeed, the audience may be extensive for these events given the centrality of minutes to many business meetings).

In other cases, talk is a private affair, for the ears of others in the conversation only. The students in Angela's study, for example, recorded conversations that took part in homes and break times in the complementary school and these data complemented those interactions recorded in the classroom setting. Rampton (2006) too recorded private conversations held by students during lessons as well as in break times. Frances recorded police officers interviewing witnesses: these interactions, not normally recorded, could also be classified as private.

Collecting interactional data

Interactional data is normally collected using a small recording device with an internal microphone, such as a mobile phone, or a video camera. These devices are either operated by the researcher or by the participants themselves. Often it is sufficient to put the recording device next to the participants who are to be recorded and then to switch the device on. However, if, like Angela, you want to collect private interactions, it is better to ensure that each speaker has a recording device and is individually 'mic-ed up', which is better done at the beginning of the data collection period. Static video cameras, however, are not such a good idea as you risk missing important shots as participants move in and out of the picture. Furthermore, it is very difficult to watch footage shot with a static camera. Instead, the researcher or assistant should operate the video camera, varying the shot when appropriate.

It could be said that once a microphone is present, all interactions become platform events as there is an audience for the interaction in addition to those present. This reality also has ramifications for the data collected as participants may behave in different ways from usual. Stubbs (1983) argued that because being studied 'is not a normal situation for most people', it is likely that, 'in extraordinary situations people produce extraordinary language' (p. 225). In other words, language produced is not natural.

Both Angela and Fiona's data show a number of occasions where participants refer directly to the recording devices, as in the following extract from Fiona's data. The trainer is admitting to the trainees that she has misunderstood an activity that T1 did in his class:

Extract 4

1. Trainer: Oh never mind then never mind I thought they were different
2.   oh so that was just for drilling
3. T1:   Yeah
4. Trainer: Oh well then that's fine yeah

```
           [
5.   T1:       They were all when when when they they were
6.             presented with the sheets it was just like a version () of all of this
7.   Trainer:  Oh that's fine sorry I thought they were different okay well
8.             done strike that erm
9.   T2:       From the record
10.  Trainer:  From the records yes ((laughs))
11.  T2:       From the tape
12.  Trainer:  ((Laughs)) erm (.)
```

When the trainer realises she has made a mistake, she apologises and moves to withdraw her criticism when she says in line 8 'strike that erm'. This legal phrase is completed by T2 when she adds in line 9 'from the record', which the trainer reiterates and positively evaluates, 'from the records yes' (line 10). At this point, T2 jokily suggests that the criticism should also be wiped 'from the tape' (line 11), directly admitting the recording of the feedback into the discussion. The trainer responds to this by laughing.

The extract is interesting as it occurs in the middle of the feedback session over half way through the course. It might be expected that by this point in the research process and the particular feedback conference that the recording device would have been forgotten by the participants. However, T2 clearly orients to the device. Speer and Hutchby (2003) argue that rather than seeing this orientation as a problem, testifying to the inauthenticity of the data (cf. Stubbs, 1983), it should, 'be seen in its own terms: as "natural interaction involving a tape recorder"' (p. 318) and the analyst's attention should be drawn to 'the event as it unfolds, rather than wondering about some missing "more natural" event that would otherwise have taken place' (p. 318). The question then becomes 'why does T2 mention the recording at this point?' rather than 'are these data authentic?' (Fiona's take on this is that through making a play on words, T2 helps manage a problematic situation in which the trainer's face is threatened. Making light of a situation through linguistic play is a feature of T2's talk in the feedback data.) Taking this analytic perspective allows the researcher to acknowledge that recording interactions, like writing field notes, is not a neutral activity but one which helps to constitute the participants and their talk. As Speer and Hutchby contend, recording devices are 'bound up in the very constitution of the supposedly pristine world to which researchers wish to gain unmediated access' (p. 334).

Like most researchers, there are times when we would prefer that the presence of the microphone (or the observer) was ignored as much as possible. We have found that adhering to a few basic principles can be helpful in this regard. If participants are used to being recorded, if their practices are mundane, and if the recording device is unobtrusive, they are less likely to be distracted by it. It is also helpful to build up a relationship with participants before recording if possible. Frances, for example, only began recording after spending a good deal of time negotiating her way into the field and becoming comfortable with the staff involved in delivering information about rights.

If participants are happy to have their interactions recorded, the question becomes what to record. Some researchers decide on the 'as much as possible' approach. This has real implications for data analysis, however, as huge amounts of recorded data require huge amounts of analytic time, not least in terms of listening and transcribing (see Frances's case study for a description of this process). It is more efficient to plan recordings according to the research questions which guide the study. In Angela's case, for example, interactions are not recorded in the participants' regular high school classes, not because this was not a possibility but because the focus of the study was the complementary school and the linguistic practices therein. As Erickson (2004b) has so elegantly demonstrated in his chapter, 'Seventy-five dollars goes in one day', it is not usually the amount of interactional data that makes a case but its analysis. It is to analysis that we now turn.

Analysis of interactional data

Once the interactional data have been collected and stored, the researcher must decide how to analyse them. This is a very difficult process to describe as it is never linear or straightforward. What we offer here are some broad guidelines to support the initial stages. Other examples can be found in the case study chapters which follow.

For most researchers, the first stage of analysis will be listening/viewing over and over again. This might be accompanied by transcribing, but not necessarily. The purpose of this first stage generally is to identify themes. Some researchers have called this 'unmotivated looking' (Psathas, 1995) but in fact it is usual to approach the data with some ideas about what you are interested in, drawing on your research questions. Nonetheless, it is very important at this stage to be open to the data and allow them to speak to you. In Angela's case study, for example, she describes how the theme of 'aspiration' emerged, despite the research team not having identified this area for attention.

Another way to begin an analysis of interactional data is to identify what Agar (2008) calls 'rich points' (p. 31). Rich points are sections of data which stand out as being unusual in the interaction in some way, which seem to the researcher different or difficult to understand. Carey Jewitt, whose work with educational multimodal data has been extremely influential (see, for example, 2008), explained that she would watch hours of classroom footage with her team until something in the data caught their collective analytic eye. These rich points then became their focus (personal communication). Snell and Lefstein (2012) describe how a change in a teacher's approach to teaching writing became for them 'a critical case' (p. 10) as it threw into relief everyday practices of teaching writing. This 'X-factor episode' (p. 10) became the focus of their interest.

Drawing on a theoretical framework can also help the researcher to begin analysing interactional data. These theoretical frameworks are what Sara in her case study (drawing on Blumer, 1954, and Rampton et al., 2004) calls 'sensitizing concepts'. They guide the researcher in looking in particular directions rather than 'provid[ing] prescriptions of what to see' (Snell and Lefstein, 2012: 11, citing Blumer, 1954: 7).

In her study, Fiona draws on the theoretical concept of face (Goffman, 1967; Arundale, 2006, 2010) to help her to uncover the developing relationships between the trainers and trainees. She examines the interactions on a turn-by-turn basis, highlighting power shifts, contestations, agreements and capitulations. For example, in the following extract, the trainer uses hedging to reduce the force of the criticism she is making:

Extract 5

Tr: think it would have been nice to have seen a little practice stage just straight after your pronunciation stage just just where they had say part of the the idiom and on a card and they just you know I mean it could have been as simple as just saying the idiom to each other with the pronunciation stressing

T1: Yeah

An unpacked version of this criticism would be, 'have a practice stage after the pronunciation stage'. The question for Fiona was why did trainers consistently hedge criticisms and what happened when they did not? Her rich points then became those where the norms of delivering criticism with hedging were disregarded, as in the following example:

Extract 6

Tr: If you a:sk the learners (..) if you actually a:sk the learners and you had some feedback from them and you were doing a lesson where there was the opportunity for students to te:ll you what they felt about the lesson () and they said that () fine () but you're not ba:sing it on that at the moment you're ba:sing it on your **own** (.) ideas that you are coming into the class with and that is not appropriate

Here, the trainer's criticism is what Brown and Levinson (1987) call 'bald onrecord' (p. 75). The trainee is told that what he/she did was not appropriate. Using the concept of face helped Fiona to focus on the contextual circumstances that led to this exchange.

One of Angela's sensitising concepts is Mikhail Bakhtin's theoretical and practical notion of 'heteroglossia' (1981), which helps her to understand the social, political, and historical implications of bilingualism in practice. Heteroglossia, as conceived by Bakhtin (1981), describes the diverse and constantly changing discourses which speakers bring to interaction and the tensions and conflicts that these discourses engender. An heteroglossic analysis, therefore, understands linguistic diversity not merely as the co-existence of discrete linguistic systems, but as participation in an historical flow of social relationships, struggles and meanings. When research team meetings are examined through the lens of heteroglossia, competing voices emerge as salient, as does the pervasiveness of reported speech as researchers represent the participants with whom they are working (Creese and Blackledge, 2012). In the following extract, for example, one of the researchers is talking about the students in the complementary school in which he is carrying out his research. The students are learning Turkish:

Extract 7

Researcher: I think we all face as teachers why are we learning this sir, why, why do we need these languages for, and as with Chinese you can say well look you might make good money out out of this in the future, but you can't use this in every language, they will say no, English is enough so

The value of heteroglossia can be seen when analysing the researcher's's narrative. First, it is played out as a dramatic interaction of several voices. Reasearcher voices the students as they contest the value of learning the community language. Then teachers of 'Chinese' are voiced, as they argue for the economic value of language learning. However, the researcher then represents the voices of the students (of languages other than Chinese), when she says 'no, English is enough', representing the resistance of the children to learning Turkish, simultaneously situating the localised voices of students in Manchester and London in the context of global economics: 'Chinese' has value as a language of the global economy, whereas Turkish does not. In a short utterance, researcher plays out the debate in the ventriloquated voices of the protagonists and heteroglossia as a sensitising concept allows us to recognise this ventroliquation.

An approach to analysing interactional data which has proved productive for a number of researchers in linguistic ethnography is Conversation Analysis. First developed in the 1960s as a way to 'investigate social order as it was produced through the practices of everyday talk' (Liddicoat, 2011: 4, cited in Paltridge, 2012: 90), CA is now used to analyse all kinds of spoken interaction, from institutional discourse (see, for example, Drew and Heritage, 1992) to the talk of second language learners and their teachers (see Walsh, 2011). Although conversation analysts are often accused of epistemological absolutism (see Baxter, 2002), other researchers are less rigid in their approach, 'borrowing' tools from CA and using these to investigate their own data (see Paltridge, 2012).

In CA, naturally occurring talk must always be used and this (not the transcription) constitutes the 'data' (Hutchby and Wooffitt, 1998). Researchers must move from the data to the hypothesis rather than the other way around, and the focus must be on sequences rather than on isolated turns or utterances (Hutchby and Wooffitt, 1998). A defining feature of CA is that it sees interaction as structurally organised: each speaking turn relates to what has gone before and anticipates what will follow. Talk is patterned and these patterns can be labelled. The value of such labelling is that it allows the analyst to see how conversation is ordered and can account structurally for conversational breakdowns or 'troubles'.

As a result of 'empirically based accounts of the observable conversational behaviours of participants' (Markee, 2005: 355), CA studies have uncovered a number of formal features of talk such as turn taking, pausing, latching, and pre-ferred and dispreferred second part pairs, amongst other things (for guidance on doing CA, see Ten Have's, 2007, excellent introduction). These formal features provide a useful starting point when examining both mundane conversation and institutional talk, which is the focus of both Fiona and Frances's research. However, as Richards (2006) argues, 'the emphasis in the analysis ... is not on how interactants obey the relevant rules, but on how they jointly construct the conver-sation and their shared understanding of what is happening in it' (p. 13). Analysts adopting a CA approach must, then, pay attention to how talk unfolds and not examine utterances in isolation. Like Bucholtz (2003) and Moerman (1988), Fiona and Frances would also argue that uncovering interactants' shared understandings of what is happening in the talk can be supported by drawing on ethnographic data, and this is what they both do.

CA begins with examining talk on a turn-by-turn basis, relating each utterance to what has gone before and what comes immediately after. In order to do so, spoken interaction is very carefully transcribed, including information about pausing, interruption and interactional feedback, with 'a ferocious attention to detail that not all researchers can muster' (Richards, 2003: 28). This is because the construction of talk provides as much information about meaning and context as its content.

Many linguistic ethnographers are attracted to CA because its focus on linguistic form in interaction when combined with ethnographic detail can add to analytical rigour. When reporting findings, the researcher can provide linguistic evidence for the claims he/she makes, addressing the criticism often directed at ethnographic work that it is overly reliant on the researcher's interpretation of the research site. It also provides a set of relevant rules for how people behave in conversation; breaking these rules alerts the analyst to a trouble spot that might bear further investigation. However, learning to do CA is a long and continuous process. While a range of books guide the analyst in how to gather and transcribe data and some basic things worthy of attention (e.g. turn taking), there is no substitute for dis-cussing data with others, particularly those who have expertise.

Reflexivity and interactional data

As we have shown, interaction is an important data source for many involved in linguistic ethnographic research. For some, the status of interactional data is even greater: they form the 'core' data, with data such as field notes, interviews, texts and artefacts playing a 'supplementary' role (see Lefstein and Isreal, in press). To these researchers, supplementary data help to contextualise the interactional data but are not accorded the same level of analytic attention.

We do not hold this view. There are a number of reasons for this. First, we believe that linguistic ethnography's strength derives from its support of combining different data collection and analysis processes rather than separating them out. Indeed, it is in combining the approaches that robust and nuanced findings emerge; each data set works with and for the other data sets so that it is difficult to imagine how findings could be arrived at without having gone through this process (see the case studies for how this works in practice, and also Chapter 9). Second, not all involved in linguistic ethnography collect interactional data: Sara does not have recordings of think tanks' meetings, for example, in her case study. Suggesting that interactional data are the core data problematises Sara's work, although we believe it to be robustly linguistic ethnographic. Finally, we suspect that this focus on interactional data as core comes from researchers' antecedents. Many coming from a background in applied linguistics research, where talk is a central concern, will already be comfortable with analysing interactional data. For them, ethnographic approaches are 'useful for contextualizing the event but not worthy of the same level of attention as the core, recorded data' (Lefstein and Isreal, in press).

On the other hand, the centrality of observation to researchers coming to linguistic ethnography from ethnographic antecedents cannot be over-emphasised and recorded talk will never take the place of immersion in the field. For these researchers context is a complex achievement 'emerging, interactionally grounded' (Auer, 1996: 45) and open to interpretation, for which observation is required not merely desired.

Luckily, we view these tensions between different researchers as to the status of data as productive rather than problematic. They allow us to pursue theoretical discussions about what linguistic ethnography is (and isn't) and how researchers working under this umbrella wish to be seen. We return to this important debate in Chapter 10.

WRITTEN TEXTS AS EVIDENCE IN LINGUISTIC ETHNOGRAPHY

Text types

Like interactional data, there is no limit to the type of texts that are admissible as data in linguistic ethnography. In the case studies, policy documents, diary entries, police rights notices, annual reports, reviews and charity commission submissions are all analysed. Taken with interactional data/interviews/field notes/interactions/ photographs, written texts can serve to provide another perspective on the site under scrutiny, and producing analytic insights that might not otherwise be possible.

One type of text common in linguistic ethnography is that produced by research participants. For example, Sara used a personal diary from her time during her employment at a think tank to throw light on think tank practices as part of a process of autoethnography. The entries proved vital in enabling her to examine and retell events and activities in order to generate new insights and understand broader social phenomena around think tanks' work. In a different study to the one presented in this volume, Angela reported on two texts produced by students in a London secondary school (Creese, 2003). The first text accused the school of racism; the second challenged this interpretation. Creese uses the letters and the interactions occurring around them, recorded as field notes, to show how teachers and students negotiate and contest institutionality and racism.

For researchers taking a linguistic ethnographic perspective in literacy studies (see, for example, Tusting, 2010; Lillis, 2008) written texts and people's practices around these texts are as central as interactional data or ethnographic data (Tusting, in press), as they not only provide evidence of how cultures and institutions are produced and reproduced but also uncover how powerful discourses are circulated and accepted. For these researchers, any written texts with which participants interact are valuable and can support development of understanding of 'the social, cultural, material, institutional, and ideological contexts of literacy' (Warriner, 2013: 532).

Collecting texts

Going into the field you may know the written texts and artefacts that interest you. If these are participant generated texts, you will need to find a way to collect them which does not inconvenience the writers or audiences. Having access to a scanner or copier will ensure that texts are returned to their owners quickly. If the texts are digitally produced, participants might be willing to email them or place them in a virtual cloud. Whichever, it is important to remember who owns the texts and to check first that these people are willing to share them with you.

Ethnographers usually collect whatever is available and in use. Blommaert's advice is to 'take everything that closely or remotely looks of interest' as 'even if it doesn't tell you much on the spot, it can always become a very relevant bit of data later on' (2006: 53). Chilton (2012) describes how she systematically gathered texts in her research on family literacy, language and numeracy programme. She argued that because talk is often mediated by texts, the ethnographer needs a systematic approach to collecting and organising this data especially to make clear the connections between the data sets. Chilton collected 72 texts during her fieldwork which she went on to subject to categorisation. She ended up with four text categories: teaching, assessment, providing information and providing evidence. These can be seen in the table Chilton produced of texts collected and analysed (2012: 112), shown in Figure 2.3.

Documents collected – categorised by use

Document	No.	Teaching	Assessment	Providing information	Providing evidence
				Administration	
Letter to parents – offering a place	1			✓	
Family Learning leaflet	1			✓	
Register (parents)	1				✓
Register (children)	1				✓
Scheme of Work (parents) – draft and final versions	2				✓
Scheme of Work (children) – final version	1				✓
Tutor's Induction Checklist & Learner Confirmation	1				✓
Family Literacy course details sheet	1			✓	
Enrolment Form	1				✓
Equality and Diversity Statement	1			✓	✓
Learning Charter bookmark	1			✓	✓
Evidence for Accreditation – Demonstrating Speaking and Listening Skills – Record Sheets (2)	2		✓		
Worksheets (18) – locally produced (4); externally produced (14)	18	✓	✓		
Handouts (16) – locally produced (2); externally produced (11); realia (3)	16	✓			
Activity sheets (for parents to do with children) (4)	4	✓			
Accreditation evidence sheets (9)	9		✓		(✓) free writing
Individual Learning Plans	1				✓
Parenting Strategy Parent/Carer Consultation	1				
Photographic Consent Form	1				✓
Skills for Life Initial Assessment (2)	2				✓
Weekly sessions reminder (informing parents what has been covered each week)	1				✓
Information, Advice and Guidance Information	1			✓	✓
End of Course Review	1				✓
End of Course Evaluation Form	1				✓
Summary of Children's Evidence	1				✓
Tutor's Self-assessment Report	1				✓
Total	72				

Figure 2.3 Texts collected by Elizabeth Chilton in the field

A third kind of text you might collect is that written by participants for the researcher's benefit. For a project on the experiences of newly arrived international students, for example, Fiona and her colleague, Sue Garton, asked a number of students to keep a blog detailing encounters in which they used English (Copland and Garton, 2011). Originally, they were concerned that participants would not complete the blogs as there was no extrinsic motivation for them to do so. However, a large number of the potential participants took part and completed blogs regularly and fully. In retrospect, Fiona and Sue think that the blog writing acted as a support for newly arrived students, through recognising that anxiety about English language use was common and providing a platform for the students to voice their concerns. In other words, the participants benefitted from the blog writing. As a principle for eliciting written texts, this is not a bad one. If the participant can see some intrinsic meaning in the text production, outside its value as data, then both the participant and the researcher will gain.

Analysing texts

The approach to text analysis will depend to some extent on the number of texts available. If these are copious, corpus analysis can be powerful. Corpus analysis is a relatively recent analytic approach requiring a number of texts (the corpus) to be inputted into a computer software package, which can then run a number of analytic programmes depending on the focus of the research. A common application of corpus analysis is to identify the frequency of a word or phrase in the texts, which indicates, for example, its importance. This approach develops the researcher's understanding of language patterning in the genre under scrutiny, which provides vital information on how texts are constructed and how ideas are represented.

A second application of corpus analysis, and one more pertinent to the concerns of discourse analysis in linguistic ethnography, is to identify 'recurring linguistic features, which can be examined in their immediate linguistic contexts' (O'Keefe and Walsh, 2012: 160). This is done through conducting a KWIC (Key Word in Context) analysis, often called a concordance line. In this process, all instances of a key word are extracted from the text(s) under scrutiny and given in order. The key word is presented in the centre of each line and a specified number of words (usually 4 or 5) precedes and proceeds.

Sara used a KWIC analysis of the texts she collected for her case study. Using the software *Antconc*, she produced a KWIC analysis for *independent* as shown in Figure 2.4 (please note that in order to preserve anonymity, some sections of the screen shot are covered).

As Sara shows in her case study, the corpus analysis was useful in two ways. First, it allowed her to hone in on how particular words and phrases were used by think tanks through uncovering what she calls 'prominent emphases'. Second, the analysis complemented the more conventional datasets of documents, diary

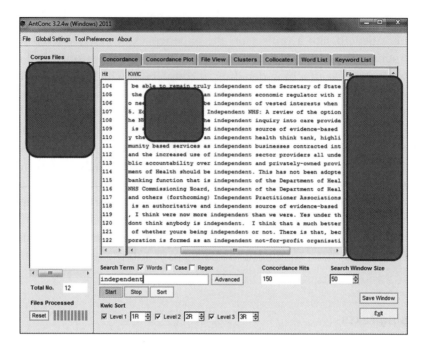

Figure 2.4 KWIC analysis of 'independent'

entries and interview transcripts, allowing her to move between them to examine the 'language, activities and settings of think tanks' work'.

Written texts can also be analysed using the notion of sensitising concepts introduced in the section on analysing interactional data. Sara used this approach with the policy documents produced by the think tanks, drawing on the Goffmanian notion of front and back stage (1959), and the concepts of sacred and profane language (Degeling, 1996). In the front stage, language is 'sacred' in that it is fixed, formal and modernist. It 'relates to claimed values which players share' (Degeling, 1996: 111). In the back stage, language is 'profane' in its informality, idomaticity and vagueness. It includes 'the selective use and release of information; agenda setting; mobilisation of bias, and efforts by participants to build coalition of support behind their specific interests and concerns' (p. 111).

Sara shows how policy is formally presented front stage in written texts using 'sacred' language. Back stage, away from the public eye, profane language is used to persuade and cajole and importantly 'to open up potential for negotiation about health policy and how this policy is negotiated and discussed'.

Reflexivity and written texts

Written text analysis often comes under the sphere of discourse analysis and there are many excellent guides to a range of analytic frameworks in this tradition (see, for example, Gee and Handford, 2012; Paltridge, 2012). However, picking a framework which seems to best suit the text(s) under consideration needs to be done with care. Cook (2011) argues that discourse analysis is not merely linguistic analysis but rather concerned with 'all elements and processes which contribute to communication' (p. 431). These include the text, the cultural context of language use and the psychological context of language use (see too Paltridge, 2012). Indeed, he suggests that in their joint focus on language and context, discourse analysis and linguistic ethnography could be synonymous (p. 437). We certainly agree with Cook that discourse analysis is no longer clearly identifiable with a single theory or method of analysis. However, we also feel that its long association with a focus on text, its lack of early ethnographic antecedents and, as Cook mentions, a tendency (albeit traditional) to make a distinction between text and context, mean that it remains distinct from linguistic ethnography, in concept if not reality. Indeed, with Cook we believe that discourse analysis has lost its traditional meaning and that it is now, 'so built into the fabric of applied linguistics that any analysis of language in use is discourse analysis of some kind' (p. 440): it has become a victim of its own success. Nonetheless, when exploring discourse analytic frameworks, researchers are advised to consider the epistemological underpinnings of each approach and to be aware of how each treats text, and the cultural and psychological contexts of use. These will need to be addressed in any research methods section.

CONCLUDING COMMENTS

In this chapter we have taken four data sets common in linguistic ethnography and explored how they might be collected, analysed and discussed. In doing so we are aware that we have not attended to other data sets which researchers have found valuable in doing linguistic ethnographic work, such as digital texts, film and photography. However, we hope that the approaches to data collection and analysis explored here might have relevance for these areas and be useful to researchers working with these kinds of data.

KEY READINGS

Blommaert, J. (2005) *Discourse*. Cambridge: Cambridge University Press.

Garton, S. and Copland, F. (2010) 'I like this interview, I get cakes and cats!': the effect of prior relationships on interview talk', *Qualitative Research*, 10(5): 1–19.

Hammersley, M. (2003) 'Conversation analysis and discourse analysis: methods or paradigms?', *Discourse and Society*, 14(6): 751–81.

Rampton, B. (2007a) 'Neo-Hymesian linguistic ethnography in the United Kingdom', *Journal of Sociolinguistics*, 11(5): 584–607.

II

Doing Research in Linguistic Ethnography: Building the Case

THREE

Case Study One: Reflexivity, Voice and Representation in Linguistic Ethnography

Angela Creese

SETTING THE CONTEXT OF THE STUDY: BACKGROUND INFORMATION, RESEARCH QUESTIONS AND FINDINGS

Over the years, one of the central research aims I have pursued in investigating multilingualism has been methodological. This means my interest has been partly in investigating the investigation. This kind of reflexivity is usual in ethnography where it is common practice for researchers to describe the tensions they face in the field and their reconciliation of contradictions encountered. This chapter describes processes of reflexivity in a team of ethnographers who were funded to research the multilingual practices of young people in and around community-led language schools. I describe the practices and routines we as a team have established for making reflexivity a regular point of consideration in our ethnography, particularly in the analysis phase. I talk about the iterative practices of individual researchers as we collected and pooled data and jointly constructed arguments in a team. Our different experiences, histories, and voices are constituted in and through team dynamics and in the kind of research tasks and outputs we set ourselves. My account describes our team's approach to analysis across our data sets. In order to achieve this I will be discussing some of the methodological approaches we have developed for working in multilingual ethnographic teams.

It is worth acknowledging at the beginning of this chapter that not everyone has the possibility of working in a research team. Within the academy it is still the lone researcher's ethnographic journey which is the default position of this research design and several metaphors exist including the 'the lone adventurer'

(Salzman, 1989), 'lone ranger' (Erickson and Stull, 1998) or 'lone wolf' (Mitteness and Barker, 2004) to describe such a process. However, research councils increasingly look to fund teams of researchers to investigate social issues and I have gained from working with groups of researchers and the range of experiences and histories they bring to team work. Indeed, working in teams has become my default mode of doing linguistic ethnographic research. Because of this, a feature of our grant applications seeks answers to processes of knowledge construction in multilingual teams and it is worth describing these processes because the journey from single ethnography to team ethnography is not without issue.

Although this is a single authored chapter, I will be drawing on my experiences of working with others and will make 'voice' both a descriptive and analytical category in my discussion of team processes. The individual voices of the researchers became an important resource in the interpretation, analysis and writing up of data. As such, the researchers' voices were as crucial to the generation of knowledge as the research subjects themselves. And because of this I believe it is worth paying detailed attention to the construction of knowledge when working in teams.

Research aims and findings

The project I report on here is the UK case study of a larger European grant[1] on which I was employed as a field researcher. A full report can be found in Blackledge et al. (in press). Each European case study looked at a different educational site. The UK Birmingham case study investigated Panjabi complementary schools which are community-run, often small-scale organisations staffed by community groups for the teaching of Panjabi. The school we worked in met on Saturdays in two sites. The Birmingham case study is a continuation of our research on complementary schools first started in 2002 and which has continued uninterrupted into 2014 (Creese and Martin, 2003; Blackledge and Creese, 2010; Blackledge et al., in press). Our most recent study set out to meet five objectives and these are described below. Under each project objective a short summary of the project's findings are provided:

- *We set out to investigate the range of language and literacy practices of multilingual young people in four European settings.* A major finding of the project was the need for new conceptualisations of language to describe and explain the linguistic practices of our participants. We found the concept of 'languages' was not adequate to capture the resourcefulness of people to respond to socially diverse and rapidly changing social landscapes. We established that the mixing of

[1] Adrian Blackledge (PI) with Co-investigators, Jan Blommaert, Jens Normann Jorgensen and Jarmo Lainio. Researchers: Angela Creese, Liva Hyttel-Sørensen, Carla Jonsson, Kasper Juffermans, Sjaak Kroon, Jinling Li, Marilyn Martin-Jones, Anu Muhonen, Lamies Nassri and Jaspreet Kaur Takhi, *Investigating Discourses of Inheritance and Identity in Four Multilingual European Settings* (AHRC/ Humanities in the European Research Area, 09-HERA-JRP-CD-FP-051) 2010-12.

languages – 'polylanguaging', or 'translanguaging' – was not problematic, but was rather 'natural' and 'automatic'. For example in classroom language learning contexts teachers adopted a pedagogy which included transliteration, translanguaging, and translation to respond to the bilingual lives of their students and we observed that this approach was viewed positively.

- *A second aim was to explore the cultural and social significance of language and literacy practices of multilingual young people in four European settings.* To respond to this aim we started not by asking 'who is speaking what language to whom' but rather what linguistic resources were being deployed, and why. In addressing this aim we became very interested in the use of linguistic signs and what they pointed to in terms of their historical and social significance. Following the work of Bakhtin (1981) and Silverstein (1976) we looked at how signs were put to use by our participants and observed how even the use and interpretation of small linguistic signs could have large social consequences for participants. We saw this in the classroom where small differences in pronunciation empowered some teachers' practices while disempowering others' (Creese et al., 2014).

- *A third aim we set out to investigate was how the language and literacy practices of multilingual young people were used to negotiate inheritance and identities.* One of our main findings in relation to this aim was about authenticity in relation to our participants' interpretation of culture and heritage. Later in this chapter I illustrate how high educational achievement became an identifiable cultural theme in the interactions of young people and teachers. Being a highly successful student, attending the 'best schools' and seeking well-paid professional employment was an identity position to which our key participants aspired. We also saw the endorsement of aspiration in the institutional discourse of the Panjabi complementary school which spoke of such aspiration as cultural heritage.

- *A fourth aim, and one which prompted this case study chapter, was to develop innovative, multisite, ethnographic team methodologies using interlocking case studies across national, social, cultural and linguistic contexts.* This aim required us to document and engage in collective critical reflexivity in our linguistic ethnographic accounts and multilingual team approaches. We have argued that multi-site, multilingual, ethnographic investigation enabled us to develop understandings of contemporary social, cultural, economic and political processes from multiple perspectives. This chapter serves to illustrate some of these methodological processes.

- *A fifth aim set out to contribute to policy and practice in the inclusion of non-national minority languages in the wider European educational agenda.* We believe our research findings have implications for European policymakers in the areas of education, community relations, international affairs and public opinion. As local, national, and European governments seek to tailor policy to the needs of individuals and groups, they need to understand people's identities not in terms of apparent or visible categories, but rather as emic positions which are self-identified, dynamic and negotiable.

RESEARCH DESIGN

The Birmingham case study team comprised of three researchers: Jaspreet Kaur Takhi (JKT) employed as a field researcher on a full-time fixed-term contract; Adrian Blackledge (AB) who was also project leader for the much larger European team of 14 researchers; and Angela Creese (AC), employed as a field researcher. Angela and Adrian both had tenured faculty positions. As a team we worked closely with teachers and administrators throughout the project and after it ended. To this day we retain a good relationship with the Panjabi complementary school in Birmingham and are invited to provide in-sessional activities for staff and to visit for further research. The data collection stage of the project was divided into three phases over the school years 2010–11:

- Phase 1: Observation of all 15 classrooms and collection of field documents (four months).
- Phase 2: Selection of two classrooms for further intense observation; identification and selection of key participant teachers and young people; audio recording of key participants in complementary school and at home (four months).
- Phase 3: Interviews with key participants young people, teachers, administrators and parents (three months).

As field researchers Jaspreet and I visited the Panjabi school most Saturdays for a year where we observed classes, wrote field notes and set up both audio recordings during class time and for later recordings at home and elsewhere. We separately visited all 15 classes over the initial four months of the project before deciding as a team on two focal classrooms for more detailed observation and recording. In each of the two focal classrooms the teacher, assistants, and two young people were given audio recording devices for self-recording. Each week we downloaded the recordings of nine classroom key participants from home and classroom recordings.

The process of selecting key participants was handled through our continued immersion in the field as well as through ongoing discussion with the teachers. Key participant-teachers were contrasted by their migration histories, language trajectories and teaching experiences, while young people were selected in the age range 13–17. Included in our key participants were also three administrators, resulting in 12 key participants in total. Key participants were crucial in the design of the project as they agreed to wear microphones in and out of class. Participant recordings at home usually captured the interactions of families, siblings and peers and these become further participant voices in the project. The two field researchers, Angela and Jaspreet, had equal responsibility for collecting data for the two classrooms and their key participants. The work was split so that Jaspreet took the morning class and Angela visited in the afternoon. We did not follow our key participants to their homes. Data collected there was without the researcher present.

DATA COLLECTION

Ethics

Before we commenced the research we went through the University of Birmingham's ethical clearance procedures and extended this to include Criminal Records Bureau (now the Disclosure and Barring Service) checks. Once we received clearance we began negotiating access and sought approval from the school's senior management team. We issued information letters to all parents and children in the Panjabi school explaining we would be undertaking observations for a set period in all classes. We gave short introductory talks to students and where possible addressed parents directly during assemblies, prize-giving events and parent conferences. In addition, we required signed consent from all key participants in our study along with other class members if they took part in audio or video recording. Because children were involved, we obtained signed consent from parents. In other words, we followed standard procedures.

However, ethical issues needed constant attention throughout the life of the project. In particular, the clarification of research aims required persistent explanation. Our interests in identity, language practices and heritage appeared rather opaque to our research participants who anticipated a research interest in pedagogy and evidence of 'good' and 'bad' practice from a team of academics working in a School of Education. Despite our best efforts at printed and verbal information, our participants did not always fully appear to understand the questions we were asking – at least not entirely, and especially not at the beginning of the research project. Teachers were nervous we might be there to inspect their classes and we spent a lot of time reassuring our participants that we were not there to judge them. We saw it as our responsibility to counter these ubiquitous inspectorial discourses by developing relationships of trust. We worked hard at letting teachers know that our note-taking was not the same as inspectors' note-taking. We showed examples of our field notes to teachers and administrators to counter fears about inspection. We came to appreciate that understanding the project's research aims was gradual, demanded sensitivity and required openness. I would say that we came to view consent not as a one-off bounded event, but rather as a series of iterative conversations which spilled into different phases of the project.

Over the course of the project we came across a lot of ethical grey areas which needed contemplation, mulling over and negotiation. One such area was project participation. On the face of it, who is in the project and who is not should be fairly straightforward. However, our experience tells us otherwise. Whereas, 'key' participants were easy to define and collect consent signatures from, other participants caught up in the research were not so easy to identify and gain consent from. We set fairly strict parameters about where our key participants should and should not undertake audio recording. For example, we asked them not to record in their mainstream schools. Such data would have been fascinating but we did not have agreement with teachers, parents or pupils in mainstream schools and so we asked the key participants to avoid recording there. Despite our warnings, some of our participants did not heed this advice. One young person took the digital recorder into school where it was stolen. He was very upset by this. We, too, were worried by the potential repercussions, but the machine was never found and the matter faded away. However, it became an important lesson for us and we talked with the key participants in more detail about the ethics of recording. We made it clear that any data collected beyond the agreed contexts would be discarded. Another participant recorded on a bus and this also raised issues of third party data (D'Arcy and Young, 2012) which sees people unknowingly caught up in the research. Again, we discarded these audio files. We decided to include as evidence only recordings taking place in the complementary school setting or the family home where parents had given consent for recordings in that setting, or outside of the home where recordings were with parents and had also been agreed. Mostly these included family recordings of interactions at times which suited the family, such as family meals or regular routines like the brushing of hair or driving to or from complementary school. However, even with these rather strict limitations, there were still instances which caused ethical dilemmas. For example there were occasional recordings of interactions within the family home which included friends rather than family members. We had not received signed consent from these people. However, we decided to use these recordings as a data source because the audio files contained verbal evidence of agreement to participate. Later, during transcription we further protected participants by changing all names.

A crucial consideration in conducting language research is ethical representation of the voices of the researched. However, less attention has been paid to ethical representation of the voices of those conducting research. There are ethical issues too in the employment, development, and mentoring of researchers in the team. Factors at play in this dynamic include the relative employment status, gender, ethnicity, and age of members of the research team. All funded research projects are situated in structures of power and finance. There are always structural hierarchies, some of which are institutionalised, such as in employment contracts or professional status, while others are less institutionalised but still pernicious, embedded in discourses of 'reputation' and 'fame'. Teams involve doctoral researchers, new-to-research researchers, post-doctorate researchers and experienced researchers. Within teams, there is gossip, insecurity, jealousy but also friendships, trust, generosity and admiration. The circumstances of individuals in the team obviously play an important role in shaping team dynamics. In pursuing our goals we quickly understood that what constituted 'the team' varied. There are teams within teams (research assistants; co-investigators; case study teams; administrative teams) who meet separately from larger teams. Some teams are fleeting (addressing a particular issue and then dispersing), some are medium-term, brought together through the funding mechanism of research councils, while others last beyond funding periods, exemplifying a legacy of successful collaborations. Working in a team requires ongoing and constant attention to such ethical considerations, particularly if a senior researcher is mentoring a more junior colleague. Consideration of ethical behaviour – in terms of exploitation and vulnerability – therefore extends beyond the research site and research participants to somewhere much closer to home. I learned we have a duty of care also to those we work with and employ as well as to those we do the research with.

The data

In our linguistic ethnographies over the last 12 years, we have typically collected six kinds of evidence. These comprise: field notes gained through sustained observations; audio recordings achieved through key participants carrying small digital recording devices with lapel microphones; video and photographs of classroom practices and participants collected by the researchers; ethnographic and semi-structured interviews recorded by the researchers during and at the end of the data collection period; field documents including teaching materials, students' school work, school correspondence with home, policy statements, and website information all collated by researchers; and researcher generated narratives and interactions. Rather than describe each data set in detail, I use this section to talk about data collection in teams and how this differs from working individually. In particular I focus on the first and the last of the above list. That is, doing participant observation in teams and how team processes themselves become an additional source of data.

Doing participant observation in teams

In any one team there is usually a range of skill and comfort about doing observation. In my experience people who join the team with a background in linguistics are often sceptical or nervous about observing. More familiar with the tools of discourse analysis, they may lack confidence in going into the field site, particularly to do unstructured ethnographic observation. This may feel too fuzzy, too open, and not scientific enough. They will want to know where to look, what to write, how to behave, when to start and when to stop observing, how much to write down, when to write it down and when to write it up, how much to change between drafts, etc. Those who are not ethnographically trained will later have anxiety about how to analyse the field note data and use it as evidence in making arguments. Such anxiety points to the need of a programme of training and development in linguistic ethnographic research methods.

Certainly doing observation is not a straightforward activity and requires knowledge and skill. Like any skill, it also gets better with practice. It is also clear that different researchers observe differently. This depends on who the researchers are themselves and how they are positioned in the field. For example, the bilingual researchers are sometimes asked, often at the very last moment, to step in to provide teaching cover when the regular teacher is absent on the day. This can open up opportunities as it allows the researcher to participate more with the students, other teachers and the school administrators. However, it also presents challenges, particularly less time to observe and take notes while the classroom action is in full swing. So while full participation as a teacher provides good access to the research site, it puts pressure on the researcher who has to juggle roles. Ideally we seek an arrangement which allows observation with some participation and this can require careful negotiation. These issues tend not to arise when the researcher is monolingual or at least not linguistically proficient in the language being taught as they are not called upon in the same way.

One way that researchers are prepared for observation and field note writing on the project is to work in pairs and exchange field notes. We make the most of being part of a team by choosing to observe the same site either in pairs at the same time or immediately one after the other. For example, Jaspreet and Angela on the Panjabi project sometimes visited the same classroom together, took notes individually, typed them up and then sent them to one another for further commentary. Or we visited each class separately in a morning session but swapped over at the break time so that we were viewing the same students, materials and teacher. We made the most of our differing experiences and backgrounds as researchers. For example while Angela has many years' experience doing participant observation, Jaspreet was new to ethnography and the writing of field notes. While Jaspreet was bilingual in English and Panjabi, Angela was not. Both had many years' experience of complementary schools; however, Angela's involvement had been as a researcher while Jaspreet's had been as a student. Although having more than one researcher in the research-site needs to be carefully negotiated with research participants, we found using pairs for shared observational events produced rich comparative data.

Field notes in the team

We used team processes of field note writing to blend the data collection and data analyses stages. We made the reading of our individual weekly field notes a regular weekly task and we talked about them before we next went into the school (Creese et al., 2008; Creese, 2010b). This meant we used them as a resource for the following week's observation. For example, Jaspreet may have noticed a practice which she wanted Angela to look out for. Or Angela may have needed some advice from Jaspreet about language or a cultural festival. Field notes were also a source of regular discussion in team meetings. They served as crucial data to develop, contest, accept and refute the development of arguments. The regular review of our field notes reminded us of the inseparable stages in ethnography of building relations in the field, data collection and analysis. When we read our field notes over, the empathies of the different researchers, Angela and Jaspreet began to stand out. Often field notes served to document these explicitly. Later on in this chapter we provide an example of this from Angela's field notes.

In team ethnography, field notes are not simply background or contextual data. They constitute a primary data source and because of this we subject them to the same level of microanalysis as other materials (see account below). As primary data they are quoted and commented on analytically in final written-up accounts. Because field notes represent the voices of our participants as well as the researchers' own voices, I believe they can be used to introduce 'a greater narrative range' (Tierney, 2002: 385) into our final published texts. Anyone reading field notes in a published article or book should immediately get a sense of the people involved and the social context in which the activity takes place. They should conjure up for the reader the lived-stuff of the social environment.

Researcher narratives and recordings

So far the data sets I have described are recognisable. Participant observation and the writing of field notes are common practices in linguistic ethnography. However, at this point I depart from the typical to describe how the researchers themselves become a source of data. I illustrate how researcher narratives and interactions are used to make arguments about multilingualism in society. This means that data in our project include not only evidence about our research participants but also evidence about the construction of multilingualism and monolingualism in the research team. This kind of intense reflexivity created new data sets for further investigation. Although reflexivity is usual in ethnography, it is mostly used to document how the researcher's backgrounds shape relationships and representations. Reflexive processes rarely serve as primary data for analysis itself. We believe that documenting a multilingual team researching multilingualism adds to the richness and complexity of doing research about communication in linguistically diverse contexts. In other words our linguistically diverse teams serve as a good source for understanding linguistic diversity. Below we describe two ways we do this.

Audio recordings of team meetings: As described in detail later in this chapter, Adrian, Angela and Jaspreet would regularly listen to and discuss data together. We have done this across our different projects. Team negotiations are at times predicated on fiercely held beliefs as researchers present themselves and their research participants in ways which cannot help but be informative and evaluative. Often we recorded these team discussions; sometimes we made transcripts and subjected them to detailed analysis. The analysis of interactions in team meetings showed researchers adhering to positions, disagreeing with others, shifting their arguments, changing their minds, offering compromises and building consensus. Credentials of bilingualism, community engagement, advocacy and scholarship saw us debate what we would write about, how we should write it and for whom we should write. We have used the analytical frameworks offered by linguistic ethnography and theories of reflexivity and heteroglossia to describe these processes of making meaning out of data in team discussions. We have argued that analysing team interactions and voices in this way added a further layer of complexity and richness to linguistic ethnography (Creese and Blackledge, 2012).

Researcher vignettes: These descriptive and analytic narratives are accounts which highlight our different perspectives in the field and in the team. Vignettes are short accounts of ourselves in which we write about how our own backgrounds shape data collection and analysis, in particular, in terms of the relationships we form.

They are written midway through a project. Typically they deal with researcher positionality, field and team relationships and language. We find avenues to publish the vignettes in full to provide different and individual narrative accounts of the research (Creese et al., 2009; Blackledge and Creese, 2010; Creese, 2010b; Creese, 2011; Creese and Blackledge et al., in press). We see vignettes as examples of 'text production' which explicitly locate the author in the text (Tierney, 2002) and, like field notes, achieve a more dynamic, accessible and public representational strategy of both ourselves and those we observe.

Data storage and readiness

Data storage happened on two levels. As a field researcher I kept my field notes organised locally. I tended to store this both electronically on my personal computer and as hard copies in a ring folder. Jaspreet did the same. However, we also needed a central system for sharing our notes with one another as well as making them available to the full European team. Jaspreet managed the overall storage of data for the Birmingham case study. We created a system we all understood and uploaded word, audio, video and photo files weekly. We found that we were reliant on our University systems for storage. This sometimes meant considerable disruption as software licences changed within our institution. At one point we had to migrate the entire data set over from one data storage system, set up for research, Microsoft Sharepoint to another, this time a teaching platform, WEBCT. The transfer caused quite a bit of anxiety about data being lost or not available. Even more recently we have been warned that this data will all be lost unless we save it elsewhere because the University is moving to a new teaching platform, CANVAS. Our experience tells us that facilities within our universities for data storage are not as long term as we might hope.

Data were stored in varying degrees of readiness. 'Raw data' were regularly posted in the form of audio and video digital files without accompanying transcripts, while field notes were only added once they had been typed up. As audio files were transcribed, the transcripts were filed alongside the audio files so that for analytical and presentational purposes we could easily locate and use the two files together.

ANALYSIS OF DATA

In ethnography, data analysis happens at different stages and levels, and at each point requires more detailed attention using increasingly sophisticated theoretical and analytical tools. To exemplify this process in our Birmingham team, I take one particular theme, 'aspiration' which emerged gradually as a theme during the investigation. That is, we did not start with it. Our research questions were about language, literacy, identity and heritage and we could not have anticipated an interest in aspiration and educational achievement at the beginning of the journey. Rather, it emerged as our interest in identity and heritage developed. Below we provide an account of how we turned our 'gaze' onto this particular theme. Through our analysis we saw it as emically relevant to our participants because it recurred in our field notes, audio recordings and interview transcripts. The iterative process of looking, relooking and looking again at data sets is described below. I take each of our major data sets in turn (observational fieldnotes, interviews, and interactional transcripts) to describe the processes of argument construction and knowledge production in our team.

Analysis of field notes

One of the distinctions between team ethnography and working as a single ethnographer is that field notes change from personal and private documents to documents shared and commented on by others (Creese et al., 2008). In other words the researchers in our teams share field notes from the beginning. This doesn't mean that researchers lost all rights to privacy in their diaries and field notes. They of course retain control over what they distribute to other team members. Between the rough jottings of first drafts and the more refined, detailed typed-up

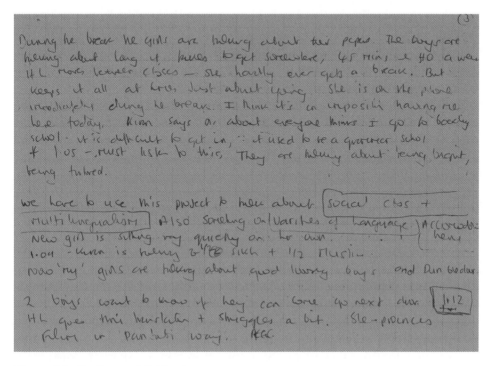

Figure 3.1 Draft one of field notes

version of second drafts changes can be made. The text shown in Figure 3.1 is an example of my field notes. It is shown here because it contains an example of my interest in aspirations and education. At the time of writing this field note I had no idea of the analytic status it would develop or the analytical attention it would be given.

As a reader you will struggle to read and make sense of these notes. They were not intended for anyone other than me. And yet, when I look at them, I see they are more detailed and fleshed out than the field notes I typically produce. Usually my first drafts contain more abbreviations, shorthand text, half-finished sentences and jottings of words to remind me of things of interest to write up in more detail at second draft. These field notes are fuller because the class I was observing was holding an examination and I was bored and had more time to write and reflect. However, I still make use of the shorthand I learned when I took a secretarial course in my mid-20s. There are spelling errors and abbreviations and they are written for my eyes only.

These scribbles reveal an interest in the break-time conversations of the young women in class, two of whom were our key participants and wearing a lapel microphone. In the notes I refer to them as 'my girls'. I record in these rough notes a discussion about which schools the girls go to and the way they describe these schools. I could not hear them very clearly from where I was sitting as they took their break in the classroom but I marked my field notes to index a link between field notes and audio recordings. I knew I could use these field notes as a resource for selecting audio files to listen to later on. Also, rather unusually in this first set of field notes, I provide a meta-commentary on the project and mention the need to follow particular themes. I specifically mention social class and multilingualism. There is also an interest in translation and pronunciation, two other themes which were to gain significance as the project developed.

So full are my first draft of notes, that there is very little change between the first set of field notes and the typed-up second. I produce a short extract here from the longer typed up notes (Figure 3.2). These were typically produced a couple of hours after the first set. That is, I tried to type them up late Saturday afternoons when I got back from the complementary school. Although this wasn't always possible, I continue to this day to follow my professors' advice from Graduate School that second drafts should be typed up quickly to retain and add detail.

Although typed up, this is still a rough document and written with a limited audience in mind. I wrote these field notes for myself, Jaspreet and Adrian only. The language is not refined or academic. In redrafting between rough notes and typed up draft, I am making decisions about what is interesting and relevant and what gets carried forward. The first draft, for example, includes a comment about boarding schools which is also included in the second draft. But I still had no way of knowing the repercussions of putting things in or leaving them out. For example between first and second drafts, I left out information about researcher

---

19 March Field Notes (AC)

1 p.m. a break is given. During the break the girls are talking about their papers. The boys are talking about money and time! Hema goes into the next class to make sure all is OK. She keeps it all going. She looks at her phone during the break and texts something.

*Kareena says something about everyone thinks she goes to grammar school. She explains it used to be a boarding school and it's difficult to get in cos everyone wants to go there. Should be worth listening to this section of recording as they are all talking about 'being bright', 'being tutored'.

My rough notes say we have to use this project to talk about social class and multilingualism. Also something on varieties of language and perhaps 'accommodation theory'. That should keep us going! New girl is not invited over to join in with the 4 girls who seem to be quite good friends now. She sits on her own. Later they include her.

*Girls are also talking about 'a half Sikh and half Muslim girl'. Also talking about a good-looking boy and Dumbledore and when the next Harry Potter film is out. The 2 boys want to know if they can go next door but Hema says no, break is over.

Hema goes over the translation and appears to struggle a bit – either reading it or translating it. I can't tell. She reads 'film' in Panjabi as 'filim'.

Figure 3.2 Draft two of field notes

imposition. In the first set, I was concerned that my presence was disrupting the mock examination being conducted by the teacher. In the second draft I do not dwell on this. In terms of what is added, further detail about grammar schools is included. Grammar schools had caught my attention, as had the girls' interest about different kinds of schools. One of the main differences between the two sets of field notes are the phrases, 'I write in my notes' and 'that should keep us going'. Both phrases are added for Adrian and Jaspreet's benefit. The first indicates that I would like the meta-comment to be noted by others in the team, while the second comment is a light-hearted point in which I position myself as somebody who is involved for the long term in the project. However, it is important to point out that despite the attention to this particular set of field notes for this case study chapter, my field notes at this point in the cycle had no particular significance to anyone. The 19th of March 2011 was not a key moment in the life of the project. This set of field notes was just one of 42 field-note documents, with each set consisting of between two and nine pages of single-spaced A4 typed-up observations. A single entry about one theme in one set of field notes does not constitute data. The aspiration and education theme had no particular salience at this point (19 March) – only a note that it warranted further consideration.

It was in the later stages that field notes received a different level of attention. After fieldwork ended, we approached field notes again in a different way. In these later readings, as Emerson et al. (1995: 142) point out, 'the researcher's stance toward the notes changes: the notes, and the persons and events they recount, become textual objects (although linked to personal memories and intuitions) to be considered and examined with a series of analytic and presentational possibilities in mind'. In the later readings we adopted the ethnographic process of 'finding data' as we engaged in searching, defining and identifying categories and themes which were 'statable' (Erickson, 2004a).

Our analysis of the field note data was undertaken by one researcher, me in this instance, who read the entire set of field notes with the intention of generating categories grounded in the details of our observations. Over a three-week period I read the 42 sets of field notes from each of the three researchers in chronological order, generating categories through a bottom-up reading. These categories were partly led by our research aims but open to other themes which appeared to us as emically important to participants. I looked for patterns in our field notes. I counted instances of occurrence. I looked for contrasts to better understand these patterns.

I did not feel completely isolated in making these decisions. As a team we had begun to have a feel for what was interesting and relevant across our data sets. However, such decisions are never anxiety free and there is always the pressure to balance evidentiary detail with coherent argument as well as to reduce the material to make it more manageable. Once the categories were generated from the field notes, a new analytic document was produced. This new 38-page single-spaced Word document was organised by themes and populated with extracts cut and pasted from the second drafts of field notes from the three researchers. During this phase of field note analysis I would say our field notes had moved from evidentiary material collected in the field to data. This is because the field notes had undergone systematic and rigorous analysis. An analytical commentary had also been introduced to organise them.

From the final analytic reading, four main headings were produced each with a series of sub-headings. The main headings were 'institutional voice', 'researcher positionality', 'classroom practices' and 'social practices'. The table of contents from our final reading of the fieldnotes in shown in Figure 3.3.

Aspiration appears as a category twice; in section 1 and 4. Under category 1 aspiration is about the institution's public voice. Under category 4 it is about the aspirations of young people, classroom assistants and teachers as evoked in their classroom and home interactions. Across the original 42 sets of researcher field notes there were 'enough' instantiations to interpret aspiration as significant. Researchers believed they were noting an emically important feature of social life significant to both young people and teachers. Some examples of the aspiration theme emerged from original field notes. Typically, when we extracted examples from the longer compiled set of field notes we tagged them for month and researcher. This allowed us to link field notes to classroom audio recordings

1. **Complementary school and institutional voice**

   Reproducing mainstream educational discourses
   Institutional networking, aspirations and entrepreneurism

2. **School/researcher relationships**

   Researcher relationships in the field
   Controlling the research process
   Researcher anxiety

3. **Classroom practices**

   Comprehensive orientation
   Pedagogy
   Classroom competition and tests
   Teaching assistants
   Language use and teaching and learning
   Grammar and accent
   Student behaviour

4. **Social practices and classroom routines**

   Greetings
   Break times
   Kinship and respect
   Religion
   Race/ethnicity/gender
   Work, education and aspirations

Figure 3.3 Table of field note contents

and retain the researcher's voice. It also allowed us to see if all three researchers were commenting on similar themes:

- I chat to Simran about school, she had 2 exam results back this week – both Maths in which she attained an A and an A* – so she's quite academic. (15.1 JT)
- They are talking about School options and this leads to discussion about studying medicine or dentistry and which earns most money. (20.11AC)
- HL tells me there are two students from the 'grammar school' attending her class. Their father asked her 'can you teach them any Panjabi?' Hema makes the link between their grammar school status and achievement. She seems very proud they are now in the A level class. (25/9AC)
- Teacher writes on the board 'future plans'. I hear lots of discussion of being a doctor, dentist, lawyer, journalist, artist, commander in army, producer, DJ, football player, chef. ... There is a discussion about not wanting to be a teacher. Sandeep tells the assistant he wants to go to Cambridge University. One kid says to his partner, 'what if I want to work at Asda – I don't know what I want to work as'. (20.11AC)
- The talk starts. It starts with Kiran, who works at an agency called Connexions which helps young people form career paths. Little boy named Arjun says 'I want to be a dentist because my dad is' – influence of parents on future careers. We hear many other professions; doctor, archaeologist, army. They talk about role models and different types of role models that one person can have, family, friends, celebrities, religious figures. (9.4JT)

In these short field note extracts we see researchers noting young people's and teachers' ideologies about good and bad schools and worthy and questionable careers paths. The field notes document the reproduction of distinctions about schooling and workplace success. These issues appeared important to our research participants and therefore salient to us. As researchers, we saw a pattern there. Establishing a pattern in ethnography is both a quantitative and qualitative endeavour. Quantitatively, we counted many references to aspiration across our different data sets. Qualitatively, we saw the interactional attention our participants gave the theme. As Erickson (1990) argues, in [linguistic] ethnography researchers strive for rigorous accounts of participants' subjective meanings and this involves looking closely at their communicative practices. What we saw was the attentiveness our participants gave to developing this topic. Using the field notes, we were able to make an assertion about our participants' social practices.

Activity 1

So what's the point?

(These activities come from the original class I took with Fredrick Erickson in 1994, Education 906, Qualitative Data Analysis and Report.)

1. Using either an existing set of field notes (or those produced through Fiona's second activity in Chapter 4) identify a pattern in your data.
2. Make an assertion based on the pattern you have discovered.
3. Return to your field notes and identify a typical instance that illustrates the assertion you have made. The instance will also provide evidence that what you are asserting to be the case in the setting actually did happen, at least once, and preferably was an instance of a frequently recurring type.

Analysis of interviews

Two researchers, Adrian and Jaspreet conducted interviews. Interviews in the project can be described as semi-structured and were always audio-recorded, usually in our participants' homes. We choose to conduct semi-structured interviews later rather than earlier in the data collection period because the observation stage was used to establish relationships. Interviews were conducted after field visits had ended because researchers and participants knew one another better. This kind of scheduling, a common approach in ethnography, allowed our observation and field notes to inform the questions we raised in interview.

Jaspreet was central to the collection of interview data. She was able to draw on her personal and social capital in relation to participants when conducting interviews. These included her age, family history, ethnicity and bilingualism.

She had developed very good relationships with the young people in the study and was invited into participant family homes where she interviewed bilingually. Adrian and Jaspreet also jointly conducted interviews with two senior male participants using the same interview schedule. Even in these later stages of the project, dynamics of social power and status continued to operate and Jaspreet preferred Adrian to participate in the interviews with two older and senior men.

The interviews were conducted through working from a series of prompts generated from the research questions and emerging themes. The prompts varied according to whether the interviewee was a teacher, a young person, a teaching assistant, a parent, or an administrator. An example of prompts is shown in Figure 3.4

Interview schedule

1. Background

   - Talk a bit about yourself
   - Where were you born, where did you grow up?
   - Family history of migration
   - Family – parents (jobs), siblings
   - Education in your family (self/parents/children)
   - Family leisure activities, travel
   - What hopes and dreams do you have for your family?

2. Language use

   - Tell me about the languages you speak
   - Your own experiences as a language learner
   - Tell me about the different accents/dialects (both English and Panjabi) you use and who you use them with
   - Do you speak differently in different contexts – at weddings, gossiping with friends, evening family meal, extended family/friends dinner
   - Mixing languages
   - How is language use changing across generations?

3. Language teaching and learning (at complementary school)

   - Rationale for school
   - Your role at school
   - Curriculum at school (content/heritage/culture)
   - Pedagogy/teaching strategies, e.g. language separation, translanguaging, transliteration
   - Role of TAs and teachers
   - School as social opportunity
   - Panjabi and 'identity'

4. Culture/heritage

   - Family stories told across generations
   - Tell me about your grandparents

Figure 3.4   Example of prompts used in interviews

Jaspreet was encouraged to depart from the prompts as the participants wished. Which language the interview was to be conducted in was also negotiated beforehand, although a flexible bilingual approach was common for both researcher and participant. Once interviews were conducted, data were stored digitally. Jaspreet then transcribed and translated each of the 15 interviews in full. The intimacy of the original conversations and the lengthy and time-consuming process of listening and transcribing the interviews led Jaspreet to speak about the participants in familiar ways. She was personally moved by many of the family and individual narratives of struggle, which she connected to her own history and family experiences. She saw this connection as both beneficial but also challenging as she describes in her researcher vignette below:

Extract 1

However sometimes this has proven a bit tricky with some of the children opening up to me about the family lives in interviews. As a researcher I must remember that although I get on with them, I am not their friend, but someone that is there to do a job. This proved difficult for me sometimes but eventually I became comfortable with the lines I keep within. (JKT, researcher vignette)

In this short vignette extract Jaspreet describes a tension. She realised her youth allowed her a closeness in relation to the teenagers and this created a relaxed and open relationship. She saw this as an asset but one which also needed paying attention to. As the vignette indicates, she also wished to retain some professional distance. When the three of us listened to the interview narratives they evoked memories for each of us and we used team meetings to also talk about our family experiences and histories. These discussions not only contributed to the emergence of themes for further analysis but also played a part in constituting trust and openness in our team. This in turn produced an environment for talking creatively about emerging ideas.

As a team we approached the bulk of the interview data in a similar way to that of the field note data. That is, one member of the team, Adrian, took the responsibility of reading across all interviews to provide a summary. Adrian listened to each of the 15 sound files accompanied by the interview transcript provided by Jaspreet. He used the process of listening and reading the transcript to write 15 summaries. These summaries were still detailed but also involved data reduction. For example, original interview transcripts were on average 7000 words in length while the accompanying summary was 1500 words long. Adrian wrote the interview summary using the general headings of the semi-structured schedule above while expanding and introducing new themes:

- profile (age, job, length of time in UK, place of birth, family members);
- family;

- education;
- aspirations;
- language learning;
- language use.

The theme of aspiration and education were included under 'background' prompts in the original semi-structured interview. However, they emerged as important during the actual interviews and gained higher and separate status in the interview summaries. An example of the aspiration data is provided below in two formats. The first is an example of the interview transcript between Jaspreet and the mother of one of the key participants.

Extract 2

JKT: ke tussi India tho aaye si ‹*that you came from India*›

Mother: (in Panjabi) you know people think that I am some sort of solicitor or social worker or something but really I am nothing right? But slowly slowly my parents moved over to Walsall and I got married [the family were from] Middlesex. My husband then took us to Hertfordshire near to London. He used to work in the city. He has a very good job and even though I wasn't educated I managed to get a job because I was confident and no one could tell that I was dumb

JKT: you're not dumb

Mother: because I had confidence because I had confidence

Son: you're not dumb

The second is Adrian's summary, which shows his interest in this discussion which he notes as an emergent theme.

Extract 3

Social positioning/aspiration: Parneet's mother appears to view educational success as one of the most important things for her children to achieve: 'Education is so important I think. So I do encourage them to study as much as they can.' . . . A recurrent concern in Parneet's mother's narrative is that of how she is viewed by others. She refers to herself as 'dumb', but she relies on confidence and determination. She says 'you know people think that I am some sort of solicitor or social worker or something but really I am nothing right'. (AB interview vignette; truncated)

The summaries served to reduce data and make explicit the themes we were developing. Although Adrian directly quotes from the interview, the comments are now glossed with an analytical explanation. We use a similar analytical approach in analysing both field note and interview data. For both data sets original extracts are cut and pasted into a new document which contains an analytical commentary and is organised around themes.

Analysis of interactions

After the data collection ended and around twelve months after the project started, Jaspreet started to listen to the key participants' audio recordings in class and at home. She organised her first analysis of the audio data by taking one key participant at a time, listening and making notes of interest about the recording. She did this on her own. She did not transcribe or translate at this point. She brought these notes to our weekly or two-weekly research meetings. At the meeting, Jaspreet would talk about the audio file using her notes. This process allowed us to debate what we found interesting or not about the data. Sometimes we recorded these meetings. Listening to the participant audio files for the first time was always fascinating. The audio files of our key participants contained recordings from home and other domestic settings between family members, between peers and siblings where we had not been present. We were therefore often listening to our key participants for the first time in intimate contexts which were very different from the classroom. However, recordings were also of classroom recordings where we had been present, although not necessarily part of the interaction (as in breaktimes). An example of the notes brought by Jaspreet in relation to an audio file is shown in Extract 4 (there was no transcript at this point). Jaspreet had identified 19 March for team listening – the same date I had tagged for further listening in my field notes.

Extract 4

Jaspreet's notes for discussion of audio files at team meeting

Parneet talks about her cousin who has been tutored privately since Year 3, and still didn't get into a grammar school. Her parents were really upset. P. also comments 'she wasn't very bright anyway'. Education and school is always a key topic of conversation in the breaks. P. talks about her brother who used to come to Panjabi school. 'He was better at languages than me.'

In the above document Jaspreet provides a summary of the audio recording she had listened to prior to the team meeting and ensuing discussion. Jaspreet's preliminary selections of data before arrival at these meetings were crucial in shaping our ongoing analysis. In this sense she was like any other doctoral or lone researcher in that she decided what to carry forward. We can say this was similar for Angela with the field notes and Adrian with the interview data. The difference in our team was that we all had access to the data sets, were all familiar and invested in them, but took the analytical lead on only one. The huge amounts of data we had collected meant we couldn't each individually trawl through all the raw material. Instead our summaries served us shortcuts for team members to refer to and link back to the original when following a research idea for publication.

Jaspreet's selection of audio files for further analysis was obviously consequential for our linguistic ethnography. However, these decisions were not isolated, entirely individual, random or arbitrary. Time in the field, the reading of field notes, the writing of vignettes, the readings of previous work, and early and ongoing discussions in groups with other researchers all served to support individual researchers in decisions of what might serve as material for further analytic scrutiny. Teams working well build up confidence in making these decisions whether they are in the analysis of interactional transcripts, field notes or interview transcripts. As a group we decided which sections of the audio to transcribe and once this decision was made, Jaspreet would do this back in her own office. When transcripts were ready, we used our next meeting to listen again, but this time following, checking and adding detail to the transcript. We did this as a group. The transcript for the in-class discussion of 19 March about aspiration is given below:

Extract 5

[Jasvinder is new to the class and sitting alone. She does not know either Kirsty or Parneet]

Kirsty:	[whispers:] do you think we should talk to her?
Parneet:	[whispers:] don't look at me
Kirsty:	[whispers:] what's her name?
Parneet:	[whispers] she's called Jas something
Kirsty:	[whispers] Jasvinder? What, Jasvinder?
Kiran:	[whispers:] she's all alone
Kirsty:	[to Jasvinder:] Jasvinder, what year are you in?
Jasvinder:	year nine
Kirsty:	same [laughs] you know my school's like right next to yours (7)
Parneet:	[laughs] [whispers:] uncomfortable silence
Kirsty:	[to Jaspvinder:] were you in a different class before?
Jasvinder:	uh?
Kirsty:	were you in a different class before?
Jasvinder:	no I just got taught by this woman
Parneet:	[laughs:]
Kiran:	everyone thought you would go to a grammar school
Jasvinder:	I used to go to like a private school but
Kiran:	mine's just a
Kirsty:	hard to get into
Kiran:	yeah it's hard to get into but you don't have to have a test because it used to be a grammar school, but it's not any more
Kirsty:	grammar schools are changing into academies aren't they, but they'll still be hard to get into anyway
Parneet:	[mockingly, to herself:] academy
Jasvinder:	I think it's better if you have that because it pressures children as well, it pressures people you know if they try for grammar and they don't get in, I think it's not fair

Kiran: hmm
Parneet: what do you mean it's not fair?
Jasvinder: it's not fair how they are put under all that pressure and they don't get in
Parneet: oh yeah
Jasvinder: and then their parents are just disappointed
Parneet: my cousin had like loads of tuition and she didn't get into any of her schools
             and her parents were like really upset because you know they spent so
             much, they'd been tutoring her since year three, she's been tutored since
             like year three but
Jasvinder: it's not always about tutoring it's about their, it's about them
Parneet: yeah but she wasn't really that bright anyway so [laughter]
Kiran: she has got tutored though
Parneet: hmm
Jasvinder: she spent lots of money as well
Parneet: I never got tutored

Jaspreet always attached the relevant set of field notes to the recording to provide additional contextual information. My field notes from 19 March were presented and included in the discussion of the transcript above during our team meeting. The interplay between field notes and transcripts is worth mentioning again here. It is clear that the transcript above provides much more detail than the original field notes. We can read about the young women's views of school hierarchies, tensions around tutoring, cleverness, etc. The transcript gives a rich sense of who the young women are and their interactions are fertile pickings for discourse analysis. The field notes are sparse by comparison. However, they were fundamental in constructing the arguments which we eventually developed for publication. First, the field notes tagged the audio file for further attention. As shown earlier, Angela's field notes asked for this interaction to be transcribed, which Jaspreet did. The detailed and micro analysis of the transcript we eventually produced was supported through the contextual evidence provided in the notes. My observations over nine months meant we knew a good deal about Parneet and Kiran, two of our key participants. This knowledge shaped our understanding of their interactions and the discursive data. Second, analysis of field notes established schooling and competition as regularly occurring topics. The field notes became our evidence that the theme was emically important to our participants. The context provided by field notes and interviews supported the transcript and gave it rigour, depth and history. We came to the transcript with lots of other information to hand and this is one distinguishing feature of linguistic ethnography in relation to other discourse analytic approaches. Third, the field notes served to remind the researcher (and reader) of their own presence in the field and in the interpretive process. This is because field notes are more explicitly authored in ways that transcripts are not. They tell us that participant observation and interpreting data is a social activity done by a researcher(s) in the real world. Discourse analysis can have a

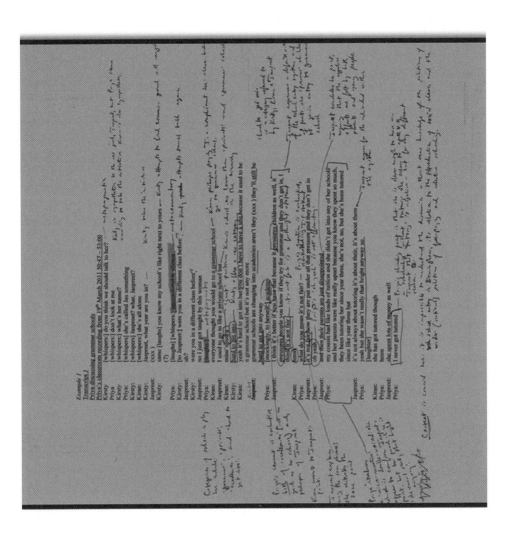

Figure 3.5 Preliminary analysis of aspiration theme

way of concealing the researcher's role in constructing data or at least not making it entirely explicit.

During team meetings about the transcript our discussions were wide ranging and extended beyond what we saw on the page. Often we would refer to theory which we thought might have some relevance to the transcripts. The bringing together of theory and data can produce moments of imagination which serve for further analysis, application and argumentation. For our team these have been varied and we have drawn widely on traditions in linguistic anthropology, literary theory and sociology. Into these team meetings we also introduced general knowledge and popular culture which we thought might be relevant. For example, the theme of aspiration generated much discussion about our understanding and hierarchies of different schools in Birmingham. We also talked a lot about our own educational backgrounds, social class and attainment. At this point, everything was up for discussion.

We were excited by the audio sound files but we had not constructed them into data yet. This typically happened with a publication in mind, and saw one of us, Adrian, Angela or Jaspreet, begin to lead on an article. At this point the audio file, cut to match a particular transcript underwent further analysis. Figure 3.5 gives an example of how Adrian went about analysing this interaction.

Figure 3.5 shows Adrian's intensive engagement with the text. Although the print and notes are too small to be read in the original, and colour is not available in this book, we reprint the text here to give a flavour of the kind of engagement the individual researcher has with the text. He used a variety of symbols to mark his interest. Adrian first glued an A4 print-out of the transcript onto an A3 piece of paper. This allowed for very wide margins. He then listened repeatedly to the transcript. The use of different coloured pens, underlining, borders around words and phrases and comments in the margins were the devices he used as he moved between audio and transcript. Sometimes he left the text to follow other leads the participants provide. This meant looking up references to Birmingham schools, or media characters in youTube postings or TV programmes or returning to field notes and interviews. Some comments in the margin introduced technical terms such as 'metapragmatics', 'micro narrative', 'evaluation', 'recontextualized', 'positioning'. These notes indicate Adrian making connections to a research literature he sees as relevant. There are notes to self to provide more contextual information when it comes to writing up. For example at the bottom of the page he has scribbled:

Extract 6

Context is crucial here: it is impossible to understand the discussion without some knowledge of the politics of school entry in Birmingham, its relation to the (re)production of social class, and the wider (national) politics of fee-paying and selective schooling.

In this comment, we can see the intertextual nature of data construction in teams which reference earlier team discussions and other data sets. However,

Adrian's own history is relevant here. He grew up in Birmingham and attended Birmingham schools; he taught in Birmingham schools; and his children were educated in Birmingham schools. His own researcher identity is not to be discarded. His running interpretive commentary in both the right and left margin is where Adrian makes interpretations of the young women's interactions but also reveals further information about himself in the analytical process. One example at the end of the transcript uttered by P. has a box around it with the following note made:

Extract 7

P.'s clinching point is that she is clever enough to have won a scholarship without tutoring. She seems to agree with J. that tutoring is negative – but for very different reasons.

Adrian's analysis of the interactional data is done alongside other data sets. While analysing this transcript other texts are also on the table side by side waiting for inclusion, rejection and possible further analytical scrutiny. These include other interactional transcripts, field notes and interviews. Each requires the other to help make the argument. From this analysis and the gathering of relevant data sets, an article begins to be drafted. From here on in, another whole time consuming and lengthy process of interpretation and analysis begins as the author(s) starts to write up. The publication process is underway.

Activity 2

Presenting a key quote to instance and warrant an assertion

1. Review audio-recordings to identify another pattern in your data.
2. Make an assertion based on the pattern you have identified.

Write out this assertion. Follow it with an exact transcription of the quote. Leave in the detail the person used. If tone of voice, pacing, or volume was important for meaning try to show this in the way you transcribe the quote (see Chapter 8). Provide interpretive summary in which you explain the meaning of the quote on the basis of form and context of the quote itself (e.g. word choice, tone of voice). Add contextual information from your field notes that clarifies its significance.

Discourse analysis in linguistic ethnography

The account given here of a team constructing analytic categories provides concrete details of our research practice. These explanations of our analytic procedures show the importance we give to interaction in our linguistic ethnographies. As we code from the bottom up, we start to argue for themes across the data sets. Our approach to discourse is ethnographically informed and is predicated on the view that research into language and culture should be a single object, socially constructed in discursive action (Hymes, 1968, 1974, 1980; Blommaert, 2005). Viewing discourse as always 'densely contextualised' (Blommaert, 2005: 15) allows data to drive us in particular directions in a constant dynamic of inductive and deductive processes. Blommaert and Rampton propose that 'it is far more productive *analytically* to focus on the very variable ways in which linguistic features with identifiable social and cultural associations get clustered together whenever people communicate' (2011: 1) than to start with ideological constructs. In being driven by the ethnographic materials we have collected, we are required to search for the clusters, themes and patterns in the 'here and now' of the situated interactional data while paying attention to the historical, social and political dimension. Heller (2011: 40) notes that '[t]he challenge … is to capture both the ways in which things unfold in real time, and the ways in which they sediment into constraints that go far beyond the time and place of specific interactions'. The researcher in ethnographically-informed discourse analysis interprets the meaning-perspectives of the people studied, through drawing on wider texts in circulation in much the same way as an interpreter does when translating the discourse of a speaker or writer. The movement between the local and the wider context can be found in the early work of Gumperz who argued we need 'closer understanding of how linguistic signs interact with social knowledge in discourse' (1982: 29). In relation to our arguments about aspiration we framed our analysis drawing across social, cultural and linguistic theory including Agha (2007), Bakhtin (1981), Bourdieu (2000) and Silverstein (1985).

REPRESENTATION AND WRITING UP IN TEAMS

As a team we write for different audiences including teachers, policymakers, funding bodies and academics. Because we believe that knowledge is constructed through team conversations and that we all jointly 'own' the data, we try as much as possible to cite all researchers even when they have not been available to contribute or comment on drafts. Citation takes several forms including listing as joint authors, recording as contributors and footnoting. However, this is not without problems. Former researchers may no longer be contactable or willing to be involved in the research. People change jobs, take different directions, and may not be committed to written dissemination. Publishers also have a role to play as many do not take kindly to long lists of authors, in our case up to nine authors (see Creese and Blackledge et al., in press). Publishers may be put off multi-authored books and papers because of contractual and reimbursement costs.

We write together in several ways. Sometimes one individual will produce a draft and invite others to comment critically in relation to argumentation, literature, data, and overall structure. This is a highly engaged and critical process and results in many drafts and discussions. At other times, we co-write, sitting together in front of the computer, usually in pairs but sometimes in threes. Sometimes we assign different sections to one another and splice it together once each has completed their section. Each approach requires a willingness to engage in critical and sometimes harsh peer review developed only through working well in a team.

In terms of the thematic analysis I have described in this chapter, Adrian led on this but, as I hope we have shown, we were all involved at all stages of the research in the ideas that flowed through data collection, analysis and to writing up. In the team we believe that data is not owned by any particular researcher even when the researcher has heavily invested in data collection in the field. Team processes require data to be shared and developed. In team ethnography data are jointly owned. A published version appears as 'Discourses of aspiration and distinction in the local school economy' (Blackledge et al., 2014). An extract from the final paper is given below.

Extract 8

Much of the educational and sociological research on aspirations thus far has focused on interviews, focus groups, and survey questionnaires. The insights gained through these studies make a valuable contribution to understanding young people's educational and professional aspirations. In this study we too draw on interviews, but combine them with audio recordings and observational field notes, in a linguistic ethnographic approach which affords a rich understanding of processes of negotiation and transformation in family discourses about education. (Blackledge et al., 2014: 173)

The extract mentions the integrated nature of data sets and I'd like this to be the 'clinching' point of this case study chapter. Interactional recordings, interview transcripts, field notes and other materials all provide evidence once they are constituted as data through rigorous analysis. They underscore our confidence as linguistic ethnographers in producing reliable and trustworthy accounts.

--- **Activity 3** ---

Think about your own research project. In what ways would it benefit from team working? How would different perspectives enhance your data collection and analysis?

CONCLUDING COMMENTS

In this chapter I have described how teams of linguistic ethnographers come to make meaning out of the materials they collect or create in the field. In demystifying the processes of analysis in linguistic ethnography I have described how data are created and made to cohere into arguments brought about in team discussions where noticings are made and connections developed. Overall, I have described our team's efforts to address an ongoing research aim which is to develop innovative multi-site, ethnographic team methodologies using interlocking case studies across national, social, cultural and linguistic contexts. I hope the account I have provided illustrates that team linguistic ethnography is a rich and reliable approach to acquire new understandings of contemporary social, cultural, economic and political processes.

KEY READINGS

Blackledge, A. and Creese, A. (2014) 'Heteroglossia as practice and pedagogy', in A. Blackledge and A. Creese (eds) *Heteroglossia as Practice and Pedagogy*. New York: Springer. pp. 1–20.

Emerson, R.M., Fretz, R.I. and Shaw, L. (1995) *Writing Ethnographic Fieldnotes*. Chicago: Chicago University Press.

Erickson, F. (1990) 'Qualitative methods', in R.L. Linn and F. Erickson (eds) *Research in Teaching and Learning: Volume Two*. New York: MacMillan. pp. 77–194.

Wortham, S. (2008) 'Linguistic anthropology of education', *Annual Review of Anthropology*, 37: 37–51.

FOUR

Case Study Two: Researching Feedback Conferences in Pre-service Teacher Education

Fiona Copland

SETTING THE CONTEXT OF THE STUDY: BACKGROUND INFORMATION, RESEARCH QUESTIONS AND FINDINGS

As I describe in my vignette at the beginning of the book, I was a trainer on pre-service teacher training courses for many years. The course, the CELTA (Certificate in English Language Teaching to Adults) is validated by Cambridge ESOL, a branch of the University of Cambridge. This course, and others like it, is considered the baseline qualification for teaching English to speakers of other languages (TESOL) in private institutions in the UK, such as International House, and in teaching centres around the world, such as the British Council. According to Brandt (2006), around 10,000 people a year take programmes such as the CELTA, so although it is not part of mainstream UK government-funded teacher education, it is the bedrock of the TESOL industry, an industry which is estimated to be worth £1.3 billion in invisible exports to the UK economy (Graddol, 2006). Many graduates of the CELTA make a career in TESOL and go on to take the Diploma in English Language Teaching to Adults (DELTA) and then a Masters in TESOL/Applied Linguistics.

When I carried out the research at the Chamberlain Centre, an institution that specialised in adult education, the CELTA was a 120-hour programme which included input sessions on how to teach English, guided observation of experienced teachers and, most importantly perhaps, teaching practice, which trainees had to pass. Teaching practice lasted 90 minutes and was divided between two to four trainees. Each taught a section of the lesson, so that by the end of the programme each trainee had taught for six hours.

After teaching practice, there was a feedback conference. The feedback conference can take many forms (see Copland, 2008), but on the courses in which I was involved, the trainees and trainer discussed the lesson for about an hour evaluating its positive and negative aspects. During this time, knowledge about best practice in TESOL was also disseminated to trainees by trainers and trainers sometimes indicated the extent to which the trainee had been successful/unsuccessful in teaching the lesson.

The longer I was a trainer, the more fascinated I became by the feedback conference. Because there were three to four trainees in each group with only one trainer, I found the dynamics and participation structures of particular interest. I came to realise that some trainees were more successful in the feedback conference than others and often what happened there shaped the trainer's view of the trainee. It also seemed apparent, from conducting feedback sessions myself and watching other trainers, that no matter what kinds of micro activities we conducted in the conferences, they all contained the same fundamental components which trainees needed to understand in order to negotiate them successfully.

At the time of conducting the research, there were few studies of feedback conferences in general (although notable exceptions included Waite (1995) and Vásquez (2004)) and of CELTA feedback conferences in particular (though see Wajnryb, 1998; Farr, 2006). I felt the time was ripe for putting this 'hidden from view' event (Heritage and Sefi, 1992) under the microscope. Based on the reasons given above, I eventually settled on the following research questions:

What are the generic features of this feedback event?
Which hegemonic positions are enacted and reproduced by trainers at the Chamberlain Centre?
What strategies do these trainers and trainees use to introduce, maintain and negotiate power in their feedback sessions?
Are these trainers and trainees adequately prepared to take part in the feedback event?

My findings have been reported in three articles in particular (Copland, 2010, 2011, 2012). In brief, I found that feedback conferences followed generic conventions and that participants demonstrated resistance to feedback and to other participants by troubling the limits of these. Particular ideas about language learning and teaching were circulated in the feedback conferences and these ideas drew, to a great extent, on the trainers' own experiences and beliefs and, to a lesser extent, on the CELTA syllabus. Power was mostly in the hands of the trainers, although wily trainees were able to introduce their own agendas and get their voices heard. There was no training to support trainees in taking part in feedback, and this might be detrimental to trainees who, for whatever reason, are unused to discussions of this type. As a result of the research, I suggested that preparation for feedback should form part of the induction processes of CELTA (and other) programmes.

Having briefly described the study and the findings, the remainder of the case study, is dedicated to uncovering and unpacking the nitty-gritty details of decisions I took as the research progressed, with particular regard to research design, data collection and data analysis. My purpose in sharing is not to suggest that all my decisions were right or that my research design was flawless, but rather to show how a research idea becomes a research project: a process which involves commitment, confusion, hard work, and many steps into the unknown.

RESEARCH DESIGN

The research design for the project was influenced by both academic and pragmatic considerations. Academically, I wanted to focus in detail on the feedback conference. Pragmatically, I had to work around the Centre where I was collecting the data and my work commitments. In order to meet the demands of the former, I observed and recorded the feedback sessions on two CELTA courses. The first, a semi-intensive course over 10 weeks, involved two trainers and four trainees. The second, a one-month intensive course, involved two different trainers and five trainees. I interviewed the trainers before they started work on the CELTA and after it had finished (these were recorded). I also held a focus group meeting with the two different groups of trainees at the end of each of the courses (also recorded). In terms of data, this provided 16 hours of recorded feedback, field notes of 16 hours of feedback, eight hours of interviews and two hours of focus groups, as can be seen in Figure 4.1.

Pragmatic considerations meant that I had to follow two different CELTA courses, one part-time (two days a week for 10 weeks) and one full-time (Monday to Friday for 4 weeks) as the Centre did not have two of the same types of programme running. Work commitments meant that I could not observe and record every day but I was able to negotiate research leave twice a week. However, pragmatic considerations also worked in my favour: I had worked at the centre for many years and had a very good relationship with the Head of English and colleagues there. This meant it was easy to negotiate access and my researcher status, although my relationship with the Centre and the trainers in particular threw up some ethical issues, to which I now turn.

COLLECTION OF DATA

Ethical considerations

I had to resolve a number of ethical issues before, during and after collecting the data. My first issue concerned consent from the trainers. The problem was not getting consent; indeed, given the fact that I knew all the trainers well professionally and socially, this was easy. Rather, the question was, and remains, is it ethical to recruit participants who are so well known to the researcher? What choice do such participants really have when it comes to taking part or, later on, withdrawing, given this

Trainers and trainees	First interview	Second interview	First feedback observation	Second feedback observation	Third feedback observation	Fourth feedback observation	Group interview
Eileen	✓	✓	✓	✓	✓	✓	
Madeleine	✓	✓	✓	✓	✓	✓	
Ned	✓	✓	✓	✓	✓	✓	
Lauren	✓	✓	✓	✓	✓	✓	
Group 1 trainees							✓
Group 2 trainees							✓

Figure 4.1 Record of data collection

close relationship? And given that a great deal of research in education in particular has a critical function, is it fair to expose colleagues and friends to the approbation of others? These concerns had to be balanced with the importance the research might potentially have in the future to trainers and, perhaps more importantly, to trainees, particularly given the paucity of research in this area. Kubanyiova (2008) suggests that such dilemmas are common in situated applied linguistics research, particularly when focusing on a particular case, or cases, as this study did. She characterises the problem as one where the 'definition of what constitutes the '"greater good" largely ignore[s] the relational character of situated research' (2008: 506). In other words, macroethical concerns, obtaining approval from the institution(s) and gaining consent from participants, override microethical concerns such as ensuring no harm is done to those taking part in the research project.

I designed the research so that these issues were approached in three ways: first, I tried to make sure that the trainers were as informed as possible about the nature of the research and their part in it. This took the usual form of holding an information session about the research and then giving the trainers time and space to complete, or not, the consent form. Second, during the research process, I tried to be sensitive to messages I picked up from the trainers, messages which might not be available to a researcher who did not know his/her participants as well. For example, chatting with trainers outside the research site, I learnt which trainers minded having a video camera in the room and which did not and I altered the data collection accordingly. Third, in the post-course interviews, I asked the trainers to give feedback on the data collected and to explain their own positions and views on what had happened in feedback. This was integrated into the data analysis and the subsequent publications.

However, it would be naive to think that addressing ethical concerns is something only done pre-data collection. As the research progressed, a number of other issues arose which had to be addressed. For example, early on in the research, I observed and recorded a very emotional and tense feedback conference. This became for me what Guillemin and Gillam (2004), cited in Kubanyiova (2008), call an 'ethically important moment'. I had to decide whether to include this in my study given that a number of participants may have felt exposed and even compromised if the data were made public. On advice, I contacted the participants individually and via email (so that they had time to consider a response) to ask if they would like me not to include the data from the conference. All participants gave their consent and seemed much less concerned than me about the data circulating. I then included it in my original PhD work. However, I remained uncomfortable with using the data as I did not feel the participants had understood, in the way I felt I did, the potential ramifications of revealing what had happened in that session to an academic and professional audience. In the end, I decided not to write about it in work I sought to have published.

The work I have done as a researcher around this ethically important moment – thinking, contacting, rethinking, considering the context of the research and then deciding – demonstrates an important principle of ethics: reflexivity. I had permission from the institutions to conduct the research, and permission from the participants to use these particular data (in other words, I was 'safe' in terms of ticking the boxes of ethical research). I could have used the data in published work with no repercussions (and they were very good data indeed). But thinking, discussing and rethinking brought me to the understanding that the data did not need to be fully in the public domain. Had I published, I would have put my own concerns as a researcher above my moral responsibility to my research participants, and, for me, this is unethical. Kubanyiova (2008: 506) suggests that researchers should display 'microethics of care' in situated research of this kind so that the researcher develops a moral approach to the participants and regards them not as the subjects of the research but as 'specific individuals, located in specific situations that require actions based in care, responsibility, and responsiveness to context' (Haverkamp, 2005: 149–50, cited in Kubanyiova, 2008: 506–7). In this particular instance, I feel I have made the right decision as a researcher, but more importantly, as a human being.

Finally, in terms of ethics, I had to decide what to do about publications. As we all know, academics are under huge pressure to publish their research and are in danger of losing their positions if they do not do so. Publishing data becomes an ethical dilemma, however, if the researcher knows that what will be published could potentially damage the research participants. This is particularly the case, I feel, in research on teacher education, as in most cases there is some criticism, overt or implied, of the practices of teachers or trainers. It has also been suggested that nothing should be put into print that could not be said to the participants face-to-face (de Laine, 2000), and this I have found a useful rule of thumb. However, as Kubanyiova (2008: 515) points out, if the welfare of the research participants is always prioritised above the contribution to knowledge that the research might make, 'there is a risk that this type of situated research ... could never contribute fully to the advancement of theoretical knowledge in any discipline'.

In the end, researcher reflexivity must again be called upon and a decision made which addresses both considerations. It is important to write with sensitivity to the feelings of the research participants, although these may at times contradict each other, to demonstrate empathy with their positions, and to acknowledge the influences and constraints under which they work. This is not to say that nobody will ever be upset with what you publish, but if you are sure you have paid attention to the microethical dimension, you should be able to discuss with these participants your decision to publish. This is the path I have tried to follow in publishing findings from this and consequent studies (although see Bourgois (1995) for an in-depth ethical discussion around the importance of publishing ethnography which exposes horrors without censure, despite the dangers it may bring).

You will have noticed that this discussion concentrates on the trainers rather than on the trainees. This is because the analytical focus was on their practices: trainees were subject to these practices rather than being the instigators of them. For this reason, trainees were not examined in the same critical way as trainers, either ethically or analytically. That is not to say that ethical questions did not emerge in relation to trainees. Nonetheless, these were easier to resolve and so did not create the kind of tricky dilemmas reported here.

Researcher positionality

Coffey (1999) dedicates a whole book to exploring the complexities, contradictions and challenges of being an ethnographer working in the field. Many of the discussions centre round what she calls 'the ethnographic self', that is, the real person with emotions, needs and desires who is doing field work. She argues that 'Fieldwork involves the enactment of social roles and relationships, which places the self at the heart of the enterprise' (1999: 23). These roles and relationships can be conceived of as 'positionality', that is, how the self is performed and perceived.

Goldring (2010) eloquently describes the issues he encountered with positionality when researching gay married men in a Manchester self-help group. As a former gay married man himself, he could empathise with many of the emotions and problems this group faced in their everyday lives. As a researcher, he had to find a way to be both part of the group, a confidant and friend, and a researcher of the group, a difficult positioning which, in the end, he was not able to sustain. As a former employee of the Centre in which I did my research, a former course director of the course team I researched, and a good friend to the four trainers, I had similar, though perhaps not as sensitive, issues to negotiate. Although I had not worked at the Centre for some time, there was anxiety amongst the trainers about my new role as researcher. One trainer wanted me to give feedback on the feedback he/she delivered to the trainees which would have positioned me in the role of 'expert trainer', one I was anxious to avoid. Another felt I would be casting judgement on his/her performance, which again, I was not interested in doing. It took a number of meetings, formal and informal, and the first interviews, to explain the purpose of the research and to gain trainers' trust in me as a researcher. At the same time, I retained my friendship inside and outside the research site with the trainers. Coffey (1999) describes in some detail a friendship she developed with a research informant, Rachel, during her own fieldwork in an accountancy firm. However, this friendship came to an end when Rachel disagreed on what had happened in the field, interpreting events differently. Luckily, my friendships have remained intact, which is due, in part at least, to their having been firmly established before starting the research.

A more challenging job, in some ways, was to persuade myself of the change in my role. It was difficult for me to believe that I had enrolled on a PhD and was conducting research in the field. I was nervous about my positioning, worried that I would make a mistake with the technology or miss something important or not be taken seriously. Developing my researcher persona took time: it is noticeable that in the early interviews with trainers, for example, I make excuses for my lack of experience and downplay my interviewing skills. In later interviews, I am much more sure of myself and what I want to know and the interview proceeds more smoothly. While I tried to position myself as the researcher when doing the observations and interviews, my other 'membershippings' (Richards, 2006) were often made relevant, by me and by the research participants (see Garton and Copland (2010) for a discussion).

It was easier to be the researcher with the trainees. As none of them knew me, I was able to foreground this position and explain the non-participatory approach I wanted to take to the research. They knew I was focusing on the trainers' practices rather than on theirs, and they did not seem concerned that I was in the room. Indeed, I often joined in with the trainees to some extent. This joining in usually happened before the feedback conference formally began, when the trainees and I were in the room but the trainer had not yet joined us. While they accepted me as the researcher, they were also aware that I was a former member of staff who had worked on the programmes. They often asked me about assignments, job opportunities and for my own experiences of teaching abroad. I, in turn, asked about their motivations for doing the course, what they had done formerly, and on the intensive course, or how they were coping with the very hot weather. I sympathised with the amount of work they had to do, the demands on their time and their attempts to understand how the rather complex assessment worked. As I did not watch their lessons, I was not quizzed for my opinions on how well they had done, and this was a benefit as they knew I could not influence their assessment. Occasionally I also met the trainees by chance outside the training room. Once I comforted a trainee who was very upset by the lesson she had given and tried to reassure her; with another, I talked about the differences between the CELTA and government-sponsored teaching courses, with which I was also familiar. With the trainees, then, I was seen primarily as a researcher but also as a source of information and a sympathetic ear.

I was, then, positioned in different ways and at different times by the trainers, the trainees and even by me. As Coffey (1999) explains, this range of roles is not unusual and nor is the number of complex negotiations in which the ethnographer must engage in order to develop relationships and remain in the field. What is particularly difficult, however, is to 'acknowledge and critically (though not necessarily negatively) engage with the range of possibilities of position, place and identity' (Coffey, 1999: 36). Developing relationships is vital and requires the researcher to take opportunities and to find the time to talk openly to participants during data collection. However, I think it is more difficult fully to address Coffey's demands regarding position, place and identity while in the field, as requirements on the researcher's time and attention are so strong. Novice researchers should take comfort in the notion that research is not only field work – reflection, reading, scrutinising and analysis are all vital elements, and all suitable spheres for engaging with these concepts.

Researcher voice

The researcher's voice in ethnographic work has been problematised by writers on ethnographic practice. Traditionally, ethnographies were given by writers who did not write themselves into the narrative. However, in recent times, it has been recognised that the ethnographic account is highly influenced by the ethnographer, who brings a range of biases, ideas, emotions and feelings to the research. Furthermore, emerging approaches to research (such as feminist research) and developing sensibilities (such as post-modernity) have influenced how ethnographers present themselves in texts. Some recent ethnographies, then, have included a strong biographical element (see, for example, Donnell Johnson, 2004), while others, as Hertz (1997) suggests, are 'presenting the author's self whilst simultaneously writing the respondents' accounts and representing their selves' (Hertz, 1997, cited in Coffey, 1999: 132). Arnesen summarises current thinking on the self in ethnographic research in her discussion of interviews:

> As a researcher, I am part of the text and provide direction by my questions in the interviews and the decisions I make regarding the form and the context of the text. I am well aware that there are many alternative ways to interpret the interviews and to present the text. My role is an active participant influencing how the tale is told. I am a person positioned between what actually happened and the account of it. (2003: 95)

In applied linguistics research, however, where the unit of analysis tends to be spoken or written text, it is more unusual for the writer's voice to be explicitly heard. While the occasional 'I' or 'we' might slip in when focusing on a decision, for example, voice is implicit rather than explicit. My approach followed Hertz (1997): I wrote myself in to the study, in order to describe its motivation, to document my emotional reactions to particular feedback conferences, and to uncover my own biases. The following extract from my thesis demonstrates this approach.

Extract 1

In the interests of reflexivity, I cannot ignore my personal response at this point. My field notes show that I was slightly outraged by Patrick's stance:

> *I find Patrick's position quite arrogant given he has only been teaching English for 3 weeks and Lauren has been teaching for at least ten years! His language is interesting - he almost sounds like the trainer 'we'll have to agree to differ' and 'I think the distinction is quite important'. Where he does have the high ground is when he says 'they got it they did see the difference', as he is in a privileged position as teacher*

> (Lauren field notes, 250706)

I felt that Lauren's epistemological position was strong and that Patrick was, literally, wrong.

While such an approach is open to accusations of being confessional (Pillow, 2003), it also enabled me to be honest about my relationship with the research participants and recognise that I had strong feelings about the roles of trainers and trainees and about teacher training at this level. Taylor (2002: 4) acknowledges such realities when she argues, 'objectivity is not attainable because people's perceptions and interpretations are inevitably selective and shaped by the understandings they bring to any situation'. In other words, this ethnography was a long way from presenting research from a seemingly neutral perspective.

─────────────────── **Activity 1** ───────────────────

You have decided to conduct a linguistic ethnographic research project in a context with which you are very familiar, and where you have friends/family as well as colleagues. What kind of ethical issues would conducting research in this context throw up? How would you resolve these? What would you do if during the research you uncovered/ recorded something that was analytically fascinating but which might compromise one or more of your participants?

THE DATA

For my project, I collected the following data: observational field notes; recordings (audio and video); interviews (recorded) with trainers; and focus groups (recorded) with trainees. As mentioned in my vignette, I originally found field notes the most challenging. Coming from an applied linguistics background, collecting, transcribing and analysing spoken data was familiar. However, making observational notes, which had to be written up into field notes soon after, was a new experience. Like many new to this type of data, I worried about what I should write, how I would know if what I wrote was relevant and, perhaps more than anything, the nakedness of the field notes – they laid bare my prejudices and opinions, undermined any attempt at neutrality (which, I believed at the time, was important) and highlighted my ignorance of ethnographic procedures. To me, writing field notes was like performing on stage: you had to be aware of your performance and simultaneously free of it. There were few models around which I could 'copy', and the advice from seasoned researchers tended to be about logistics (see, for example, Berg, 1998; Silverman, 2001; Richards, 2003), or discussed field notes in an abstract way (for example, Emerson et al., 1995).

As suggested above, the first stage of producing field notes is observation, which may or may not come with the opportunity to make notes. Luckily, I had this opportunity (although many ethnographers do not) as I sat at a table away from the group, as can be seen in Figure 4.2.

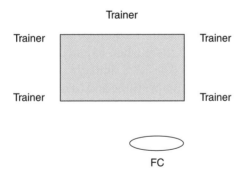

Figure 4.2 Typical seating arrangement during feedback

As I observed, I kept in mind my research questions, not because I was looking for definitive answers to these but because I knew from hours spent observing teachers professionally that unfocused observation can be unhelpful as well as exhausting. That is not to say that I did not jot down other aspects that captured my attention but rather that I focused my observation on particular aspects of feedback practices.

The second stage requires writing up. When I first sat down at my computer on the evening of my first day of observing the feedback conference, my observational scribbles in front of me and my head full of ideas, my only real problem was knowing where to start. I soon found, like Erickson (1990), that:

> Write-up stimulates recall and enables the researcher to add information to that contained in the unelaborated, raw notes. Write-up also stimulates analytic induction and reflection on relevant theory and bodies of research literature. There is no substitute for the reflection during fieldwork that comes from time spent with the original fieldnotes, writing them up in a more complete form, with analytic insights recorded in them. (p. 147)

I was also new to interviewing but I was more confident with this method of data collection than I was with writing field notes. As I state above, I also became more successful at interviewing as the research process went on. Some of my most successful interviews came towards the end of the process when I re-interviewed trainers and showed them sections of video or transcripts of the feedback talk for discussion and comment. Insights were gleaned at that point that significantly contributed to later data analysis (see Copland, 2011) and to my understandings of the feedback conference as a situated social genre. Later I too became very interested the co-construction of interviews, in particular how prior relationships with the trainers affected this (see Garton and Copland, 2010).

Data storage and readiness

As a new researcher, I was surprised by the huge amounts of data that the research generated and found organising them quite stressful: retrospectively, I think lack of time facilitated my natural inclination to store data in a somewhat disorganised way. My feeling was that as long as I had the recordings/field notes/interviews on my computer, I would be able to locate them when required. However, this was inefficient and dangerous (my backing up skills were similarly chaotic) and it would have been much more effective to set up a proper filing and labelling system in advance, and, as with field notes, attended to saving files as soon after the field visit as possible, building in time to the fieldwork schedule for organising data. I am much improved now in my approach to storing data (though not perfect) and try to make sure that copies are stored virtually, in my case in 'Dropbox', as well as on the hard drive.

Making data ready for analysis was similarly challenging. I stayed on top of the field notes, and, after each visit to the site, dedicated some time the same day to writing them up. This ensured that when it came to the end of the data collection process, I had one data set that could be considered 'complete' in that a whole set had been produced.

However, the recordings presented a different challenge. In order to analyse the feedback conferences generically, and to present the talk in the thesis, I needed to transcribe the feedback and the interviews. This took an extraordinarily long time. In the end, I hired a transcription service to transcribe the interviews and, after some deliberation, to complete the feedback conferences transcriptions. Although this approach would be criticised by some (transcription is analysis), I believe that for the initial genre analysis of the feedback conferences and the content analysis of the interviews, the transcriptions prepared by the transcription service were good enough. It was later, when I came to micro analyse sections of the talk that I spent some time working on the prepared transcripts, arriving at the level of delicacy required for this type of work (for more on this issue, see Chapter 8).

Activity 2

Think about your place of work or your place of study. Identify an area in which people gather (perhaps a common room or the mail room). Spend one hour in this space making observational notes. You are responding to the following research questions:

What relationships are developed in the communal area?

What kind of talk do people engage in?

Go back to your workstation and write up your observational notes (this should take about one hour). What differences are there between your observational notes and your field notes?

Underline sections of the field notes where you respond to the research questions. Highlight sections where you develop ideas you have noted briefly in your observational notes. Circle those sections which show preliminary analysis. How could you use field notes in your next study?

ANALYSIS OF DATA

I agree with researchers who argue that analysis begins from the moment you start to collect data; after all, you are at this stage selecting what is relevant to your interests and to your research questions. However, this level of analysis is almost intuitive rather than deliberate as we tend to go with gut feelings about what is important. The real problems with data analysis come when you sit at your desk surrounded by your data and wonder what you are to do with them all and how you are going to make sense of them. In this section, I would like to show the steps that I went through to conduct analysis on the different data sets. These steps can be seen in Figure 4.3, though it would be wrong to suggest that the process followed an entirely linear progression or that I had decided on these steps before beginning the analysis. Rather, this figure represents a retrospective account of the organisation of data analysis.

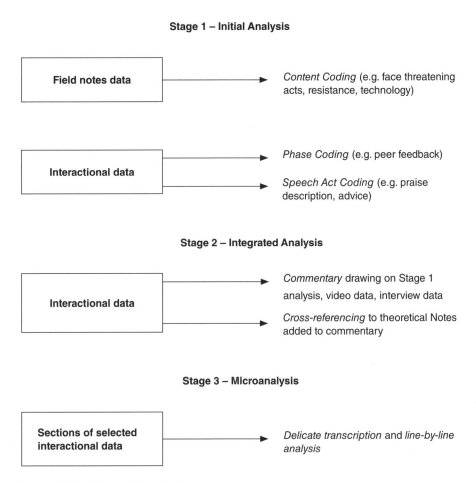

Stage 1 – Initial Analysis

Field notes data → *Content Coding* (e.g. face threatening acts, resistance, technology)

Interactional data → *Phase Coding* (e.g. peer feedback)
→ *Speech Act Coding* (e.g. praise description, advice)

Stage 2 – Integrated Analysis

Interactional data → *Commentary* drawing on Stage 1 analysis, video data, interview data
→ *Cross-referencing* to theoretical Notes added to commentary

Stage 3 – Microanalysis

Sections of selected interactional data → *Delicate transcription* and *line-by-line analysis*

Figure 4.3 Stages of analysis

Stage 1 - initial analysis

As can be seen, the initial analysis involved working with the field notes and feedback data. I began by coding the field notes. This was a pragmatic decision as I had not done this kind of analysis before and felt that the field notes comprised a manageable data set. As with most analysis of this kind, I decided on some of the codes before beginning the analysis as my notes had been influenced to some extent by my research questions. For example, as I was interested in power I decided that 'face threatening acts' would be a useful label. Other codes, however, emerged as the analysis went on. For example, 'technology' was obviously an issue as I was constantly referring to it! The content analysis served one important function in particular; it helped to reveal my concerns as a participant observer, making me more aware of where my sympathies and prejudices lay, and helping me to develop a reflexive attitude to the research site and to my data.

In Extract 1, above, I presented an example from my field notes in which my feelings and thoughts are overtly described. However, in many other extracts, my beliefs are more implicit than explicit, as in Figure 4.4, which also included my codes and notes.

In the first section of the field notes, I make fairly strong judgements about what I observe although I refrain from openly praising or criticising the trainer or trainees. I use the appraising adverb 'clearly' in the notes, which I underline in the analysis, to signal my positionality (that I align with the trainer). I then also explicitly side with the trainer's evaluation of the trainee's lack of preparation when I write 'but not too harshly, I felt'. There are other implicit judgements in this text – Simon folding his arms is problematic in some way to me as I highlight it and make a note to 'check the video' for evidence of him folding his arms. Then, when I write 'it was clear that Madeline did not think that practice was enough' I interpret Madeline's actions as being critical of Simon (using 'clear' again, this time as an adjective, to signal this position). In the final section, I turn my attention to the notion of 'practice' in class (which I am implicitly contrasting with 'presenting new language', using my emic understanding of training practices). I first question my own ideas about practice in

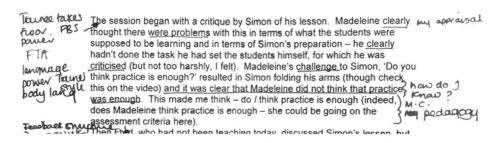

Figure 4.4 Extract from coded field notes

class, something not immediately relevant to my research, and then contrast my reflections with the more relevant beliefs of the trainer, speculating that the assessment criteria might have something to say about the role of practice in CELTA teaching.

My point, then, is that close analysis of the field notes ensured that not only was content coded but that my view of what I observed was acknowledged and taken into account. Indeed, eventually I arrived at a dual coding system: colour codes on the left referred to how the participants behaved and those on the right (in pink) revealed my own views and prejudices.

The second part of Stage 1 was an analysis of the transcripts. This I did in two ways. First, I wanted to understand the extent to which feedback could be considered a genre, using 'formal communicative/semiotic characteristics that make a chunk of communication recognisable' (Blommaert, 2007c: 4). To do this I looked for what Waite (1995: 33) calls 'phases' in feedback. Waite uses Scheflen's definition of phase, which I also adopted (Scheflen, 1973: 65, cited in Waite, 1995: 33):

> When two or more people come together they engage in a common activity. These activities form a context for the relations, which become phases in the sequences of activity. Each phase is a context for the particular kinds of communicative behaviour which each participant contributes.

Phases, then, are sections of feedback in which certain types of talk are engaged in by participants. I identified five phases. I then colour coded the font in the transcripts according to the phase of feedback. The phases I identified were: other talk about teaching (grey font); peer feedback (blue font); trainer feedback (green font); questioning (pink font); self-evaluation (red font). Of course, these were very broad categories, but their very broadness ensured that the phase analysis was workable (that is, all the feedback talk was an example of one or other of the phases).

Identifying phases was helpful in showing how feedback was organised on a macro level: although the order of phases was flexible and often overlapped, phases were a fixed feature of all conferences. However, phase coding created a very broad scheme and further drilling down was needed in order to understand how talk was organised. I applied a second level of analysis that I called 'speech act coding'. I labelled the talk produced by participants according to what its primary purpose seemed to be (this analysis was quite subjective as in many cases utterances seemed to have a number of different functions). Speech acts were colour coded (this time in blocks of colour). So positive evaluation provided in the peer feedback phase had a blue font but was shaded yellow. As I struggle now for labels to describe the myriad colours I used (unfortunately, the publisher could not stretch to colour printing!) the complexity of the analysis becomes apparent (see Figure 4.5 below).

Phase	Typical Speech Acts
Black font = OTHER TALK ABOUT TEACHING PHASE	Clarification (grey shade) Institutional talk (lilac shade) Empathy/humour (generic) (purple shade)
Blue font = PEER FEEDBACK PHASE	+ve evaluation (praise) (yellow shade) −ve peer feedback (criticism) (mustard shade) Suggestion/advice (teal shade) Empathy/humour (purple shade) Expressing belief/drawing on experience (red shade) Clarifying point in peer's lesson (dark grey shade)
Green font = TRAINER FEEDBACK PHASE	+ve evaluation (praise) (yellow shade) −ve evaluation (criticism) (mustard shade) Organising talk (turquoise shade) Empathy/humour (purple shade) Suggestion/advice (teal shade) Expressing belief/drawing on experience (red shade) Clarifying point in trainee's lesson (dark grey shade)
Pink font = QUESTIONING PHASE	Nominating/organising question (turquoise shade) Probing question (black shade)
Red Font = SELF-EVALUATION PHASE	+ve evaluation (praise) (yellow shade) −ve evaluation (criticism) (mustard shade) Description/explanation (blue shade) Trainee accepts evaluation (aubergine shade) Expressing belief/drawing on experience (dark green shade) Trainee rejects evaluation (light green shade)

Figure 4.5   Grid showing colour coding

This analysis provided useful findings about how feedback conferences were organised, who spoke about what and when, and how pedagogic knowledge was transferred and negotiated. The analysis also began to shape the genre analysis as it revealed the 'conventionalised expectations' used 'to shape and construe the communicative activity' (Rampton, 2006: 128) that participants were engaged in. Furthermore, the colour coding showed that certain speech acts were more common than others; for example, there were few 'red font/green shading' sections, which represented a trainee rejecting evaluation. Accepting or rejecting evaluation evoked power relations, a key focus of my study.

Stage 2 – integrated analysis

At the end of the first stage, I had coded field notes and colour coded transcripts (and had a much better feel for my data). However, both these data

	[
J	(laughs)
C	to see it working in and and see how it could be fixed I mean in the ideal world I'd have fixed it before I got there but erm I sat there for hours trying to visualise () how

	[
S	mm
C	it's going to work () and I struggled I I sort of canned the entire lesson three times ()
	[
J	mm
C	and tried to find something else
	(.)

L	Right (laughs)
	And then went back to it
L	Uhuh () yes it's one of those erm () looking at the logistics of things is often quite difficult I think () isn't it
C	And I I just couldn't get it but I think I might have got it now (laughs)
L	Okay so Stuart I'd like you to think of erm () a good thing () that you'd like to say about Calista's lesson
S	I thought she dealt very well with late-comers rearranged the groups perfectly () erm
C	That's what I always say about you (laughs)

	[
J	(laughs)
S	No no cause I like I that was one of my major criticisms recently that I that I didn't (..) er and I I thought the time with moving like people to this table and when you got sheet to come round that was spot on
	(.)
L	And a question
S	And a question
C	What was your lesson about (long laughs)

	[
S	right actually no I've got a I've got a que I've got a question-mark here it says purpose of survey
C	Oh () it was to establish exactly how green they really were (.) we ran out of time
L	Do you mean language purpose
S	Erm
C	Oh right sorry
	[
S	well n no I don't know no not language purpose because I I think you know a lot of language was used in (.) everyone getting the results () but then when it was being filled out on the board (..) erm where is it (....) yeah cause I I guess I felt that they all had () the same numbers as each other written down
C	They sh they sh they should have () done I think
	[[
S	so that they you know what I mean though I mean sort of six zero six zero () I thought () they already had that down you know what I mean

(Continued)

```
      [
C     yeah
C     It was too it was to that was to illustrate the the six out of six  () two out of three ()
                                                                    [            [
S                                                                   mm           mm
```

Figure 4.6 Example of integrated analysis

sets were separate entities, as were both analyses. I needed to find a way to integrate the data sets so that the analytic points in one set supported and developed the analytic points in the other. What is more, I had to find a way to use the data from the interviews, which I had not as yet analysed. My solution was to use the colour-coded transcripts as the base data set. I then went through each feedback conference carefully, adding codes and comments from the field notes, cross-references to interview data, and notes from video footage, where available, through the 'Insert Comment' function on Microsoft Word. These notes created a commentary on the feedback, sometimes providing explanatory comment and sometimes describing what was happening physically. An example of this integrated analysis can be found in Figure 4.6, which is provided for illustration only.

The point I wish to make from this figure is that this commentary is analytical in that it attempts to develop the colour-coded analysis by providing contextual detail and participants' perceptions (including my own) on the development of the interaction. This process took many weeks, and involved re-listening to the audio tapes and video tapes and checking my labelling.

It was during the integrated analysis stage that I re-read articles/chapters which I had found helpful and read recent papers which were relevant to my topic. I looked at my own data in terms of others' findings, cross-referencing accordingly. I was influenced by Rampton (2006: 404) who argues:

> Cross-referencing to theoretical literatures might lack the parsimony of structural modelling, and disturb the impression of uncontaminated naturalism that ecological descriptions sometimes convey, but there is no reason why it should entail a retreat from the disciplines of empirical data.

Indeed, I felt that this stage of my analysis enabled me to see patterns across the data and also alerted me to sections of the transcribed data that had not seemed pertinent first time round. I feel I can claim, like Rampton, that without this literature, 'a whole argument would fall apart and the data would regress to a set of separate piles' (p. 405).

Stage 3 – microanalysis

'Microanalysis' is the 'open-ended immersion in the situation being investigated' (Rampton, 2007b: 2) and requires that 'you launch into the process of detailed transcription, inhabitation, description and analysis' (p. 3). Microanalysis entails repeated listening/viewing of the data, a detailed and informative transcription, and a line-by-line (Richards, 2003) analysis of the data, asking questions such as '"Why this now?" "What else could have been done here and wasn't?"' (Rampton, 2007b: 5).

Perhaps one of the most difficult decisions in terms of microanalysis is choosing salient sections of data. Analysts can be accused of cherry picking sections to make a particular analytical or theoretical case. Researchers must make it clear why particular sections have been chosen – is it because they are typical, atypical or salient in some other way (see Erickson, 1992). Jewitt (personal communication) reports that in her work she chooses sections of video to transcribe and analyse after repeated viewings of the whole tape (in her case, of classrooms). In my case, I chose sections that demonstrated typicality in terms of genre (through identifying repeated instances of the same phenomenon or pattern) or that showed how the conventions of the genre were being challenged (atypicality). I also chose sections where either the negotiation or the demonstration of power were particularly apparent. In terms of analytic tools, I then used Conversation Analysis (CA) and Politeness Theory (PT) to show how face, a key construct in PT, was negotiated on a move-by-move basis (see Goffman, 1967, and Brown and Levinson, 1987, for classic introductions to face, and Arundale, 2006, 2010 and Haugh and Bargiela-Chiappini, 2010, for recent exemplifications). In the following section I show, through a worked example, how PT developed my analysis and how the linguistic analysis was supported and expanded by the ethnographic data.

DISCOURSE AND ANALYSIS IN LINGUISTIC ETHNOGRAPHY

As stated above, one of the phases I identified in the feedback conference was 'peer feedback'. This entailed trainees giving feedback on each other's lessons. Sometimes they would offer positive feedback and sometimes negative. They would also give advice, show empathy/humour, draw on their own lessons and clarify points (see Figure 4.5). The initial analyses had shown that although encouraged by trainers, negative feedback was not common. This made the sections of feedback, in which negative evaluation was given, salient. I applied Politeness Theory to these sections to discover how trainees constructed their negative comments and how others reacted to these criticisms.

Extract 2 below, is an example of negative feedback, followed by an analysis using Politeness Theory. Fred, a trainee, is providing feedback to Hannah, another trainee: the criticism is that the activities Hannah introduced in her lesson were not distinct enough. However, it takes some linguistic work to make this point:

Extract 2

F: I was just going to say that sort of the distinction between sort of the two last
    activities wasn't really very clear at all one sort of ran in to the other one and they
                                                    [
H: mm
F: didn't really kind of know what was going on and things until you started
    going round sort of explaining and things like that
              [[[
H: mm   yeah   yep

Fred introduces his criticism using a distancing device ('I was just going to say that'). The past progressive form here coupled with the adverb 'just' shows Fred downplaying his criticism (he does not say, 'My criticism is …'), which he then introduces ('the distinction between … the two last activities wasn't … very clear at all one … ran into the other one and they didn't … know what was going on'). However, he surrounds the criticism with 'softeners', that is, vague phrases that have the effect of reducing the severity of the criticism ('sort of'; 'sort of'; 'really'; 'sort of'; 'really kind of'; 'and things'). Fred then mitigates the criticism with a positive comment ('until you started going round … explaining') to show that not everything that Hannah did was, in his opinion, wrong.

Holmes and Stubbe (2003: 146) suggest that 'hedging and attenuation are important resources in managing problematic talk' and Fred seems to show, through the extensive use of these devices, that he knows what he wants to say is difficult. What is more in praising immediately after criticising, Fred uses what Tracy (2008: 187) calls 'positive jewelry' so that the feedback is not wholly negative. Fred, then, does a good deal of 'face work' in order that his negative evaluation is accepted by both Hannah and the group.

For her part, Hannah says little but she does provide acknowledgment tokens ('mm', 'yeah', 'yep'). Acknowledgment tokens can have a range of functions, but in this case they seem either to show agreement with Fred's comments or to indicate that Fred's comments are acceptable within the genre of feedback conference (after all, Hannah could have interrupted or contradicted or even agreed effusively with what Fred says, but does not). Fred's cleverly negotiates providing negative evaluation through employing appropriate face-saving devices. He does so effectively and successfully.

Politeness Theory, then, can support the researcher in understanding how participants negotiate face on a move-by-move basis, and this analysis can provide an empirical foundation for claims then made in the central discussion around power. However, the linguistic analysis can only show *how* face is negotiated; it cannot explain *why* it is necessary. In order to better understand this dynamic, the analyst needs to look across the range of data sets and their analyses. The integrated analysis of Fred's feedback was crucial in this regard. First, it included a reference to my field notes where I comment on Fred's bravery in giving negative feedback and the skill with which he did so. There was also a comment about the focus group data where Fred had described his feelings about feeding back to peers. I went back to all the data sources for a more detailed look.

The field notes overall contained a number of comments around peer feedback, noting how trainees seemed to struggle to do it, and how much of their feedback is descriptive rather than 'critical' in nature. They also noted how in some cases trainees reacted badly to negative feedback delivered by peers while in other cases they reacted well, as in the case in Extract 2. In other words, peer feedback was experienced in different ways. This led me then to look at other phases of peer feedback for differences and commonalities in face negotiation. My findings, perhaps unsurprisingly, were that negative evaluation tended to be quite short and when it was tentative and hedged, feedback was generally received well by trainees (in other words, trainees seemed at least to accept the feedback). Also, trainees often referred to a similar weakness in their own teaching before proffering negative evaluation. As with hedging and other distancing devices, this self-evaluation had the effect of mitigating negative evaluation, as if the trainees wanted to share in the blame as well as deliver it.

The sections in which negative evaluation seemed to be contested by trainees (red font, green highlight) were far fewer in number but generally the discussion went on for longer, and the trainee providing the negative evaluation often backtracked to some extent or noted that the opinion was personal once the evaluation had been refuted. In one case, a trainee refused to take part in peer evaluation (see Copland, 2012 for a detailed discussion), which, apart from being atypical, alerted me to the potential tension in peer evaluation and the trouble it could cause for trainees.

Examining the field notes and feedback data in detail drew out the complexities of peer feedback, and the different approaches trainees took to taking part, or not, in the peer evaluation. This was invaluable in helping me to produce detailed and nuanced analyses. However, the *why* question remained only partially answered. I now turned to the focus group data, to further explore this crucial ethnographic question.

Trainees in both focus groups suggested that they found peer evaluation difficult, but for a variety of reasons. The trainee, Simon, who had refused to take part in one feedback session and in another had had his negative evaluation refuted by a peer, was particularly interesting on the topic. When I raised peer evaluation, he stated:

Extract 3

Trainee S: I felt that () we generally exchanged like compliments and stuff after the lesson after the first few () and that repeating those was in front of the trainer wasn't really worthwhile and I didn't feel that I could make any criticisms

FC: Right you didn't have any to make or you didn't want to make any
Trainee S: No I had them to make but I didn't feel I could make any
FC: Right wh why didn't you feel you could make them?
Trainee S: Just cos I didn't think they'd be received () um (..) I didn't think they'd be recei::ved () ((*rising tone*)) positively () maybe that's a bad expression

Simon, the trainee in this extract, suggests that negative evaluation was not welcomed by his group of trainees and this discouraged him from offering this kind of feedback (he suggests he did not engage with positive feedback either as this was generally performed outside the formal environment of the feedback conference). His comments point to the importance of relationships within the group: in his opinion, negative feedback was not well received and so for him, there was no point making it.

In the same focus group, another trainee points to a different reason for finding peer evaluation difficult.

Extract 4:

Trainee J: It feels sometimes like we're expected to give feedback on each other's teaching, but we don't have the knowledge that the, erm that the tutors do, so you're kind of felt like you're pushed to give feedback and at the same time you're often, you know, you feel like you're often wrong about your feedback because you don't have the same criteria to base your decisions on. So sometimes it feels quite, it feels a little uncomfortable to me sometimes

This trainee produces a three-point argument to explain her position: she does not have the expertise of the trainer; she feels forced to give feedback even when she feels unsure of its value; and she is not given criteria on which to make her judgements. In other words, she lacks confidence in her own opinion.

In the other focus group, trainees gave two reasons for not taking part in feedback. The first also focused on judgment, but from a slightly different perspective:

Extract 5

Trainee F: I mean we kind of give feedback to each other and things, but sometimes the feedback we give is ..sometimes we can say, sometimes we can say, 'Oh I thought that was really good, the trainer would say it wasn't ... good

Here Fred, the trainee who gives the negative feedback in Extract 2, suggests that his view of strengths and weaknesses in lessons did not always concur with the trainer's, and although he does not explicitly say this stops him from giving feedback, it could account for the care he takes when doing so. The second reason given is that trainees find problems focusing.

Extract 6

Trainee H: And because it's like erm, it's like an exam isn't it, really, you're being exam-
              ined how you teach, so you're a bit nervous and sometimes you can't always
              take in what, yourself

Not being able to focus on peers in the lesson because of nerves was a common reason given by trainees during my time as a trainer and reiterated here.

Taken together, these comments show trainees' discomfort with the peer evaluation phase of feedback. Trainees feel variously that their comments are: not valued; not based on expertise; not the same as the trainer's; and difficult to make because of lack of concentration. Underlying each opinion is a complexity of power relations (with the trainers, with each other, with the group, with the Academy). The first trainee, S, seems to feel powerless in his group; the second trainee, J, feels forced to give feedback; the third, F, recognises that the trainer's opinion is more valuable than his; and the fourth, H, recognises the need to perform successfully to be positively evaluated. Of course, these are individual trainees' reported perceptions, but they are no less valid because of that. Importantly, how these power relations are locally managed are made manifest in the feedback conferences as it is here that 'individuals negotiate with the status that they and others have been allotted or which they have managed to achieve, and which within particular contexts they can contest or affirm, through their use of language and through their behaviour' (Mills, 2003: sec. 2:2). The answer to the 'why' question, then, is rooted in power relations.

In this section I have shown how using Politeness Theory as a discourse analytic tool can uncover the ways in which participants construct talk and negotiate status with others. However, I hope I have also shown that this tool is only one aspect of the whole linguistic ethnographic enterprise. In my approach, it is the dialogue between data sets and their analyses, continuously reiterated, that uncovers the detail of motivation and action in feedback.

Activity 3

Here is a section of data from a feedback conference. It is in the trainer feedback phase and Trainer 2 is criticising Trainee C's teaching of which verbs are commonly followed by a present participle ('ing' form) such as 'I enjoy eat**ing**', and which verbs are commonly followed by an infinitive form (to + verb) such as 'I want **to go** home'.

1. Trainer 2:   actually at no point (.) I know you put them in two boxes =
2. Trainee C: = I did explain the 'ing'
3. Trainer 2:   but at no point did you explicitly say look or raise their awareness about
4.   the fact that some of them go with 'ing' and some of them the =

(Continued)

(Continued)

 5. Trainee C: = I didn't yep
 6. Trainer 2: = infinitive and that you know that is an issue
 7. Trainee C: It's a fair cop
 8. Trainer 2: yep
 9. Trainee C: ((laughs))
10. Trainer 2: yep yep (.) yep
11. Trainee C: ((laughs))
12. Trainer 2: yep yep

- Make notes on the text. As you do so, answer Rampton's (2007b: 5) questions: Why this now? What else could have been done here and wasn't?
- In what ways does the trainer negotiate face issues? In what ways does the trainee?
- What else would you need to know in order to uncover the power relations in this extract?

(For a discussion of this extract, see Copland, 2011.)

REPRESENTATION AND WRITING UP

Professional audiences

Although the products of research are often aimed at an academic audience, much research in the social sciences can also have meaning and value for a professional audience. This audience might range from research participants to policymakers, from the media to practitioners. Each audience requires the researcher to consider carefully how research is represented and communicated. This is not a matter of dumbing up or dumbing down, but rather a matter of making the research accessible and relevant so that it can have the impact of which it is capable.

I have shared data in presentations to practitioners, mostly teachers and teacher trainers. My experience of doing so has not always been positive. Generally I have found that practitioners can be quite critical of their colleagues, and make negative comments about their feedback practices. I think this is because they have a good understanding of the professional context and relate the data to their own professional lives. They are also used to being evaluative. Furthermore, trainers will often use the data to forward their own agendas rather than to discuss the features I have introduced.

Recently, when giving professional talks, I have concentrated on features in my data that highlight what I consider to be good practice in feedback. In particular I show how knowledge is constructed in a dialogic way, that is, through talk that is collective, reciprocal, supportive, cumulative and purposeful (Alexander, 2005). The following extract is a case in point. I usually begin by introducing the context (that Eileen is the trainer and Hannah and Fred are both trainees and that they are talking about Hannah's lesson). You should recognise lines 18ff. as they have been discussed in some detail in the section above:

Extract 7

1.	Eileen:	Okay and something that you weren't so happy with
2.	Hannah:	Um I wasn't happy because I didn't give them a chance I think enough of a
3.		chance to practise making sentences using those verbs and verb patterns
4.	Eileen:	How clear were they did you think about that last activity
5.	Hannah:	I think um it there was a little bit of confusion possibly um for the last
6.		activity um but as I was explaining it in groups they seemed to understand
7.		what to do I think there was a bit of a problem they weren't really listening at
8.		the beginning and then I just felt a bit nervous I thought oh they're not really
9.		listening to me okay let's sort of go in groups and then try and explain it that
10.		way
11.	Eileen:	Right cos () how did you think you'd given your instructions were clear to
12.		start with
13.	Hannah:	Um no I don't think they were they could have been clearer I was just a bit
14.		worried bout time and I was like oh time's running out what shall I do um ()
15.		so that's possibly why ((laughs))
16.	Eileen:	What you feel
17.		[
18.	Fred:	I was just going to say that sort of the distinction between the two
19.		last activities wasn't really very clear at all one sort of ran in to the other one
20.		and they didn't really kind of know what was going on and things until you
21.		[[
22.	Hannah:	mm mm
23.	Fred:	started going round sort of explaining and things like that =
24.		[[
25.	Hannah:	yeah yeah

After getting trainers to read through the data extract in groups (it is essential that an audience is given the time to get to know data; reading it out loud can be an efficient and fun way to accomplish this), the first thing I ask trainers/educators to look at is topic nomination as this indicates whose agenda is being addressed. In this extract, Hannah nominates the topic (the verb phrases, line 3) and this is discussed throughout. It is her topic. I then focus on questioning by asking how many questions are asked and who asks them. This helps the audience to focus on Eileen, the trainer, who, rather than telling Hannah how to improve her lesson, asks her questions about what she did. While it could certainly be argued that Eileen is hijacking the topic to some extent, questioning rather than telling allows Hannah to contribute again, this time in a long turn, to explain her thought pro-cesses (as the teacher of the class, Hannah is in a privileged position in terms of understanding classroom interactions and dynamics).

Fred is the next focus in the discussion; I usually ask how he gets the floor. What I want to reveal here, which is atypical in my data, is that Fred interrupts the trainer. He then delivers a negative evaluation of Hannah's lesson (see above), which is also atypical (although valued by trainers). We then discuss how Eileen's approach in the conference may have influenced Fred's confidence and also the dialogic feel of the discussion.

One of the joys of presenting to professionals is that they draw on their own experiences when discussing the data and they often notice features which as a researcher you have missed. Importantly, the discussion might impact on practice, which, as an applied linguist, I am keen to promote.

In my experience, it is necessary to be very selective about what data you choose to share with different communities of users. As I have discussed above, there are ethical concerns to be considered as well as issues of access. In the next sections, I would like to focus on sharing data with other researchers and with participants in two different forums.

Sharing data with academic colleagues

Many university departments hold regular data workshops. I was not working in such an institution when I was conducting this study but I shared sections of my data at a workshop held on the Ethnography, Language and Communication course I described in my vignette. I submitted my data for this workshop as I felt opportunities such as these were relatively rare and would help me to assess whether my own interpretations were shared by others as well as giving me alternative readings of the data. I chose a piece of data which seemed to be troubling the boundaries of the generic conventions but which I was struggling to analyse. I was absolutely delighted with how the workshop developed, despite the fact that some readings of the data contradicted my own ideas, as I felt I developed critical capacity through the process. Other colleagues, however, were not as pleased when they submitted data for examination. They felt that either the data were not well understood or that there was a criticism of the research participants.

The moral of the story, of course, is that if you do share data in a workshop forum, you need to be ready to have your ideas and analyses challenged, developed and even contradicted, and this is not always a pleasant experience. On the other hand, such an experience will be useful in developing robust claims from your data, as you will know where the problems are and where objections might be made.

I would also advise that you choose your data carefully. Transcriptions are notoriously difficult to read and you need to be able to provide enough useful contextual detail without either boring or confusing your colleagues. Having said that, one of the most rewarding data workshops I have attended, given by Joke Dewilde, required us to read transcripts that included talk in Norwegian and Somali, which were then translated into English. At first, this seemed almost impossible to process, but as the workshop went on, our understandings developed and we found the different languages did not impede our ability to say useful things about the unfolding talk.

Sharing data with research participants

The most successful data-sharing experiences I have had have been with the participants in my research. In the post-observation interviews I took sections of the transcribed data, or the audio/visual recordings, and showed them to the trainers. I took extracts that I found either puzzling or which seemed to trouble the boundaries of accepted behaviour in the feedback conferences. This experience not only provided a more emic perspective on the interactions but also provided a space for me to reflect on my own interpretations and assumptions (see Copland, 2011). Importantly, it allowed me to share the research with the trainers and trainees and to give them a stake, however limited, in the research process. What is more, a number of the participants seemed to find the data personally useful, using it to reflect on their performance in the feedback and to better understand the other participants.

Sharing data with participants is not a novel approach (for example, see Lefstein and Snell, 2011) although it is not common either as much transcription and analysis happens once the researcher has left the research site. Nevertheless, it is worth considering timetabling data sharing at the research design stage. I certainly found it valuable.

CONCLUDING COMMENTS

In this case study I have described some of the processes I went through during my study, the problems I faced and the questions I had to answer. I am not claiming that I always made the best call during this research journey but my hope is that by laying some of these issues bare, I can reassure readers that insecurity, unpredictability, confusion and moral dilemmas are all common in research of this kind and should therefore be faced at least thoughtfully if not always calmly (see, too, Hey, 2002).

I have also shown how Politeness Theory as a discourse analytic tool can be used to examine linguistic data and uncover how face is negotiated between participants in interaction. I hope too that I have made the case for showing how other data sets and analyses can support a deeper understanding of face, in particular how it links to power relations.

The final section of this chapter has considered three different audiences for research findings and how data might be selected and presented to them depending on purpose. As research in the social sciences in general moves towards more participatory models, sharing data will become more common, but this will bring its own challenges in terms of interpretation and presentation.

KEY READINGS

Copland, F. (2011) 'Negotiating face in the feedback conference: A linguistic ethnographic approach', *Journal of Pragmatics*, 43(15): 3832–43.

Holmes, J., Stubbe, M. and Vine, B. (1999) 'Constructing professional identity: "Doing power" in policy units', in C. Roberts and S. Sarangi (eds) *Talk, Work and Institutional Order Discourse in Medical, Mediation and Management Settings*. Berlin: Mouton de Gruyter. pp. 351–85.

Kubanyiova, M. (2008) 'Rethinking research ethics in contemporary applied linguistics: The tension between macroethical and microethical perspectives in situated research', *Modern Language Journal*, 92(4): 503–18.

Roberts, C. and Sarangi, S. (1999) 'Hybridity in gatekeeping discourse: Issues of practical relevance for the researcher', in C. Roberts and S. Sarangi (eds) *Talk, Work and Institutional Order Discourse in Medical, Mediation and Management Settings*. Berlin: Mouton de Gruyter. pp. 473–504.

FIVE

Case Study Three: Ethnography and the Workplace

Frances Rock

SETTING THE CONTEXT: BACKGROUND INFORMATION, RESEARCH QUESTIONS AND FINDINGS

The police station is many things. It is a place for making enquiries about such apparently trivial matters as security marking of personal property. It is a place of detention for some. It is a place to recount unpleasant events seen, heard or experienced; a place of confessions and revelations. It is a place where journeys through the criminal justice system begin, from which return is impossible. Yet beyond these public images and experiences, the police station has another side. It is a place of banter and gossip; where snacks and crosswords pass the time. It is a place for career progression, meetings and email. These latter examples recognise the police station as a workplace. By distinguishing the diversity of activities and actions which occur in this setting, we can begin to see the police station in all its complexity; we see institutional life, rather than just an institution (Palomares and Poveda, 2010: 194). As I reported in my vignette at the beginning of this book, my PhD work focused on language and policing, specifically the communication of rights in custody and the interviewing of witnesses. I have since expanded my experience of researching policing, particularly contact between police and the public, by studying call-taking, interview training, complaints against police and written communication with witnesses. I will draw on my varied experiences in policing environments in this chapter but will focus on the custody setting, a microcosm of police work, for three reasons. First, because custody was my own entry point into workplace research so it illustrates one route in and indicates the foundations of my subsequent approach. Secondly, because custody is so focal and consequential, being 'where the rubber meets the road' (McConnell-Ginet, 2011: 102) for officers and lay constituencies, in different ways. Finally, partly as a result of this importance of custody, it is a site which provides many curious challenges and opportunities for linguistic ethnographic work.

The study of policing has a relatively long history in the social sciences (for example, Cicourel, 1968), taking in linguistics (for example, McElhinney, 1995) and ethnography (for example, Caldeira, 2002; Paperman, 2003). This is set against ground-breaking research from both disciplines in institutions (for example, Smith, 2005) and workplaces (for example, Holmes, 2006). Some recent work has taken a recognisably linguistic ethnographic line to such sites (for example, Flynn et al., 2010). When I started my research on language and the police in the late 1990s, the influence of linguistic ethnography was much less keenly felt by linguists than now. Nonetheless, methods which are now recognisably 'linguistic ethnographic' proved valuable. Through the lens offered by intricate data collection and analysis, questions I originally had about how police use language in their work were translated into an impetus to understand policing work as social action. Crucially for me, questions about how comprehension works in particular policing settings were transformed into a stimulus to examine the processes and practices of and around the joint creation of meaning in that work.

To begin this case study, I will introduce police custody and some of its definitive writing and talk. Individuals who are suspected of a criminal offence are taken into custody after arrest. They can be held for a limited time whilst investigations ensue and once the time limit is reached they must either be charged or released without charge. Since concerns about policing standards came to a head in the 1980s, police custody has become increasingly regulated. As a result, documents structure and punctuate custody. The Police and Criminal Evidence Act Code of Practice, Code C (currently in a 2013 edition) is core to this as it specifies requirements for 'the detention, treatment and questioning of persons by police officers'; it is the rule book of custody. Code C details, for example, what records should be kept of detention (Home Office, 2013a: 7–8, 26–7). Code C must be available in custody suites, not only for police officers' reference, but also so that detainees can read its assertions. However, Code C is a fairly intimidating document. It comprises 68 pages of close-set type organised into numbered sections each containing decimal-numbered sub-sections followed by, and cross-referencing, annexes. Perhaps in recognition of the demands that Code C places on readers, its key content for detainees, information on rights and entitlements, is presented in two other ways. The first, although less expansive, still involves written text; a boiled-down version of Code C, highlighting key rights. When I began my research that summary document was usually, and opaquely (Rock, 2007: 105), called the *Notice to Detained Persons* (its current version is available online, see Home Office, 2014). Speech is the second mode of communication to recast Code C, most notably delivering information about the right to silence, administered through a scripted caution. My study began with a focus on this written and spoken rights language which structures and punctuates custody. However I soon came to recognise complex interrelationships between the wider custody site, people's practices and language there.

Using the wide range of data that eventually became available (see 'Collection of data', below), I was able to ask research questions about the linguistic characteristics of the written rights notice and the spoken caution but also about their use in custody and the orientations of different custody participants to them. These questions were emergent, developing as the data pool grew (Sunderland, 2010: 8). The linguistic ethnographic drive to consider and connect multiple sources of data, and the particular combination of ethnographic and linguistic elements, led me to view the data as most usefully examined using the notion of transformation. In relation to the caution, this involved examining explanations of the caution, and in the case of the rights notice, examining revisions to the notice designed to aid comprehension. My research coalesced around two sets of questions:

- First, along the theme of *syntagmatic relations* and *intertextual chains*: In relation to both cautioning and written rights texts, what changes between the 'original' and the transformed text? Is the transformed text 'like' the original in any recognisable way, and if not, why not? How does it differ and what consequences might this have?
- Second, along the theme of *paradigmatic relations* or *polyvocality*: In relation to both cautioning and written rights texts, are there any similarities among the various transformed texts produced by various speakers and writers, and if not, why not? How do transformations differ from one another and what consequences might this have?

When revising both written rights notices and spoken cautions, changes were at all linguistic levels. Speakers and writers tended to remove what are often characterised as 'difficult' linguistic features such as passives and nominalisations as well as both omitting and adding information. By identifying and discussing the changes they made with them, it was possible to discover their orientations to features which they perceived as problematic. The transformations they made had knock-on effects on power relations, interpersonal arrangements and even function. By interviewing officers and detainees and observing the policing setting using field notes and photography, I was able to go beyond 'assessing comprehension and comprehensibility', finding, for example, that officers thought carefully about affective dimensions of their explanations; that procedures which aim to explain are often appropriated for other ends by both officers and detainees; and that issues such as face are important but often overlooked in rights communication.

This case study gives the opportunity to share experiences of doing language research in policing. As Tsitsipis notes, there is quite a difference between *explanandum* (what is to be explained), in this case activities in the world of policing; *explanatum* (the explanation itself), here results, findings and publications; and *explanans* (the process which produces the explanation), research activities including the investigator's active intervention in the interpretive process. He notes that the *explanans* frequently undergoes 'convenient erasure' in positivist approaches which reify phenomena (2007: 627). In this chapter, *explanans* is instead the main focus, providing a perspective on research activities.

RESEARCH DESIGN

My initial design centred on a plan to collect and analyse naturally occurring instances of cautioning. Initial literature searches revealed that work on rights in custody had had a fairly narrow methodological focus at that stage. The established research, from psychologists, tested rights texts' standard wordings outside the custody context (for example, Clare and Gudjonsson, 1992; Clare et al., 1998). As I noted in my vignette at the beginning of this book, a conversation with a solicitor exposed the limitations of this. In context, these texts are accompanied by extensive informal talk including explanations in officers' own words. This informal talk, the naturally-occurring delivery of rights, seemed too important to ignore. Examining this talk built on the work of Cotterill (2000), who had studied police officers' self-reports of their explanations of the caution, and Russell (2000) who focused on a small number of explanations from interpreted interviews. I anticipated collecting multiple recordings of explanations of the caution and asking research questions like 'How is the police caution brokered in context?' (Lillis and Curry, 2006); 'What discourse features characterise its delivery?'; 'How do detainees respond to the caution and its explanation?'; and 'How do detainees explain the caution when asked to demonstrate understanding during police interviews?' As I began to collect data, even naturally-occurring talk seemed impoverished. I began to see the central shortcoming of language data: it invariably leaves things to the analyst's inferences. Interpretation is necessary in examining audio-recordings, interviews and written data, for example. Yet by placing multiple forms of data together and revisiting them systematically and repeatedly, the analyst's inferences can become better informed, at least and at best, something new will emerge.

A desire to go beyond only analysing transcripts led to a reinvention of my research design. Getting individual data sets to speak to the research questions and to one another was an iterative process. As Blommaert asserts, linguistic ethnography is 'an open and experimental site in which people explore and try different ways of analysing language in society' (2007a: 687). Activities like selecting salient features for analysis segue into weighing the value of different data and in turn evaluating how, and indeed, whether data sets connect. My approach ultimately fits Rampton's characterisation of linguistic ethnography as 'a site of encounter where a number of established lines of research interact' (2007a: 585). By shifting to a responsive, open research design I could consider theoretical ideas, such as metalanguage, not only in relation to naturally occurring data. My response to the rich, complex situation I was finding in custody was to draw on ways of examining language in context which opened up the various sources of information rather than closing them down. My research design evolved strategically in response to increasing data access and the questions which emerged as my understanding of custody developed. Ultimately, various discourse analytic themes such as communities of practice, face and politeness, participation frameworks and speech acts became salient through data analysis. My work had an explicitly applied focus in that one major aim was to consider whether the communication of rights in custody was successful (and from whose perspective) and even how it might be improved (and for whom). As Scollon noted, '[As analysts] we are already engaged in the action under study. We don't have the option of asking whether we're involved in action; the only question is whether we're activist about it' (2004, in Kramsch, 2009: 262). The applied contextualisation of my analysis led me to take on some critical perspectives, particularly around the notion of 'difficult' language and to draw in additional disciplinary voices, most notably from document design and information design literature but also from applied sociolinguists (for example, Solomon, 1996).

The label 'research design' suggests something perhaps more pre-determined and principled than my data collection and analysis in this project felt. This absence of a feeling of design was largely caused by data access issues, discussed in the next section.

DATA COLLECTION

Ethics, access, feasibility, relationships in the field

Data collection was a long, complex journey. Perhaps the single most obvious challenge of working, or hoping to work, in legal settings is that access is fraught and consent to use data can be elusive (Speer and Stokoe, 2014). This understatement applies to many workplace settings. Yet there was cause for optimism about obtaining naturally occurring cautioning because cautioning is generic and universal despite occurring within police interviews; it occurs quite separately from the highly personal and identifying interview proper. I began with some informal, ad hoc approaches to getting data. At the time I was a volunteer for Victim Support (a charity which helps victims and witnesses of crimes). A colleague there, a former police officer, was very interested and made enquiries on my behalf. I also approached a linguist who undertook expert witness work. I approached local solicitors' firms, where I hoped to access data through recent detainees. All of this proved fruitless. I began to fear that I would not be able to collect any speech at all. This led me to reassess what forms of data I needed and, accordingly, to reassess my methods and methodological approach.

If I was to examine naturally occurring data, a discourse analytic approach which viewed analysis of talk and text as key would have been appropriate. Instead, as naturally occurring data seemed inaccessible, I began to consider investigating the settings where those texts and practices reside (Gee, 2005: 190) and working with elicited speech from interviews with police officers and detainees. In what turned out to be the most important activity of my doctoral work, I wrote to the Chief Constable (the most senior officer) of every geographical police force in England and Wales (at the time 43 forces), by name, seeking access to data. I had realised that, unexpectedly, the Notice to Detained Persons was not a uniform text but rather underwent recontextualization in each police force having been circulated in a suggested, not obligatory, format. Therefore the most elementary form of data that I requested was simply a copy of the Notice used in each police force. This was an uncontroversial request as this text was in the public domain, being given to everyone in police custody. Practically, it was an easy request for any police premises with a custody suite. I asked for additional access on a cline of imposition. This included access to naturally occurring recordings (most imposition because of their real-world status), opportunities to interview custody participants and to observe custody.

Responses to my 43 letters were mixed, not surprising given that no 'good news story' would likely follow from this work (Bamber and Sappey, 2007), but enabled me to obtain not only the naturally occurring data that I had originally sought but also many other things. After some perseverance I managed to collate examples of the rights notice for every police force in England and Wales. I also had permission to go to one force in the north of England to interview as many officers as I wished. From two other forces, I had permission to visit in order to listen to audio-recorded police interviews. My Victim Support colleague had also been busy. He helped me to arrange incredible access to data in the form of the opportunity to go to interviews and incidents with police officers. One other police force got in touch to let me know that a custody officer there was rewriting the Notice to Detained Persons for the Home Office. That force eventually allowed me to undertake extensive observations in custody suites and interview detainees; I established a long-term research relationship with the officer in question. I also interviewed police trainers. With this range of these forms of data an ethnographic approach was almost inevitable. At this point linguistic ethnography was still taking shape under that name (Rampton et al., 2004). Towards the end of my studies, in the early 2000s, I attended early meetings of what became the Linguistic Ethnography Forum. This was instrumental in helping me to recognise that my work was not a potpourri of observations about unconnected forms of drastically different data, but a systematic study whose constituent parts, informed by cross-cutting, complementary sources and methods could offer something distinctive to the linguistic and legal study of rights in custody and to characterisations of custody as a workplace.

Ethical issues were in my mind as I prepared to gather data, as I was, at that time, involved in drafting the student-focused part of the British Association of Applied Linguists' ethical guidance (BAAL, 2000). Ethics were not straightforward in my study. At the most simple end, I interviewed police officers and detainees and was able to explain my study to them in advance and to elicit consent to participate both before and after interview, offering what have relatively recently become generally predictable reassurances of anonymisation, confidentiality and respect (Rock, 2001).

Yet, to say that this is the end of the ethical story, even in these relatively 'simple' cases, would be to overlook subtlety and difficulty which is implicit in achieving anything that might be sensibly regarded as ethical research in 'real-world' settings.

Police officers were interviewed during work time when they were available, having been willingly released from their duties by their employers. However, whenever we interview someone at work, we turn consent into something more loaded than in many other situations. If an interviewee is asked to participate by their boss, how much space do they really have to refuse? I framed my consent-talk by directly addressing the potential for officers to feel compelled to participate. Imposition during work time can be professionally and practically costly. This was a factor I also needed to address, highlighting that interviews could be post-poned, cancelled or curtailed. Questions about work can threaten participants' professional self, jeopardising their sense of their work and its value. Moreover, the impression created of individuals and the organisation they represent can poten-tially be negative if interviews achieve their aim of candid reflection. Both of these considerations were especially important in one police force where I interviewed officers, because there, a very recent, highly controversial death in custody might have made officers unusually sensitive to damaging (self-)evaluations of their work.

Detainees presented different ethical challenges, in particular around access negotiations, which focused on the timing of my interviews. Initially the police force and I explored the possibility that I would interview detainees whilst they were in custody. This would have had the advantage of them being, quite liter-ally, a captive audience, which might have provided a good rate of agreement to be interviewed. However, the ethical costs are high. People in detention might well feel compelled to participate or might do so for the wrong reasons, seeking emotional support or to pass the time, for example. As I was discussing rights, detainees might have taken our exchange as instructional; I was not in a position to fulfil a pseudo-legal advising role. It was likely that interviews at this stage would have compromised the law too. Yet interviewing detainees, whilst detained, about the texts and practices they are encountering at that time would have clear research benefits. These benefits, for me, and for the police force did not outweigh the range of costs. I therefore interviewed detainees after they had been formally released, although I was able to do this in the custody suite both as a safety precau-tion and a convenience. Here, the priorities were to make it clear that just because the interview occurred in a police station, and was brokered by an officer, it was absolutely optional and I had no connection to the police, aside from my location.

As well as these constrained data collection moments, I formed many other kinds of working relationships during this research and issues of ethics, access, feasibility and relationships surfaced differently in each. For example, I became involved in extended collaboration with an officer who rewrote the rights notice. Our work became mutually beneficial and mutually defined, we often recorded our conver-sation. He arranged further data access and I became involved in his revisions and in communicating these to the Home Office. I also entered the working lives of officers in two locations where I was not recording but making field notes. There was a delicate line between keeping my presence as a researcher in their minds and distracting them by being present. The ethnographer walks the lines of emergent relationships like these and their consequences for ethics and access.

From the point of view of anonymisation, I was fortunate not only that there are many police forces but that I worked with a good number of them, as that brought a degree of automatic anonymisation. As well as anonymising individual officers and detainees, I also anonymised the police forces themselves. My anonymisation was not simply about removing names, though this is important. Rather, I looked carefully for other features which might suggest factors like the age and background of speakers (for example, cultural references) and altered those too, in ways which, for me, stopped short of decreasing the data's value (Rock, 2001). Anonymistion was particularly important as some of the data were fed back to officers, so it was important that they could not guess speakers' identities.

Researcher positionality and voice

Negotiating positionality materialises differently according to constituency. With police forces it was a constant necessity, for example, in access discussions, as I noted above. In the early stages, clarity about what the research needed, and what it could give, was essential. I had not anticipated being able to 'offer' much that would be useful at the police force level. I gave summaries of findings and upshots to anyone who requested them but rarely knew what happened to such feedback. However, ultimately I had positioned myself such that I became involved in redrafting one of the key texts in custody, as I will explain later.

Negotiating positionality with detainees involved not aligning, nor being seen to align, with police, yet not aligning with detainees so much that they unburdened themselves of compromising information (a practical imperative) or became absorbed only in confiding about their lives (a research-driven imperative). Details which seemed minor were influential in detainee interviews. For example, appearance can shape interview responses (Bucholtz and Hall, 2008: 416) and give 'street-cred' (Thorpe, 2012: 73). My sartorial choices became increasingly casual as time passed and I came to understand the risks of indexing formality.

With police officers, the challenge in positionality in interviews was a different one. It involved avoiding positioning as a 'know it all' who had swallowed the custody rulebook or, conversely, as someone completely naïve about procedures who needed things explained from the ground up. Again, this was a delicate balance achieved through negotiation and performance of self in interview. In the following excerpt, for example, the officer has come to correctly assume that I will understand 'changes in divisions and boundaries' as well as being able to infer a meaning for 'everything like that' and that I will understand these in relation to his main topic, the changing norms of custody. Transcription conventions for all excerpts are outlined in Figure 5.3 (p.142).

Extract 1: Divisions and boundaries

everything like that I've adapted to in twenty-two years and they'll change it again I'm sure same as we've changed divisions and boundaries and everything like that you've got to adapt to it and if you don't adapt to it and- you know you just- you just bang your head against a brick wall

Officers were well aware of tensions between their participation in research inter-views as police officers and organisational representatives, and their participation as individuals with personal views. Some of them initially seemed to construe the interview as an opportunity to demonstrate knowledge of and compliance with official procedures, such as the officer who told me '[detainees are] verbally told that they have the right to a solicitor and all their other rights and then they're handed that bit of paper'. This was, of course, not what the interview was about for me. I was interested in their orientations to and lived-experience of proce-dures, not an 'official line' on them. Yet perhaps the situation of being interviewed at work, triggering a desire to 'say the right thing', creating an expectation that I wanted facts. In all but one instance, attentive, qualitative interviewing permitted progress into more personal, experiential areas.

In my subsequent work I have frequently been fortunate enough to be positioned rather constructively from the outset, as someone fluent in policing procedures who 'get[s] police culture' as one officer put it (cf. Venkatesh, 2002). I have also been positioned as having something to offer police through applied language research. Achieving and maintaining a position as disinterested, pragmatic and sensitive to officers' agendas remains vital in order to have a voice, even in one's own research. Reflecting on my position and voice in this way has been important in putting reflexivity in its 'proper place in the conducting of fieldwork, descrip-tion, and writing' (Tsitsipis, 2007: 628).

THE DATA

I wanted to collect data that would not 'reduce the complexity of social events' but would 'describe the sometimes chaotic, contradictory, polymorph charac-ter of human behaviour', the 'complexity of social events' 'comprehensively' (Blommaert, 2007a: 682). The data collected were:

Written texts:

- 43 versions of the Notice to Detained Persons as used across all regional police forces
- 1 version revised by a police custody officer

- 5 versions revised by information designers
- 1 revised version ultimately used in custody

Interviews and focus groups:

- 1 focus group with the above information designers (4267 words)
- 48 interviews with police officers (157,024 words)
- 52 interviews with detainees (120,923 words)
- 10 interviews with police trainers and custody officers (14,588 words)

Naturally occurring talk:

- 151 examples of cautioning explanations from police interviews (41,849 words)

Observation:

- Observation in police custody units (approximately 600 hours)
- Go-alongs with police patrols (20 visits) (Kusenbach, 2003)

Photographs:

- From one custody suite

Combining data sources provides a rich understanding of the sites under examination and 'an improved explanatory warrant for statements about language' (Tusting and Maybin, 2007: 581).

In workplace settings, it is sometimes impossible to access or save all data that one might wish. Busy work schedules, insurmountable concerns about confidentiality, even just poor coordination between departments can mean that one has to work with the data available rather than the data desired. In one current study, for example, I have been asked to scrutinise the effectiveness of a particular police interview training technique. Yet there is only access to training materials and simulated interviews. Neither of these data sources permits comment on any aspect of the tool's use in context so findings must be delivered with appropriate caveats (Stokoe, 2013).

Data storage and readiness

If the storage of data about real people is important, it is all the more important when those data are intensely personal, potentially incriminating or professionally sensitive. Workplace data are often all of these so storing and backing-up securely deserve attention.

Given the volume of spoken data within my custody study, I could have spent an incredible amount of time transcribing (Bucholtz, 2000). I decided that this investment was worthwhile and transcribed every interview and research conversation, not because I thought this would ensure some special relationship between the recording and the representation on paper (Mishler, 1991; Green et al., 1997) but because I found the transcription process extremely valuable. I had two word-processing documents open whilst transcribing – one where I transcribed and another where I made notes and cross-referenced the transcriptions. Whilst this did not provide complete analysis, of course, note-taking and annotating the transcripts were invaluable to identifying analytic themes for further examination. Transcription of the whole dataset, as I did, is not always justified. There need to be good reasons for undertaking such time-consuming work but also for avoiding it.

Activity 1

Imagine that you have been asked to examine a workplace process which has been introduced into an office. The technique centres on 'vertical' meetings in which team members stand up, throughout. Standing supposedly encourages them to exchange views rapidly and regularly with the intention of improving the 'big picture' of one another's work. The meetings are also intended to offer a forum to collectively negotiate the flow of work and joint and individual deadlines.

Now consider the following questions:

1. What data would you need to collect in order to investigate this setting?
2. How might you get access to data?
3. What might impede access?
4. What particular consent issues are likely here which might not figure in other settings, even other workplaces?
5. How will you record the meetings and what will be the implications of your choices?

ANALYSIS OF DATA

Interactional data

Naturally occurring interactions provide opportunities to observe what is happening on the surface of talk and to extrapolate from that surface. My academic background made this the data I was most familiar with and my touchstone when considering other sources. The custody project's naturally occurring data were audio-recordings of officers delivering the police caution to detainees, a procedure which is less homogenous than one might imagine. PACE Code C (Home Office, 2013a), the police officer's rulebook, introduced at the beginning of this chapter, tells officers that they should, at particular points in detention, recite the caution's official wording:

> You do not have to say anything. But it may harm your defence if you do not mention when questioned something which you later rely on in Court. Anything you do say may be given in evidence. (Home Office, 2013a: 28)

Yet officers are also told that they should explain the caution in their own words 'if it appears' that their interlocutor does not understand (Home Office, 2013a: 29). Officers solicit explanations from detainees, to investigate this. I examined over 800 cautioning exchanges, focusing on 151 in detail, drawn from the 'four corners' of England and Wales.

My analytic approach involved first listening to and transcribing the data as already described, which provided key themes. In order to understand the data from different vantage points, I dissected them in various ways. For example, I separated officers' explanations of the caution from detainees'. Seeing explanations divided by speaker clarified participants' varied roles and orientations. I cleaved each set of explanation further. The caution's three sentences proved surprisingly useful analytic divisions because many speakers oriented to them explicitly. Dividing the dataset, according to which sentence was being explained, revealed that not all explanations followed the sequence of the original wording and not all were complete. This division also demonstrated participants' innovative use of metalanguage to orient addressees to their explanations' structures. It would not have been prudent to examine only isolated turns, so another important focus was cautioning exchanges in their dialogic complexity. This revealed that some officers seemed to rattle off an unvarying explanation of the caution irrespective of addressee whilst others attended to their interlocutor, tailoring the explanations to what they saw as their needs.

The excerpt below illustrates how themes emerged from the data. The fact that I have selected this example essentially at random (the only constraint being not repeating data examined elsewhere) illustrates the vitality of cautioning data. In all extracts in this chapter, P indicates that a police officer is speaking and D denotes a detainee in police custody.

Extract 2: Your opportunity

1. P: I'm going to ask you some questions over an alleged offence (.) uhm you do not have to say anything but it may harm your defence if you do not mention when questioned something which you later rely on in court (.) anything you do say may be given in evidence do you understand what I //mean://
2. D: //yeah // (.)
3. P: by that =
4. D: = yeh
5. P: d'you just want to explain to me what the (.) caution means: to you
6. D: 's that I don't have to say owt unless I'm [inaud. 1 syllable]
7. P: right (.) but: (1.0) s'just ((taken)) that this i- this is your opportunity to tell me what happen:ed if y- if you don't tell us something today (.) which you then uhm mention in court hh they may question why y- um why you've not mentioned it now //and//
8. D: //yes//
9. P: this is your opportunity to tell me

At the micro level, we see the officer pausing at points which he might expect would improve comprehension: before he begins reciting the official wording and after the caution's 'difficult' long sentence, in turn 1, for example. The detainee overlaps with the officer before the officer finishes asking whether he understands. This apparent haste to take the floor gives way to silence. My transcription attributes the pause after the detainee's 'yeah' in turn 2 to the detainee, even though it is the officer who speaks next. The transcription 'hears' this as being a point when the detainee was expected to continue. Apparently minor transcription details have analytic consequences. In response to the detainee's pause, or perhaps despite it, in turn 3 the officer extends the semantic and syntactic unit begun in turn 1. By latching on (turn 4), the detainee is again quick to confirm understanding. Having thus said twice that he understands, the detainee's demonstration of understanding, his explanation (turn 6), is short and becomes inaudible. Looking beyond this single instance, we find that the mismatch between the detainee's claim of comprehension (turns 2 and 4) and his performance of comprehension (turn 6) is extremely typical of the data set. By comparing multiple instances of this phenomenon we can learn about how detainees respond to different forms of comprehension-checking (a yes/no question versus a request for explanation) and possible implications and situated significances of this. If we add other forms of data, most obviously interviews with detainees, we begin to discover what detainees make of being asked about comprehension in these ways, whether comprehension-checking serves its intended function and what else it does. The comprehension-check procedure ultimately emerged as only ostensibly about checking comprehension.

The officer's talk, suggests some issues around face threat. His formulation in turn 5 (*d'you just want to explain to me what the caution means*), uses a question about the detainee's desires as elicitation. This theme was supported by data from interviews with officers (Rock, 2007: 210–14). The most striking thing about the officer's talk, however, is his framing of the caution through one of its upshots; it offers an *opportunity* to account (turns 7 and 9). This framing was prominent (Rock, 2007: 173). The officer could be criticised for going beyond explanation. However, officers often described struggling with what was, then, a relatively new procedure, so we could also see this as a realisation of a response to workplace change. The detainee's explanation had only attended to the caution's first sentence, *you do not have to say anything*. We could argue that the officer is responding to this incompleteness by attending to the caution's caveat *but it may harm your defence*, even if casting this incongruously. This could, then, exemplify that the officer is approaching explanation dialogically, attentively filling gaps and addressing misconceptions (Rock, 2007: 215–21). Nonetheless, his explanation is not only partial but also incomplete; he does not mention the caution's third sentence, *anything you do say can be given in evidence*, at all.

Interviews

I had interviewing experience from a previous project (Lilford et al., 2001) when I began my custody research, yet doubtless my interviews in this new setting show the 'hegemony of the interviewer' as I hogged first pair parts and missed interviewees' directions (Agar, 2005: 16; Garton and Copland, 2010: 533). Likewise, I initially shared Vanderstaay's tendency to 'talk past' some interviewees 'confused and frustrated in trying to get a fix on the terms and referents we share' (2003: 377). However, like Agar (2005: 17), I found that connecting the local (data from the interviews) to the global (here, themes from other forms of data) opened up analysis. Themes mentioned in the previous section could only be taken so far using naturally occurring data. Taking just one example raised above, it *seemed* that some officers tailored their explanations to detainees, co-constructing meaning with them, but was this just my perception? What would officers themselves make of the idea of different levels of attentiveness to audience in their explanations? To answer such questions, recourse was needed to officers.

Extract 3: Keep quiet

1.	F	in the thrust of getting on with work when you're out on
2.		the streets I guess you're very unlikely to explain it (.) have
3.		you ever had to explain it at that stage
4.	P	well no (.) I think the only time I would explain it is maybe
5.		not in official jargon as I say (.) if somebody asked perhaps
6.		a question that I feel that A I can't answer or B it might be
7.		in their best interests that you know that you know you've
8.		given them the caut- I've given them the cau- 'you've been
9.		given the caution my advice would be part of that caution
10.		is you do not have to say anything and I think it would
11.		probably be in your best interests that if you keep quiet
12.		and then when we get before the Custody Sergeant if you
13.		have any questions he will probably be able to explain
14.		better than I will' (.) so probably not in a formal go through
15.		the caution and explain it all in the detail that you would
16.		before an interview but certainly as I say if I feel that uh I
17.		don't know maybe they're a juvenile or whatever but
18.		certainly as I say if I feel that maybe they're a juvenile or
19.		anything like that you might maybe go into it in a bit more
20.		depth

This officer speaks directly about the potential to tailor explanations to particular addressees, involving, for him, altering the 'depth' according to interlocutor's age (lines 18–20). Chapter 11 of Rock (2007) takes up this theme, examining how officers innovate on the comprehension-checking apparatus. This officer describes not only tailoring his explanation to the detainee, but tailoring in various other ways too. In lines 8–14, he mimics an interaction with a detainee. In his arrest scenario, he does not explain the caution's full, literal meaning but situated, pragmatic implications of just one section. He foregrounds the right to silence, as particularly salient at arrest (*part of that caution is you do not have to say anything*, lines 9–10) and labels his speech act as *advice* tailoring pragmatic aspects of the caution according to the situation. In the invented scenario, the detainee seeks information whilst the officer attempts to close things down by noting that there will come a time for the detainee's questions (lines 12–14). Thus he tailors cautioning to manage talk. This theme, of the appropriation and multifunctionality of rights talk, is discussed in chapter 12 of Rock (2007). The notion that officers might re-sequence and truncate the caution, raised also in the naturally occurring data, above, underpins chapter 10 (of that book). The officer raises further themes which span forms of data. He implies that he finds the caution difficult to explain, particularly at arrest, and notes that explanations can be in *official jargon* or not, depending on their function. He suggests that the Custody Sergeant would *probably ... explain better* (line 13–14) and has an important, distinctive role in the custody community of practice (line 12) (Rock, 2005). The diversity of analytic possibilities, in even this short turn illustrates the utility and fit of interview data.

Of particular interest to this chapter is that the questions research interviewers ask rarely determine the talk that follows ('talk' as opposed to 'answers'). This does not contradict the assertion that 'the researcher is inevitably part of, and shapes, the research that is being produced' (Tusting and Maybin, 2007: 578). Interview analysis accordingly rested on letting themes emerge, rather than tracing sets of 'answers' to particular questions.

The ethnographic interview is very different from other forms of interviewing. It should be conducted from a place of contextualised knowledge and honesty about that knowledge. This responds to the 'ethnographic imperative to understand practices as they are meaningful "from within" and to participants' (Jacobs and Slembrouck, 2010: 238). Sociolinguistic awareness is essential in recognising that, in research interviews, social identity is produced interactionally (Drew and Sorjonen, 1997: 95) leading some answers to address the situation or social identity of the interviewer, not the question, for example. Likewise, interviewers may encounter stance-taking, for example, influencing interviewees' appropriation of interactional resources (Myers and Lampropoulou, 2012: 1216). At the micro-analytic level, interviewees might orient towards question–answer sequences in rather particular ways during interviews (Grindsted, 2005: 1026), ultimately struggling to produce 'well-aligned move[s]' (House, 2003: 21) even in the most gentle interview.

Qualitative interviewing provides opportunities to explore around and behind responses. Within my interviews, for example, probing answers which superficially suggested incomprehension uncovered detainees' performing incomprehension to demonstrate disengagement with the institution. On the other hand, probing answers which suggested comprehension revealed, in some cases, detainees' attempts to conceal what they felt was poor comprehension. Qualitative interviews therefore offered opportunities to identify instances when detainees responded to some aspect of the investigative apparatus, rather than the investigative focus itself. Metalanguage in interviews (Stross, 1974; Maschler, 1994) was a clue to this, as the following extracts from transcripts show:

Interviewees:

- Evaluated the apparatus:

  o that's a good question
  o that's a difficult one to answer really
  o I think that's a fairly comprehensive look at the caution really

- Speculated on their 'performance':

  o was that any good then?
  o you'll get different answers from everybody in our office
  o do you get the same answers every time you do this?

- Speculated on the function of the apparatus:

  o so what's the idea of doing all this research is it to make [the caution] shorter?
  o I'm not quite sure how you could shorten it

- Noted difficulty in responding to the apparatus:

  o I don't know how to put it into words
  o I just can't say it if you know what I mean
  o do you mean what I would do personally or–

- Critiqued and repositioned the apparatus:

  o me talking to you and everything to me it's all an illusion you know what I mean it's like– it's madness
  o I think you're wasting a lot of time and effort on people who do it all the time because I bet you anything they just bin these

Consideration of the interviewing mechanism is essential to data collection, analysis and writing-up. As Briggs notes, if we ignore this we ignore our own role in the research process (1986: 4) whereas a focus on 'how the interview comes off' (Rapley, 2001: 317) permits more complete use of interview data. This necessitates attending to the interview data as co-constructed talk (Seale, 1998) and indeed to 'the affective, sensuous, relational, embodied and social-spatial dimensions of each interview event' (Thorpe, 2012: 52). Thus the interview moves far from appearing to be an unproblematic means for gathering 'information' or pre-existing 'facts'.

Textual data

An important focus of my custody study was written texts, their form, function and appropriations. The project considered how people in a very particular workplace make meaning from texts; examined what meaning potentials the texts have and asked how the texts relate to needs in custody. My initial analysis of the Notice to Detained Persons described it exhaustively at all levels of language. I was struck by how many of its lexical, syntactic and discoursal features were ones which scholars and plain language activists claim reduce comprehensibility. Yet I was not convinced of a simple one-to-one correspondence between eradicating 'difficult' language features and improving the situation of detainees trying to make sense of custody. A social practices approach to literacies (Baynham, 1995; Barton et al., 2000; Rai and Lillis, 2013) allowed me to observe and discuss the texts in use. I added a novel method which examined writers' understandings by considering their revisions to the rights notice. This involved both analysing the revised texts and discussing them with their authors. One of the writers in question was a police officer and the others were information designers; professional writers who aim to improve usability.

Analysing this diverse mixture of data required several routes. Rewriter interviews offered a distinctive perspective on the texts. Sometimes this was as simple as discussing rewriters' responses to 'difficult' features, but I also focussed on how the authors brought their different forms of expertise into their writing, how they oriented to readers and how they warranted their rewriting decisions. Interviews with those who had been given the rights notice in custody, raised new analytic lines to take back to the texts. Detainees did not specifically comment on fine-grained detail but drew attention to higher levels of language such as discourse structure. Ultimately, however, interviews with detainees, and police station observations, revealed that literacy events around the rights notice were more influential than the text itself.

One strand of my analysis considered the prior experience of custody that detainees brought to the rights texts. This categorisation of detainees by custody experience emerged from interviews and observation; police officers and detainees oriented to these categories. Using 'participants' own identifications' is common in linguistic ethnography (Sealey, 2007: 645). I grouped detainees into those arrested frequently, occasionally or never before. I then considered whether detainees claimed to have read the texts offered to them. This revealed that, of those who were new to custody, less than one fifth read the papers. Of the remainder, around a third did not read them. These figures were indicative, as only 51 detainees were asked about this, but they contextualised detainees' talk about reading or not reading in custody and added perspective to observations of literacy events there. Consider just one example (below). Here we join a detainee as she explains which parts of the documentation she read:

Extract 4: Not today

1. D: I didn't read this side oh hang on yeah I read that bit I was going to ask what the Codes of Practice were but I thought well I'm in a whole new world of trouble as it is so maybe I'll keep quiet
2. F: okay so it wasn't terribly clear from the papers what exactly they were
3. D: no I don't suppose it was that I mean this is just this is just telling you you can have a look at their Codes of Practice doesn't it and I was just out of curiosity I suppose you could say you want to have a look at this booklet you know Codes of Practice but I thought maybe better circumstances I might have said can I have a look but not today eh

The detainee's presentation of her motivations, in this case around reading the Codes of Practice was usefully juxtaposed with other data. For her, the circumstances she found herself in precluded reading despite her awareness of the possible advantages of reading. The interviews revealed how people's orientations to reading influenced their engagement with the institutional rights framework.

Field notes

Scollon and Scollen point out that while ethnographers share little agreement when defining ethnography 'one clear commonality is the idea of participant observation', despite its potential to 'undermine scientific cannons of objectivity and distance' (2007: 612). Being new to participant observation and field notes, I gradually realised their value so my notes became more full, systematic and, accordingly, more useful over time. I was surprised by their multifunctionality. Some essentially captured characteristics of my research task and served as a useful subsequent reminder of conditions. This can be seen in field note example 1.

Extract 5: Almost fruitless

It seems odd to be on my way home with half of a day's work done and it's only 11 a.m. It was an early start today - I phoned at 4.30 a.m. and Sid reported that there might be as many as three people to interview. They would be off to court at around 9 a.m. so I needed to get a move on. I arrived in the Custody Suite just before 6 a.m. and it was already lively. The distinctive, entirely unpleasant smell of men in the morning greeted me as ever. I found that Sid had got a bit carried away as there only seemed to be really two possible interviewees. One was one of the unusual people who declined to be interviewed - understandable, given the circumstances of being due in court, for the first time in the next few hours, but frustrating. The other was virtually monosyllabic having been in custody and, evidently, in heroin withdrawal for too long to make our interview very useful. It was harrowing to see the way he would keep drifting away from our conversation. ... A tiresome and uncomfortable visit but one which, through that one perfunctory interview, brought home, once more, the reality of 'communication' in the custody suite.

Field note 1 begins with an account of a routine visit to custody (lines 1–5) and the scene on my arrival (lines 5–10). Notes like these have, from time to time, been useful when producing accounts of the site. I used some of the material from lines 7 and 8 to provide context at the beginning of a paper on cautioning, for example (Rock, 2012: 312). Field note 1 gives way to a much more obviously useful kind of note (lines 14–18). Whilst this was at the time motivated by frustration, empathy and sadness, what Katz calls 'poignant data' (2002: 78) it became part of a tapestry of forms of data which brought home the complexities of this particular setting – and the complexities of 'comprehension' in the chaos of life. My overview at lines 19–21 reflects on this very point.

Photographs complement my field notes. I took these around the custody suite one quiet day when I had spent enough time there to understand something of how the material environment functions. Wacquant indicates the usefulness of photographs for Bourdieu. First, they offered 'efficient recording and storage' when things could not be noted in times of change; they 'served to intensify the sociologist's gaze' and finally they 'anchored and facilitated' Bourdieu's intense emotional work (Wacquant, 2004: 399–402). I was certainly not working in such distressing circumstances as Bourdieu so time in the field worked differently for me, yet the potential of photographs to store detail, to be reviewed repeatedly and to perspectivise cannot be underestimated. They provide for capturing spaces where talk and text reside. In custody, photographs reveal the place of written texts like those densely packed behind the booking-in desk in Figure 5.1.

Figure 5.1 Texts on display at the booking-in desk of the custody suite

Some of the texts in Figure 5.1 could be from any work environment (Hindmarsh and Heath, 2000: 527): a fire evacuation procedure notice; a large calendar with each day crossed through from the start of the financial year; a picture of light bulbs with a reminder to save electricity. Others are very specific to this workplace: instructions on drugs referrals; labels on lockers linking each to a cell for storage of belongings; a poster explaining how to obtain free legal advice. This clamour of texts creates a strange impression because of their mixed audiences. Most were aimed at custody suite employees, despite being displayed in a semi-public area, some targeted investigating police officers who might visit to conduct interviews or bring in arrestees and some of the texts were aimed at detainees. This space is simultaneously front and back region (Goffman, 1971 [1959]: 109) as people come and go, taking up the environment in their different ways. Such 'blurring of the boundary' between front and backstage is not unusual in institutional settings, and is reflected in performance (Jacobs and Slembrouck, 2010: 237). Figure 5.2 shows similar diversity, this time looking out from behind the custody desk.

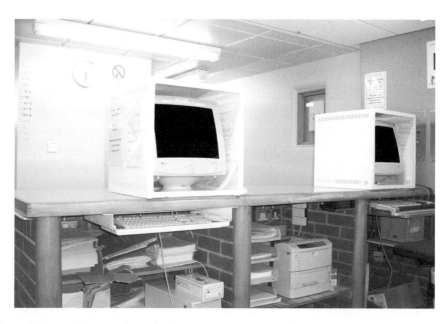

Figure 5.2 A different view – further texts on display at the booking-in desk

In Figure 5.2, we get a sense of physical space being appropriated by texts. To the far left of the photograph, running up the corner of a wall are handwritten numbers alongside small lines making an improvised height chart to measure detainees. In the foreground, below the desk, an elaborate system of stacking trays contains texts for a variety of purposes including forms for completion and the rights notice, stored ready to give to detainees.

Just as selecting key moments from naturally occurring data is a vital analytic task (Richardson, 2000), selecting fragments of life to convert into field notes and photographs is similarly demanding but usually more spontaneous.

Activity 2

Task 1: There are two data excerpts below. One is from custody desk field notes, the other from a research interview with a detainee. Consider each in turn and make some notes on its interesting features and any themes that you imagine you would pursue if you had a larger data set (you might like to do this activity with a partner, each considering only one excerpt, ignoring your partner's excerpt for this part of the activity).

Task 2: Now, consider the field note and interview excerpt together. What insights become possible by considering two forms of data which were not possible with only one? Now add Figures 5.1 and 5.2 to the mix. Do they enrich your analysis?

Field note: Custody pinball

It's been a busy Friday evening at the desk. A succession of people being booked in in various states of inebriation and with various levels of confidence. I've been struck today by the diversity of levels of experience of the detainees. A couple of young lads, late-teenagers-going-on-thirty, swagger in having seen it all before. What a contrast with the young girl who turned out to be 14 but had the air of a small child, huddled with her mother whilst she waited for the next activity in her journey through the police station. There were also interviews going on follow-ing from arrests during the day. One of the solicitors seemed fairly new to things! I still feel like the custody process is a ball which I can only see one side of. It seems that texts are such an important part of the Custody Sergeant keeping track of it all. How do they keep so many plates in the air? Too many metaphors here but the desk has seemed like part of a pin-ball machine this evening at times. In between the bursts of activity there is banter, fact-finding, instructions . . .

Extract: Nothing to hide

F: right first of all looking at [the rights notice] did you actually read [it] when you were given [it]

D: no

F: did you read them at all while you were here

D: no

F: no . . . is there any particular reason that you didn't look at them

D: I've got nothing to hide to be quite honest I didn't need to read them I am still unhappy about certain ways I've been treated but my solicitor's had to sort that out but I'm not happy with what's gone on but no I've got nothing to hide I spoke to my solicitor I've cooperated everything so I no - no problem at all

DISCOURSE ANALYSIS AND LINGUISTIC ETHNOGRAPHY

I have drawn on the rich tapestry of discourse analysis in my research, selecting the level of granularity according to the analytic task at hand, identifying particu-lar concepts for attention according to the presence, absence and significance of specific features. Billig observes that 'social scientific investigation is frequently presented as being based upon the following of methodological rules' he instead proposes use of what he calls the anti-methodological approach of 'traditional scholarship' in which 'hunches and specialist knowledge are more important than formally defined procedures' (1988: 199). This approach, which I have taken, can feel 'begged, borrowed and patched together' (Gee, 2005: 5) but certainly some antecedents are traceable in my work. Specifically, from the field of discourse analysis is an orientation which places the social and societal above the cognitive and leans towards the social and functional without completely forgetting the formal. Discourse analysis has given me an interest in structure (for example, Sinclair and Coulthard, 1975). It has provided what are now seen as basic, foundational ideas such as coherence and cohesion (Halliday and Hasan, 1976), framing (Goffman, 1975), as well as nuanced understandings of power, recontextualisation and context. Following from this, a social (as opposed to cognitive) pragmatics has brought consideration of speaker and hearer roles and the building blocks supporting their activities. Without an understanding of such ideas as speech acts, and the concept's development from Austin (1962) and, in turn, Searle (1969) and thus of locution, illocution, perlocution, and felicity conditions, I could not have made sense of the legal worlds I encountered. My work is also influenced by interactional sociolinguistics' imperative to 'bridge the gulf' between observable communicative forms, such as words and register, and the things which interactants 'take themselves to be doing' with the forms (Bailey, 2008: 2314). The notions of contextualisation cues (for example, Gumperz, 1982: 132) and conversational inferencing (for example, Gumperz, 2003: 219) have been significant. I also came to be influenced by social practices approaches to literacy which require a rich view of written information (for example, Barton and Hamilton, 1998). These approaches give a tremendous sense of the situatedness of writing (Barton et al., 2000), but also of the potential for texts to reach out into social life in novel, constructive ways. The idea that there is value in scrutinising the different ways that texts figure for different individuals in different situations steered my research methods and such specifics as my interview rationale. Conversation Analysis has also been useful especially in concepts such as orderliness (Schegloff and Sacks, 1973: 290; Sacks, 1984: 22) and preference (Bilmes, 1988: 161). Critical Discourse Analysis was drawn in, contributing a particular flavour to my sense of how local processes and practices shape and re-shape social relations through discourse, but also bringing pertinent concepts such as synthetic personalisation (Fairclough, 2001: 52) and the related idea of technologisation (Fairclough, 2010: 136). Where they were useful, in providing points of comparison and contrast, I have drawn on concepts from corpus analysis, particularly collocation (Sinclair, 1991) and semantic prosody (Louw, 1993) in considering more expansive text relations. In general terms, I have a sociolinguistic orientation, drawing in notions like style (Cameron, 2000).

There is of course a difference between being analytically open and being a methodological magpie. For me, this is where theory enters to ensure that the analyst's position is not dislodged by the diversity of positions and approaches. This is tempered by Smith's ethnographic ideal to examine the functional complex of law from the perspective of the actualities of everyday life for particular individuals, rather than from the starting point of theory and its objectified constructs (Grahame, 1998: 349–53; Smith, 2005). This highlights the value of approaching research through individuals' experiences, which can, itself, reveal novel research themes. This is exemplified in work like Kerekes and West on trust in interviews where the theme derives from the data (2006).

REPRESENTATION AND WRITING UP

I compiled multiple, extensive thematic documents as a key analytic activity. The biggest challenge of the research process for me was marshalling these into coherent accounts which might interest readers and reflect what the data had revealed. I managed this process extremely inefficiently, trawling data and thematic documents time and again. This was positive for the familiarity it gave me with the data but the time taken by repeatedly revisiting and revisiting the various sources is not sustainable. To date my efforts to work with data more efficiently have involved constructing a tighter analytic focus before approaching the data although there seems to be no substitute for detailed engagement with written data and audio files. My writing process too became drawn into the cumulative, dialogic process of connecting and re-connecting data sources such that writing also became 'a way of 'knowing' – a method of discovery and analysis' (Richardson, 2000: 516).

Writing for different audiences

Most of my writing has been for academic audiences. This is not to say that academic writing is homogeneous. Quite different approaches are required for the journal article and handbook chapter, for example. Additionally the nature of my work is such that I have different disciplinary audiences. When writing or speaking to a general (socio)linguistic audience my point of departure and focus throughout will be different from occasions with a specifically forensic linguistic audience, and different again for an audience who associate with linguistic ethnography, information design or law. Academics make such shifts not because they have anything to hide from any audience but because they want to make their work maximally interesting and relevant to each. With the forensic audience, for example, I might connect my work to that on 'difficult' legal texts such as jury instructions. With the linguistic ethnographic audience I might foreground practices, and with the more general audience, I might orient to particular theoretical constructs. Each focus brings different resonances and opportunities.

My writing has extended beyond traditional academic activities. Press releases are an increasingly important genre for academics as we are encouraged to disseminate our work in new ways to new constituencies. I have also found myself writing short research summaries for central participants and other interested parties or decision makers such as those at the Home Office, mentioned in more detail below. I have also experienced different forms of writing such as annotating the texts of authors whose work I am studying so that they can see my findings *in situ*. Writing for different audiences and for and with users has been a way of invigorating my writing.

Sharing data with different communities of users

I have been fortunate in having been able to share data with many research participants and with practitioners with interests in law and workplaces. The most satisfying example of this took place within the custody research. One of my collaborators was a police officer who had been appointed by the Home Office (the government department responsible for policing in England and Wales) to rewrite the rights notice. By working with that officer I was able to feed directly into his writing. I also accompanied him on visits to the Home Office where we discussed the text and used data to present arguments about revisions. Whilst we were unable to make all of the changes we recommended, it was satisfying to have a voice in such textual change. I have since presented data to workers within training which sought to encourage them to reflect on their workplace practices. My recent work has used discussion of data in supporting police officers in thinking anew about their text production. One of my current projects is designed entirely around dissemination. It collects examples of lay people explaining legal terms and presents those explanations to legal personnel and interpreters in order to facilitate reflexivity on lay understandings of legal terms (Rock, 2014). Such direct collaboration with practitioners is not always easy because in drawing out 'the patterned nature of language behaviours, even where this is opaque to those concerned … linguistic ethnographers need to take on the epistemic authority to make truth claims which may differ from those of their research participants' (Tusting and Maybin, 2007: 579–80). In my work, the varied positions and perspectives of those researched means that I have found myself less frequently simply contradicting the truth claims of the researched than exposing some of the participants, usually those in power, to the perspectives of others, usually lay people. I have sought to do this without creating the 'systematic bias' possible when one tries a priori to 'further the interests of marginalised, exploited or dominated groups' (Hammersley, 2006: 11). This activity of giving voice yet with the objectivity of language research in place too, has proved very satisfying.

Activity 3

The excerpt below is from an exchange between a police officer and detainee at the opening of a police interview. The detainee is 12 and his father is with him as an 'appropriate adult'. Consider how you would write up (or otherwise present) a short analysis of the excerpt for four different audiences:

1. Academic peers
2. Police officers at a training course on interviewing
3. Members of the public attending an information event about how to exercise their rights in custody
4. School children of age 14 attending a 'citizenship' class which explains the role of police in society

Extract: Use it in evidence

P: now you're Kyle's father and you're here to make sure that we look after him whilst he's in custody

F: that's right

P: I'm gonna caution you again now you do not have to say anything but it may harm your defence if you do not mention when questioned something you later rely on in court anything you do say may be given in evidence (.) do you understand the caution

D: yep

P: do you want just to explain briefly to me what you think I just said (.) what I meant by the caution

D: can (.) use it in evidence or

P: we can but the most important thing about it is that you don't have to say anything (.) you can actually sit there and be completely silent (.) yah?

D: yeh

P: you do not <u>have</u> to speak to me you can't walk out of the room but you do not have to speak to me

D: yeh

P: <u>but</u> if you do not say anything the courts when they later hear you in the court room if you went to court might say to themselves (.) well now is he talking to us now and why didn't he say anything to the police woman in the interview

D: yeh

P: and they may think he must have been guilty

D: yep

P: is that understood yah?

CONCLUDING COMMENTS

This chapter opened by pointing out that as well as being a site for encounters connected to crime and justice, police custody is a workplace for the 129,584 full-time equivalent police officers in England and Wales as well as the 65,573 police staff such as administrators and the 33,216 volunteer police officers (Home Office, 2013b). This was certainly not a workplace ethnography in the sense proposed by Edwards and Bélanger of a study of a group of workers and their relations of 'conflict and cooperation' with managers. Yet the overarching interest of such a study is to examine 'how work gets done' (2008: 292) and this gets to the root of my focus. Kramsch in her description of Scollon's scholarly influence points out how academics help each other to cumulatively develop understandings of the relationship between language, thought and action (2009: 261). Linguistic ethnography as a coalescing of complementary traditions has been for me a focal point of such development.

Underlining	Indicates stress signalled by the speaker through a change in pitch and volume.
(.)	A micropause of 0.9 seconds or less.
(1.2)	A pause of 1.0 second or more, the duration appearing within the brackets. In this case, for example, the pause lasted for 1.2 seconds.
// //	Simultaneous or overlapping talk. Words within the double slashes on consecutive lines are simultaneous.
hhh	Audible out-breath.
=	Latching on.
-	Self correction or speaker breaking off.
[ ]	Comments (for example [coughs]).
(( ))	Unclear speech (Double brackets either contain an attempt to decipher the unclear speech or, where that is not possible, an estimation of the number of inaudible syllables).
:	The vowel in the preceding syllable was prolonged.
…	Indicates that words have been removed from an excerpt, to increase intelligibility through brevity.
?	Indicates rising intonation.

Figure 5.3 Transcription Key

KEY READINGS

Blommaert, J. (2007a) 'On scope and depth in linguistic ethnography', *Journal of Sociolinguistics*, 11(5): 682–88.

Smith, D. (2005) *Institutional Ethnography: A Sociology for People*. Lanham: AltaMira Press.

VanderStaay, S. (2003) 'Believing Clayboy', *Qualitative Inquiry*, 9(3): 374–94.

Venkatesh, S. (2002) 'Doin' the Hustle', *Ethnography*, 3(1): 91–111.

SIX

Case Study Four: Ethnography, Language and Healthcare Planning

Sara E. Shaw

SETTING THE CONTEXT OF THE STUDY: BACKGROUND INFORMATION, RESEARCH QUESTIONS AND FINDINGS

Think tanks are organisations specialising in the production and dissemination of knowledge related to public policy (Stone, 2000; Medvetz, 2010). Current estimates indicate that there are over 6600 think tanks worldwide (McGann, 2013), with numbers increasing as think tanks fill a gap created by the decline of political parties and provide a forum in which experts are able to come together to coordinate policy agendas (Fischer, 2003; Stone, 1996; Medvetz, 2008). In the UK, there is an active community of think tanks. They vary in their history, focus, structure, funding and activities but all have a common desire to inform policy. Think tanks are often mentioned in scholarly discussions of public policy (Wildavsky, 1979; Fischer and Forester, 1993; Parsons, 1995; Stone, 2000) and they are increasingly visible in policymaking related to health and healthcare (see, for instance, Ruane, 2005; Player and Leys, 2011; Smith, 2013). However, to-date think tanks have not been the subject of close study, generally and specifically in relation to healthcare. Part of the reason for this is that academic researchers have rarely accessed and studied think tanks (Korica, 2011). The collective case study that I describe here set out to redress this.

Two theoretical approaches shaped the research: interpretive policy analysis, an approach to thinking about and analysing policy that is grounded in the meaning given to policy through language and social interaction (Yanow, 2000; Fischer, 2003; Hajer and Wagenaar, 2003; Wagenaar, 2011); and linguistic ethnography, an approach that sees language and social life as mutually shaping (Rampton et al., 2004). These guided the research process: the initial focus being on examining the

Table 6.1 Overview of think tanks participating in the study

	Think Tank A	Think Tank B	Think Tank C	Think Tank D
Funding source	Primarily via an endowment of c £103m, supplemented by project and sponsorship funding	Primarily via an endowment of c£65m, supplemented by project and sponsorship funding	Primarily via project- and programme-based grants and contracts	A combination of corporate donations and membership, and project-based funding
Estimated annual income	£14m	£2.5m	£6.5m	£1.1m
Staff	c. 130	c. 30	c. 85	c. 15
Time established	100+ years	60+ years	20+ years	10+ years
Field of work	Academic/media	Academic	Business/academic	Political/media
Focus	Principally on health policy and reform in the UK, including leadership development	Principally on health policy and healthcare reform in the UK	Healthcare features strongly in work programme, with a UK/European focus	Healthcare forms a substantive part of their work on domestic/UK policy issues

Source: Adapted from Shaw, Russell, Parsons et al. (2014), with data drawn from analysis of think tank activities undertaken in 2012.

way that think tanks shape health policy in England, with the following specific questions then emerging from the research process: How do think tanks frame and represent their work when they seek to shape health policy? And how do they account for and manage their decisions?

The study initially involved a UK-based organisation that describes itself 'an authoritative and independent source of evidence-based research and policy analysis for improving health care in the UK' (mission statement, 2014) and which I refer to here as Think Tank B. I worked at Think Tank B for just over two years, from February 2009, undertaking research and analysis on areas related to UK health policy (for instance, healthcare commissioning). I took up a full-time academic position at Queen Mary University of London in May 2011 (retaining an honorary appointment at the think tank, which remains in place at the time of writing), where I engaged with colleagues, Jill Russell, Trish Greenhalgh and Wayne Parsons, and we extended the study to include three other UK think tanks (Table 6.1).

All four think tanks were selected for study after conducting a review of academic and grey literature, including websites, from a number of health think tanks. From this we developed a typology of UK think tanks that have health and healthcare as part of their work programme, recording detailed information about history, mission, staffing, funding, governance, board members and more. From this we confirmed inclusion of Think Tank B and the three other think tanks as we sought maximum variety in relation to: (a) funding sources (including, for example, endowment funds, project funding, donations); (b) length of time established (from under 10 to over 100 years); and (c) principal field of work (i.e. political, media, academic, business).

We focused our case study on a programme of healthcare reforms in England that were announced by the Coalition Government in July 2010 (DH, 2010) and culminated in new legislation (House of Commons, 2012) in March 2012. The content of proposed reforms was not the main focus of our work but provided a tangible period of health policy on which we were able to focus data collection and analysis. I do not intend to give an account of these reforms here (see Timmins, 2012, for a full review). However, for those unfamiliar with recent policy changes in England, a sketch (Figure 6.1) is useful context. All four think tanks were engaged in work relating to the NHS reforms, including, either directly (in three cases) or tangentially (in one case).

Our findings highlight how think tanks in our sample appeared to seek to publicly ('front stage') position themselves as an 'independent research organisation' or 'charitable research foundation', emphasising particular activities, artefacts and actors, as well as instrumental language (for example, 'evidence-based') that allowed them to feed emerging evidence into policy and, they report, improve health services. Such positioning provided them with legitimacy in the eyes of decision-makers. Other think-tank activities (e.g. meetings with politicians and civil servants) took place 'back-stage', allowing them to link with like-minded actors and interests with

July 2010: Government proposes substantial reorganisation of the NHS in England (DH, 2010). Headline changes include abolition of administrative superstructure, with family doctors taking over commissioning of NHS care. Also a new economic regulator to oversee competition in health services provision, with 'any willing provider' from the public, private or voluntary sector allowed to supply NHS care.

July to October 2010: Consultation invites contributions from all sectors and organisations. Reponses are mixed.

November 2010: Opposition to the proposed reforms gather pace. Concerns focus particularly on the scale and pace of reorganisation and the strengthening of competition in the NHS (seen by many as a drive for privatisation).

December 2010: Government confirms that they will go ahead with legislation to implement the reforms (with few changes following consultation).

March 2011: Mounting criticism from professional organisations, research organisations, patient groups and decision-makers.

April 2011: The government announces a 'pause' in the passage of the Bill, a new Future Forum to take stock and time to 'listen, engage and amend'.

June 2011: The *Future Forum* reports, with all but one recommendation then accepted by government.

September 2011: Legislation clears the first part of the process having been amended 1,000+ times, a sign of the intensity of debate.

February 2012: The Prime Minister holds a meeting with only those who are 'constructively engaged' with the reforms. Calls for the Bill to be withdrawn continue.

March 2012: Health and Social Care Bill approved following last-minute amendments.

Figure 6.1   Overview of healthcare reforms in England

a view to influencing health policy and shaping healthcare delivery. In the context of NHS reforms, the think tanks in our sample provided (to varying degrees) broad support to government proposals to reform the NHS and, in particular, to extend market principles to publicly-funded health services. Informants appeared to work to neutralise this 'back-stage' influencing through a range of discursive strategies and accounted for their practices in terms of dominant instrumental discourse on health planning. This served to re-affirm their 'front stage' positioning as independent research organisations that provide value-free expertise to inform health policy. Readers can find a detailed account of findings in Shaw, Russell, Parsons and Greenhalgh (2014).

RESEARCH DESIGN

Retrospectively, our research design was a collective case study of think tanks. However, it did not start out that way. During my time working at Think Tank B I kept a journal, reflecting on my experiences of working as a senior researcher within the organisation. This remained a personal project until I left to take up my position at Queen Mary University of London. There my colleagues encouraged me to see my journal as an autoethnographic account of working in a think tank and to explore opportunities for more in-depth study. As a method, autoethnography combines characteristics of *auto*biography and *ethnography*. It tends to be associated with what is sometimes referred to as 'evocative ethnography' (Anderson, 2006), characterised by 'confessional tales' and a descriptive literary approach (see, for instance, Ellis and Bochner, 2000; Holman Jones, 2005; Ellis et al., 2010). Our approach was grounded in analytic autoethnography (Anderson, 2006), in which the researcher is a member of the research setting, visible as such in published accounts, and committed to

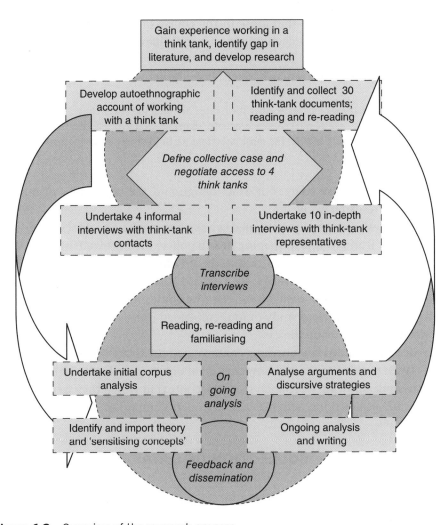

Figure 6.2 Overview of the research process

'an analytic research agenda focused on improving theoretical understandings of broader social phenomenon' (p. 375). It involves the researcher in retroactively and selectively writing about past experiences and assembling these with the benefit of hindsight (Ellis et al., 2010) with a view to 'giving voice to personal experience for the purpose of extending sociological understanding' (Wall, 2008: 38).

Figure 6.2 provides an overview of the study process as it subsequently evolved. Collaboration with academic colleagues was crucial to the study: ensuring that we did not delimit the research questions, methods or legitimate answers on the basis of a mono-disciplinary focus (Latuca, 2001); shining a light on the role of think tanks in shaping health policy through the lenses of sociology, social policy, organisational studies, political science and medicine; and enabling challenge to theoretical, methodological and analytical approaches throughout. More practically, it ensured a forum where we could share data, test out ideas, and consider issues (for instance, access) that arose in the course of the study. Those who are keen to adopt a similar approach might refer to Wildavksy's chapter 'On collaboration' (2010: 103–18).

In discussing case study research, Ragin describes how:

> researchers probably will not know what their cases are until the research . . . is virtually completed. What *it* is a *case of* will coalesce gradually, sometimes catalytically, and the final realization of the case's nature may be the most important part of the interaction between ideas and evidence. (1992: 6)

So it was with our case study: our exact design and the boundaries of our case shifted as the research evolved.

Our study design originally developed as a *single in-depth case study* (Simon, 2009) of Think Tank B and its role in shaping health policy; then evolved into a *dual case study* (involving one longitudinal case study of Think Tank B and three replicated case studies with other think tanks; see Leonard-Barton, 1990); and finally developed into a *collective case study* (Stake, 1995) examining how think tanks shape health policy through close study of four embedded units (Baxter and Jack, 2008) that, collectively, made up the case.

Our design included an ongoing commitment to focus on the particularity (Stake, 1995) of think tanks and how they go about shaping health policy in their everyday work, allowing close analysis of the context in which they were working, as well as the interactions, activities and arguments employed.

COLLECTION OF DATA

Ethical dilemmas

At the outset of the study, we drew up a protocol describing our plans for negotiating access, seeking consent, assuring anonymity, storing data and so on, and received approval from the university research ethics committee. Our study raised important questions about the nature of consent, accountability and the analytic process that meant ethics was an ongoing concern relevant to 'every aspect of the research process from conception and design through to research practice' (Goodwin et al., 2003: 567). We therefore made ethical issues a rolling issue in team discussions (for instance, reflecting on how to avoid putting undue pressure on colleagues to participate in the study).

At the time of writing, the study is not yet complete; potential sensitivities remain (for instance, about emerging findings); and I continue to have a working relationship with some of the people who have been involved in the study. This means that writing about the detail of ethical dilemmas is tricky and, in some cases, risks established working relationships. In this section, I have chosen to focus specifically on issues of negotiating access, gathering data and interpreting findings, and describe how we sought to address these. However, in order to preserve the integrity of the study and allied relationships, I do not go into as much detail as readers would perhaps like.

Negotiating access

All four think tanks that we invited to participate in the study were largely receptive, describing, for instance, how 'we are all warm to the idea of y[ou]r project' or that 'It is an honour to be asked to take part in this and we'd be delighted to do so'. By the time that we contacted them, we had already given considerable thought to our approach and sought to engage them in an ongoing process of dialogue about the study and their involvement, recognising the need for us to 'negotiate and continually re-negotiate access to the arenas where the interactions under study take place' (Gains, 2011: 58). We had thought that we might encounter some obstacles to 'studying up' (Nader, 1972). This prompted us to be clear that we welcomed input to the study from each of the think tanks (for instance, in relation to design and sampling, participation in interviews and disseminating findings). Given that some interviewees were public figures invited to participate because of the position they hold, we were clear at the outset that there would always be some risk (however small) that some people in the know may be able to identify some of our participants. To try and protect against this we developed robust anonymisation and data storage procedures (see below).

On first contacting the four think tanks, each expressed some concern about potential organisational exposure. Given the smallness of the think tank world we were clear that we could not offer organisational anonymity and think tanks were understandably concerned about the way in which their organisation might be presented in future study outputs. We sought to address this by assuring individual confidentiality; reassuring think tanks in our sample of our intentions to publish primarily academic outputs; and agreeing to share emerging findings with them in advance of publication. We also discussed opportunities for feedback and dissemination with each of the think tanks and – as far as possible – tailored our responses to their individual requests. As a result of this process, and at the request of senior staff at some of the participating think tanks, we subsequently made a decision to anonymise the names of all organisations in study outputs.

My working relationship with Think Tank B was not raised by any of the participating sites. On reflection, it likely facilitated access. From my own perspective, however, this was a double-edged sword – on the one hand enabling access and on the other raising questions about my own role:

Extract 1

'... there are areas that I'm finding it difficult to address and resolve (what is my role at Think Tank B? How can I square working with the organisation whilst at the same time studying it? What are the implications of critical findings for my role ...)'

Field note, 11 October 2011

I found that my role as both 'researcher of think tanks' and 'think tank researcher' led to my occupying two separate, yet related, worlds. We sought to address this by establishing a clear boundary between these roles that required me to collect data at certain times and in certain settings (for instance, whilst visiting Think Tank B a formal study capacity) and not others.

Gathering data

Data collection began with my journal: as I left my position at Think Tank B and the study took shape, so the status changed from personal project to auto-ethnographic account, and we therefore wanted to be clear that it would be a part of the research. As we began negotiating access, we sent a copy of the research protocol to Think Tank B, which described how and why we would draw on 'an autoethnographic account of the lead researcher', alongside other sources of data, with a view to 'setting the scene in which healthcare planning takes place and over time ... raising questions about the work undertaken and ... facilitating the analytic process of transitioning from initial review of documents and interviews to research analysis and interpretation and to connecting with wider social theory' (Research protocol, 23 November 2011).

No queries or concerns were raised about this aspect of the study, either at the outset or further down the line. Traditionally such a lack of concern might raise questions about the power differential between researcher and participant and whether people fully appreciate what being involved in a research study involves. However, our focus on those in senior positions, many with direct experience of undertaking research (including ethnography) calls into question such issues of power, understanding and accessibility (Nader, 1972; Gusterson, 1997; Odendahl and Shaw, 2001). We were not privy to the discussions that took place within each of the think tanks involved in the study; however, we were confident that they understood the nature of the research and what it involved. For an additional check, we discussed our approach to collecting and analysing data prior to the start of each interview (making it clear on the information sheet that we sent to interviewees beforehand that agreeing to interview was taken to imply formal consent).

There were limits to other sources of data that we were able to access. For instance Board papers and corporate sponsors were sometimes (though not always) inaccessible and, in a very few instances, interviews proved difficult to arrange. We discussed these issues and made judgements on a case-by-case basis. In only one case did the process involve, 'far more time and negotiation than I had envisaged' (Research diary, 6 December 2011). After four months of emails and phone calls to one think tank, we decided to include only publicly available documents and I emailed our contact to let them know. This resulted in a swift response confirming that an interview would, after all, be possible. A handful of similar instances occurred throughout the study (largely with the same site). They required us to balance our own motivations for undertaking the work and the wishes and commitments of others, and reminded us how time and tenacity can be helpful companions in research.

Interpreting data

The NHS reforms put forward by the Coalition Government (Figure 6.1) have been described as one of the most radical reorientations of the NHS since its inception in 1948 (Triggle, 2010; Timmins, 2012) and were the topic of considerable debate throughout the study. The think tanks in our sample undertook a range of activity relating to the reforms and to health policy and planning generally: Think Tank C did not undertake any work directed at emerging policy, but had been commissioned by the Department of Health to conduct relevant project work. Think Tanks A, B and D focused elements of their work (to varying degrees) on the reform process and emerging policy, as well as undertaking wider projects and, in some cases, developing programmes of work (the latter often supported by large endowment funds). Each of these three think tanks in our sample challenged specific aspects of the NHS reforms including, for instance, the potentially negative impact of price competition or the speed of implementation – overall they tended to provide legitimacy to, or support for, proposed changes (Shaw, Russell, Parsons et al., 2014). In contrast, much of the wider university department in which the research team was based was less supportive of – and, in some instances, actively challenged – the proposed reforms. Some think tank representatives expressed concerns about how this might influence our research and about accessibility of study data beyond the research team (see below), whilst some academic colleagues encouraged us to publicly critique the approach adopted by thinks tanks. This presented challenges in terms of our approach to analysing and interpreting data. We reassured study participants that others in the university were not involved in the study by ensuring effective data storage (see below); creating spaces away from the university in which the research team might together reflect on emerging data away from the spotlight of debate about NHS reform; holding two data sessions inviting colleagues from a range of disciplines and backgrounds to explore anonymised data with us; and sharing our emerging analysis with a range of colleagues to gauge the trustworthiness of our interpretations. In the first instance, we also sought to focus our analysis on the way in which think tanks work, rather than the specific content of their arguments.

Researcher positionality

My own position in relation to think tanks and think tank representatives proved challenging. On the one hand, my experience of working *with* and *for* Think Tank B provided a rare opportunity to examine how think tanks work to shape health policy and planning, but on the other my involvement with Think Tank B meant that I might be more inclined to focus on them when analysing and interpreting data. Our collaborative approach proved crucial here: discussions with academic colleagues provided a forum for reflecting on concerns about my own position as both 'researcher of think tanks' and 'think tank researcher' and what this might mean for the research; and early discussions with Think Tank B highlighted the importance (for them and us) of seeking additional cases to ensure a good balance within the study. What emerged was our collective case study design, with Think Tank B one of four embedded units. This really helped me to approach data collection, analysis and writing in a different way as it allowed me to embrace all four think tanks in our sample and provided a useful contrast within the study.

I did not ask colleagues in participating think tanks about how they viewed me in my two roles, as 'researcher of think tanks' and 'think tank researcher'. However, my sense from emails and informal discussions was that colleagues in all four organisations were largely supportive of the study and interested in the findings. For those at Think Tank B, their prior knowledge of me and my work – as well as that of the rest of the research team – suggested that they trusted me to undertake a thoughtful and balanced study. Negotiating with the other three think tanks involved recounting the trust already put in me by colleagues at Think Tank B, whilst at the same time not being seen to be aligning with one organisation or viewpoint. To facilitate this balance I tended to keep my emails fairly formal: briefly describing my time working at Think Tank B, whilst also emphasising my academic position and the formal processes that the study had gone through (for example, approval from the university research ethics committee).

Researcher positionality clearly has the potential to shape data collection. In previous work I have deliberately adopted a *naïve stance* to interviewing

(Shaw, 2006) and we initially thought to adopt a similar approach here. This changed as our research design developed and it became clear that many interviewees were in a powerful position relative to my own and, particularly in the case of Think Tank B, were known to me professionally and/or personally. I therefore adopted a more proactive and knowledgeable approach to interviewing which enabled us to position interviewer and interviewee on a more equal footing and introduce questioning 'of the logic of participants' questions and answers' (Kvale, 1996: 20).

Researcher voice

Our research has a strong biographical element to it, beginning with my account of working at Think Tank B. However, whilst I recognise the value of acknowledging my own ideas, biases and emotions within the main study, I struggled to do this in practice. On reflection, my struggle to write myself into the study related to three aspects of my work. Firstly, my dual role working with and studying think tanks – combined with ongoing working relationships with think tank colleagues – meant that it was sometimes difficult for me to reflect critically on the environments that I was in. Secondly, being based in a medical school (where research tends to be dominated by randomised controlled trials and systematic reviews) meant that writing from a biographical perspective was unusual. Thirdly, given that the study was unfunded, it was hard to find the time and space to reflect on – and give voice to – the biographical elements of my work.

So, what changed? The process of writing collaboratively helped to shift my thinking: the rest of the research team were able to stand back from my experiences, recognise the relevance of my voice as an integral part of the research process, and encourage me to write myself into emerging papers and presentations. A major turning point came at a conference in Vienna in July 2013: finding myself free from the above constraints, I scrapped the presentation I had prepared, disappeared to my hotel room and typed furiously for three hours. What emerged was the story of my own experiences of working in a think tank. I used my story as a vehicle for discussing the study with conference participants and conveying some of the questions, concerns, queries, experiences, people, values and emotions that come into play in the things that think tanks do.

THE DATA

We sought complementary sources of data that could provide detailed insight on the way that think tanks seek to shape health policy. These sources combined field texts (comprising my autoethnographic account of working at Think Tank B, alongside a research diary), interviews with think-tank representatives and think-tank documents.

Field texts

Strictly speaking data collection began on the day that I started my journal reflecting on my time working at Think Tank B (February 2009 to March 2011). At that time, my entries were not intended as 'data' and the study had yet to be conceived. My journal started as a personal project, oriented to making sense of my new work situation. Take the following extract, in which I am trying to make sense of the environment and approach to working, having been in post for close to a year:

Extract 2

I have been struck by the formality of some of the emails . . . They often bring with them the sense of a 'formal managerial request, where I am required to act in some way, my response should also be formal and thought through and this will be recorded and filed somewhere for future reference or 'good record keeping'.

This approach to managing, decision-making and communicating all has a rather strange effect on me, inspiring me to rebel against 'the system'. It makes me feel that research is dictated from 'on high' and that my role is simply to undertake and deliver rather than investigate and explore.

Field text, 5 January 2010

This extract is grounded in my experience of working in a think tank. Such entries subsequently proved helpful in appreciating the everyday activities of think tanks in our sample. As the study evolved, we therefore resituated my journal as an autoethnographic account, enabling us to examine and retell events and activities in order to generate new insights and understand broader social phenomena. For instance, returning to the extract above, this meant moving from personal narrative about certain activities ('some of the emails', 'formal managerial request', 'requiring me to act in some way') to connect with wider social theory about health policy and planning and to established (or what Degeling (1996) refers to as 'sacred') approaches to planning that are grounded in an accepted way of doing things (for instance, 'approach to managing', 'dictated from on high'). Hence what began as a personal project documenting personal experience of working within a think tank, subsequently enabled us to better understand organisational practices and activities, and link with wider social theory.

 Activity 1

Doing autoethnography

Think of a community that you identify with, such as your place of work or study. Over the next week, spend some time reflecting on your personal experiences of the community. Consider how membership has contributed to your beliefs, involved you in rituals, or influenced your behaviour.

Now write a brief autoethnography (one to two pages). Provide information about yourself, and describe the community for those who may have no knowledge of the group. Formulate a thesis which clearly identifies you as a member of the community, using one or two narrative examples to demonstrate the assertion you have made and to illustrate the community and its effect on you. Your writing should demonstrate critical reflection about your connection with your community.

When conducting the main study (October 2011 to November 2012), we supplemented my autoethnographic account with a research diary. At this point, I was no longer employed by Think Tank B (though I retained an honorary position). However, we recognised the value of observation in appreciating the context of think tanks' work. We therefore sought to document observations as and when opportunities arose (for instance, at the time of interviews). It would have been easy to frame this as a continuation of my autoethnographic account. However, my research diary was different, deliberately reflecting on the research process (for instance, issues of access), as well as capturing situated accounts of interactions with the people, artefacts and processes allied to think tanks. Take the following entry describing my encounter at the start of an interview with a senior executive at one think tank:

Extract 3

I noticed that the table in [the] room has changed . . . a childlike four-seater (dwarfed by the size of [the] office) having grown up to a twelve-seater, I assume for bigger and more important meetings? It slightly takes me aback and I wonder where to sit. I take my place at the end thinking that [they will] sit at the head next to me but, once [they are] finished with emails, [they] walk over and sit opposite me. [They] seem a long way away but maybe this is the point. It certainly sums up the tone of much of our discussion.

Field text, 1 February 2012

This extract is different from that in my autoethnographic account (Extract 2) as it documents observations of think tanks in the specific context of the research, exploring, for instance, how interviews are negotiated ('I wonder where to sit', 'the tone of the discussion'). It provided insights on the think tank environment (for instance, buildings, meeting rooms) and actors (for instance, interviewees) and provided a space to document analytic reflections (for instance, about think tank activities in relation to NHS reforms).

Both my autoethnographic account and subsequent diary (referred to collectively from here on as 'field texts') provided empirical data through which we could gain insight into a broader set of social phenomena than those provided by other data sources alone (interviews and documents, see below). Field texts were not perfect. Whilst I spent extended periods in think tank settings, documenting activities and experiences was not always feasible in light of other work commitments, and practical and emotional circumstances. However, they were sufficient to enable us to open up our analysis to the different settings, contexts, actors, activities and interactions allied to the work of think tanks, allowing us to contextualise the more detailed micro analysis of think tanks' arguments and discursive strategies.

Documents and interviews

We supplemented field texts with documents and interviews, to enable us to examine the content of think tanks arguments and discursive strategies (for instance, via formal publications); deliberate and conscious statements (for instance, about independence) at particular points in time; and reflections on the role of think tanks and their work in relation to NHS reforms. Starting with Think Tank B, we began by collecting, reading and re-reading relevant documents (including over fifty publications, annual reports, reviews, charity commission submissions, historical accounts and more).

This gave us a detailed appreciation of the work of Think Tank B. However, as we shifted to a collective case study, we sought to include other think tanks. This led us to sample 30 documents, including at least one each of the following from each think tank: a strategy document (e.g. annual report, strategic priorities); a governing document (e.g. memorandum of incorporation); and a piece of work relevant to current NHS reforms (e.g. policy briefing). We supplemented this with wider contextual material (e.g. government policy documents) in order to understand the policy and regulatory context in which think tanks were working.

Data collection in each of the four think tanks began with an informal interview with the main contact (in one instance via email) about the nature and focus of their work. These initial interviews guided access, built rapport, and allowed us to identify relevant documents. We then undertook 10 in-depth interviews with senior think tank representatives (6 at Think Tank B, 2 at Think Tank C and 1 each at Think Tanks A and D). Interviews adopted a narrative approach (Muller, 1992), allowing for an account from the narrator's perspective of the role of think tanks, and of how events and actions in relation to NHS reforms unfolded over time.

There was no fixed set of questions that was relevant to each interviewee. Instead we sought to ask broad questions (Figure 6.3) to facilitate discussion around individuals' roles, experiences and knowledge over time and the context/s in which this was situated. We supplemented this on a person-by-person basis with specific questions relevant to each think tank and its work.

At one level narrative interviews represent the personal stories of individuals. However, they also take place within a broad structural context and therefore

1. Can you start by telling me a bit about your background and how you came to join [think tank]?

2. How would you describe [think tank] and the work it does?

3. Do you regard your organisation as a 'think tank'? Which other organisations are working in the same space as [think tank]?

4. What role do you think organisations like [think tank] have in shaping policy?

5. I'd like to take you back to July 2010 when the White Paper, *Equity and Excellence: Liberating the NHS* was published. Can you describe [think tank's] reaction to the White Paper at that time?

6. How has [think tank's] response changed over time?

7. How do you think [think tank's] approach to the current reforms differs from that of other, similar organisations?

8. How successful do you think [think tank] has been in shaping policy?

9. I would like to ask you some specific questions about your own role at [think tank].

10. Is there anything else that *you'd* like to add?

Figure 6.3 Overview of topic guide used in interviews with think tank representatives

provide a useful means of picking up on the wider social and political context in which health policy and planning evolves. Narrative interviewing therefore allowed us to examine relationships among individual accounts, institutions and policy goals over time, instances of 'policy talk' and explanations of think tanks' perceived roles.

We deliberately undertook detailed data collection with Think Tank B in the first instance. Having gained an understanding of their work, this allowed us to explore some issues in depth before testing out emerging analysis with other think tanks. Hence our interpretation of documents and interviews was most heavily influenced by the case of Think Tank B, with others providing contrasting cases at a less in-depth level.

Data storage and readiness

We gave considerable thought to data management and the ways in which we could ensure the security of data relating to individuals and organisations participating in the study. This was particularly important given the breadth of data that we either had (my journal) or planned to collect (interviews and documents), and which was gathered at different times. In terms of regulatory requirements, we were concerned to meet the requirements set out in the 1998 Data Protection Act. In terms of the study context and ongoing debate about NHS reforms, we were particularly concerned to protect individuals' privacy and confidentiality and ensure a firewall around data at the university.

Initially, whilst I was working at Think Tank B, I kept my journal on my laptop. As the study evolved and I began a second journal (a research diary, kept as a separate file) so I also began to store study data on an external, encrypted hard drive. This included interviews with think-tank representatives, which I recorded with consent and then paid to have transcribed by a professional transcriber (who I have an established working relationship with that includes formal agreements regarding confidentiality and disposal of data); and think-tank documents.

There is no software that can *do* qualitative analysis. However, there are packages that can help with storage and retrieval and can also be used for making links between sections of data (Kelle, 2004). I choose not to use such software for this study as I felt that this would present a technological barrier to my engaging fully with the data set (see Tallerico, 1991, for an overview of the pros and cons). As our analytic focus on language developed, however, we needed some way of systematically searching the data corpus. We identified a free software programme – Antconc, a programme dedicated to analysing corpora – to help us to undertake analysis of keywords (a simple frequency analysis), and concordance (examining key words in context) (Anthony, 2005). We included interviews and documents in our corpus and prepared this by resaving relevant data files (largely Word documents and pdf files) as text files, which could then be systematically searched and examined using Antconc.

Collaborative research brings challenges in terms of shared access to data: whilst I stored data locally, I still needed to be able to circulate it amongst the team. Early on I gained detailed comments on my journal and research diary with team members each working on electronic copies, adding memos and sharing comments. Subsequently, we focused largely on hard copy data extracts during team meetings (selection being guided by ongoing face-to-face and electronic discussions), as well as hard copy summaries of the emerging corpus analysis.

Activity 2

Managing qualitative data

Data storage and management are important issues for all qualitative research. Take 10 minutes to reflect on the data management issues you have faced in your current research. What were the immediate and long-term consequences to your research project? How have you resolved these issues?

> Now consider how data management issues might change in any future research that you do, for instance involving different participants (e.g. politicians, healthcare professionals or patients) or different types of qualitative data (e.g. field notes, transcribed interviews, government documents, speeches, diaries)? How might you address such issues?

ANALYSIS OF DATA

To arrive at a stage called 'the analysis' is somewhat arbitrary, as we were immersed in analysis early on in the research. I therefore want to use this section to demonstrate how that analytic process involved application of a theoretical framework by focusing on specific 'sensitising concepts' that we used in our analysis. This makes analysis sound straightforward, but that was far from the case. Having done considerable theoretical and methodological work in the early stages, it was hard to then translate this into a clear analytic method.

As usual with studies adopting linguistic ethnography, we turned to the data. I began by reading and re-reading field texts, documents and interview transcripts, checking out intuitive hunches in the data, and discussing emerging thoughts with the team. At this stage we were looking for a way-in, asking 'what's going on here, and why'?

Field texts proved important in these early stages. Take the following two extracts, the first from my autoethnographic account reflecting on what kind of organisation a think tank might be, and the second from my research diary at the start of the study as we began negotiating access and participants queried our use of the term 'think tank':

Extract 4

When I was interviewed for my post at Think Tank B there was much emphasis about the similarities with a university or academic approach and I was, even at that stage, encouraged to have an honorary contract and maintain my existing links with the world of academia. The sense I gain[ed] was that Think Tank B were framing themselves as an academic research organisation.

Field text, 9 December 2009

Extract 5

I sometimes regret the title of our study: the role of think tanks in shaping healthcare policy and planning. I wonder how different the response would be if we had, for instance, focused on 'non-governmental research organisations', 'tharitable trusts' or 'independent charitable organisations'. . . These are fairly bland titles, they don't really say much and could cover an awful lots of organisations. But think tank seems to be more sensitive, hold some sort of connotations and perhaps captures something about the political nature of the work?

Field text, 6 December 2011

Such entries encouraged us to unpack the meaning that people gave to terms such as 'think tank', 'independent', 'academic' and 'charitable', and consider why think tanks were involved in a process of 'framing themselves' and their work in particular ways. This led us to ask interviewees about their use of such language and to explore the use of such language across our dataset.

We used corpus analysis to enable systematic language analysis of interview and documentary data, examining terms that think tanks did – or did not – place particular emphasis on (for instance, independence) and how, when and why they used such terms. This provided a 'way-in' to more detailed and close analysis, highlighting particularly prominent emphases (see, for instance, Figure 6.4) and allowing us to move between different elements of our data – keywords, documents and interview transcripts – to examine the language, activities and settings of think tanks' work and the interaction with health policy and planning; and to look for potential explanations for language use and the people, practices and artefacts that might support it.

Introducing sensitising concepts 1: 'front-stage' and 'back-stage'

Early analytic work focused on how and why think tanks frame their work (for instance, as independent). To guide our analysis further, we introduced the sensitising concepts of 'front stage' and 'back-stage' to enable us to explore the different contexts and settings in which such framing takes place (Degeling, 1996, following Goffman, 1959). These concepts enabled us to identify 'public' and 'private' settings and the audiences allied to them: 'front-stage' being where think tanks knowingly perform and adhere to the conventions that have particular public meaning, and 'back-stage' being where think tanks are away from the public eye and are no longer required to play such a role. By acknowledging overlap between these concepts, we were also able to explore the relationship between different settings and audiences.

Field texts opened up this aspect of our analysis, allowing us to explore the different settings in which think tank work takes place, and the interactions with individuals, institutions, artefacts and activities allied to health policy and planning (see, for instance, Extract 1). Our analysis of field texts suggested that think tank staff invested considerable time and energy in drafting and redrafting formal written accounts of their work for the 'front-stage' (for instance, formal publications, websites, conference presentations) and similar time and energy in arranging events 'back-stage' (for instance, private dinners, seminars, informal meetings).

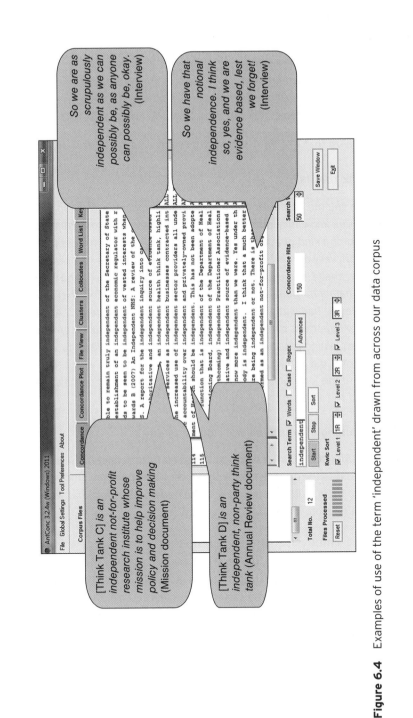

Figure 6.4 Examples of use of the term 'independent' drawn from across our data corpus

This led us to explore what purpose such settings served, through informants' own accounts of their work (i.e. interviews). Take the following example from an interview with a senior executive at one think tank, describing the significance of publicly available written accounts of their work:

Extract 6

I have come to realize that writing it down actually does matter a great deal, oddly.

Why do you think that is?

So, I think it gives you the authority. And in a lot of the process, well, people either want something to go, you know, in a lot of these processes they want something to go back to . . . and with a kind of, a kind of audit trail . . . . There's a sort of seemliness to that process. So I think, I think it's very difficult actually to influence without the sort of, without having the written analysis to underpin it, which you have published. And actually, of course, in the parliamentary discussions where our work was quoted, they don't quote a conversation they've had with you, they quote what you've written . . . And that discourse is a very important part of this. Now what is really helpful is combining that writing with the explaining personally. And also the warming people up to the fact that you're going to write, and in many cases I had prior conversations with people about how I was going to word this - sought their advice on [discussion about specific reforms]. And I changed some of the wording to, having reflected on their advice.

Okay, almost framing of what you were going to say?

Yes. So I iterated. So I did, I didn't, I didn't do things quite so sequentially. I guess I did the - and the, if, I guess the engagement with people was a two-way process where I was trying to influence them, but I was also taking their advice. So that what we would say was capable of being more influential.

This interviewee emphasises the importance of 'front-stage' written accounts ('written analysis', 'published', 'quote what you've written') in providing weight to think tank arguments ('writing it down actually does matter a great deal', 'it gives you the authority') and a tangible, traceable and citable source of ideas ('they quote what you've written', 'a kind of audit trail') that decision-makers can draw on ('in the parliamentary discussions'). These 'front-stage' accounts of work opened up possibilities for think tanks in our sample to interact with key areas of policy and influence NHS reform ('what we would say was capable of being more influential'). The production of front stage accounts involved an interactive process away from public view ('a two-way process', 'combining that writing with the explaining personally', 'warming people up'), and for those think tanks that undertook work specifically on the NHS reforms (A, B and D) involved co-production of accounts of NHS reforms on which both could then draw ('changed some of the wording', 'reflected on their advice'). This production of written accounts was visible to varying degrees in the activities of the four think tanks in our sample.

Field texts and interviews proved crucial in examining the activities, interactions and actors that were characteristic of 'back-stage' and enabled us to examine how think tanks – A, B and D and to a lesser extent Think Tank C – sought to build coalitions of likeminded people ('usually a select bunch of high powered policymakers, leads, managers', field note), and provide discrete 'back-stage' forums for debate about issues pertinent to health reform (for instance, on economic regulation).

Introducing sensitising concepts II: 'sacred' and 'profane'

We were not only interested in 'front-stage' and 'back-stage' settings, but also in the language and interaction used in these settings. We therefore introduced concepts of 'sacred' and 'profane' language (Degeling, 1996), where the former relates to language emphasising shared values considered important to the instrumental potential of policy and planning (rationality, objectivity and so on) and the latter to the more political dimensions of planning (including, for instance, agenda setting and coalition building).

This led us to examine the language think tanks in our sample employed in 'front-stage' and 'back-stage' settings. 'Front-stage' accounts (for instance, formal publications of think tanks' research) tended to employ 'sacred' language, drawing on modernist conceptions of health policy that describe the policy process as an exercise in informed problem-solving (Parsons, 2004; Degeling, 1996), and in which a problem is identified, data collected and analysed, and evidence provided to policymakers on which they can then base decisions. Each of the four participating think tanks emphasised a set of technical skills and activities (for instance, 'experimental intervention', 'examining active age management', 'evaluating the impact', 'contributing to the evidence base'), which informed precise 'research and policy analysis' that, for at least three of these organisations (A, B and D) then fed into 'the administrative machinery' of government. Whilst terms such as 'care', 'people', and 'patients' were used regularly (1771 and 576 and 457 instances, respectively, across the data corpus), these tended to be depersonalised and emphasise structures and processes (e.g. 'unwarranted variations or gaps in care', 'capture people's experiences').

By employing such 'sacred' planning discourse 'front-stage', think tanks publicly deferred to values such as objectivity and due process and, in doing so, signalled to decision-makers that they knew about and adhered to the rules of the game 'front-stage'. This reinforced think tanks' self-presentation as independent organisations, and publicly situated them as legitimate advisors on healthcare generally as well as proposed NHS reforms. It also enabled think tanks in our sample to identify, engage and interact with decision-makers in other settings, and to speak about and practise planning in ways that gave more explicit recognition to its political dimensions. Take the following extract from an interview with a senior executive at one think tank, talking about their work to engage with government proposals:

Extract 7

the battle lines had been really - I mean remain so unfortunately - but kind of, I think, retrogressively very drawn on choice, competition, public, private, these sort of really unhelpful polarities . . . And so that was when we started publishing on innovation and did a lot of work with Stephen Dorrell* on productivity and events with him and trying to find, trying to sort of gee up the conversation in a slightly different way, which is to say, you know, let's not talk about competition, but let's just talk about new and better ways of doing things because we really need them.

(*At the time of the study Stephen Dorrell was Conservative Member of Parliament and Chair of the Health Select Committee.)

Such extracts highlighted how (to varying extents) think tanks' focus on – and engage with – a small group of decision-makers involved in shaping policy ('did a lot of work with Stephen Dorrell'), emphasising the importance of relationships with decision-makers and engagement with institutional agendas ('choice, competition, public, private') in shaping NHS reform. This engagement took place in 'back-stage' settings (with field texts in particular highlighting a range of private dinners, meetings and events with a range of decision-makers). Whilst this interviewee references policy (choice, competition, etc.), their emphasis is less on gaining legitimacy (this already having been established 'front-stage') and more on opening up potential for negotiation about health policy ('let's just talk about new and better ways of doing things'). The planning language shifts from 'sacred' to 'profane' ('gee up the conversation in a slightly different way', 'let's not talk about competition') in recognition of the messy realities of *doing* policy. This 'back-stage' activity often appeared to contradict 'front-stage' performances of planning discourse.

Our analysis also identified a number of discursive strategies that think tanks employed in their work (for instance, neutralising metaphors and declarations of their independence) as a means of neutralising 'back-stage' activities and further emphasising their legitimacy to decision makers.

Summing up

The above description of our analysis presents a rather neat account. In reality it took several months to tease out the relationship between linguistic, ethnographic and contextual data and to make sense of the work that think tanks in our sample did. We adopted an interpretive approach that emphasised the role of language and interaction in shaping healthcare planning (Fischer and Forester, 1993;

Bacchi, 2000; Yanow, 2000; Shaw, 2010; Wagenaar, 2011). We brought together a diverse data set (Figure 6.2) combining my account of working within a think tank, with field notes, interview transcripts and documents. Our analysis focused on the messy realities of healthcare planning in context – the planning talk and settings that shape, enable and constrain planning. Corpus analysis initially provided an aerial view of our data: as we introduced sensitising concepts to our analysis so it provided a means of systematically searching interview and documentary data and examining how, when and why language was used in different settings (for instance, formal publications providing access to 'front stage' accounts). Field texts opened up this aspect of our analysis further, allowing us to appreciate the different settings in which think tank work takes place and the interactions within and between them.

Through close examination of language and context, we found that participating think tanks' focus on policy and planning required them to frame, shape and guide the messages that they want different audiences to receive. This meant that they simultaneously sought to engage with the political process 'back-stage' whilst at the same time employing a range of discursive strategies to emphasise their neutrality and independence 'front-stage'. This ensured legitimacy and enabled them (to varying degrees) to contribute to government proposals on NHS reform. A detailed account of theory and findings can be found in Shaw, Russell, Parsons et. al, (2014).

Discourse analysis, linguistic ethnography and interpretive policy analysis

In my vignette, I tell the story of how I came to two overarching theoretical approaches: interpretive policy analysis and linguistic ethnography. These two approaches framed our study of think tanks and guided us to hone in on particular theoretical reference points, including discourse theory (see Shaw, Russell, Greenhalgh et al., 2014, for a detailed discussion).

Interpretive policy analysis provided us with a robust and relevant foundation. This is because it focuses on 'meanings that shape actions and institutions, and the ways in which they do so' (Bevir and Rhodes, 2004: 130) and hence provides a welcome counterbalance to the instrumental approaches that have tended to dominate research on think tanks and health policy. Such approaches have guided researchers (and decision-makers) to categorise think tanks (e.g. 'media think tank', see Hart and Vroman, 2008); to understand them primarily as organisations; and to think of their potential contributions in terms of value-neutral expertise that can inform policy in a simple and direct way. But such approaches fail to account for the actors, interests and values involved in shaping policy – the very things that we were keen to examine. Interpretive policy analysis made good sense as it guided us to focus on political actions, institutions, actors, artefacts and meanings that contribute to the work of think tanks (Shaw, Russell, Greenhalgh et al. (2014) and Shaw and Russell, in press). Field theory and practice theory were relevant reference points: the former guiding us to see think tanks as operating in different social spaces, each with associated actions and rules (Medvetz, 2010, 2008), and the later to focus on think tanks' everyday activities as potentially shaping policy and planning (Nicolini, 2009; Wagenaar, 2011). For instance, Extract 6 highlights how think tanks seek to frame their work as 'academic' and led us to (a) unpack the meaning that people gave to such terms, and (b) examine the kind of activities, institutions, artefacts and language that might be employed – or practised – in this context.

Interpretive policy analysis provided an overarching approach to thinking about and analysing think-tank contributions to health policymaking. However, it tends to focus more on social institutions and interactions than on micro analysis of language and communication (Shaw and Russell, in press). We were keen to examine such language and communication in order to understand how think tanks employ policy and planning talk. Hence we turned to linguistic ethnography, which focuses on close analysis of situated language (Snell and Lefstein, 2012). Discourse theory was a particularly relevant reference point, guiding us to see thinks tanks as one actor amongst many that seek to shape policy through a combination of language, storylines, networks and discursive practices (Bacchi, 2000; Hajer and Wagenaar, 2003; Shaw, 2010).

The term 'discourse analysis' is complex and contested (Ockwell and Rydin, 2010). In linguistic ethnography it indicates 'an authoritative analysis of language use' (Rampton et al., 2004: 6), the aim being to use discourse analytic tools in creative ways 'to extend our understanding of the role language plays in social life' (Creese, 2008: 235). Those working in linguistic ethnography draw on a range of approaches to analyse discourse. Our focus on health policy and planning meant that we needed an approach that enabled us, not only to examine social interaction, but to do so in the specific context of policymaking (for instance, agenda setting, policy formation). Given the nature of policy discourse (Bacchi, 2000; Rydin and Ockwell, 2010; Shaw, 2010), we elected to focus not on specific utterances in a relatively small number of short data extracts (as is often the case in linguistic ethnography), but on the architecture of debate across a large and varied corpus of data. As I have described above, to do this we centred on policy and planning as the object of our study, and then, building on the work of Goffman (1959) and Degeling (1996), connected with relevant sensitising concepts ('front-stage' and 'back-stage', 'sacred' and 'profane') to guide our analysis. This allowed us to 'reveal aspects of social and political processes that were previously obscured or misunderstood' (Rydin and Ockwell, 2010: 168), and the argumentative structures and practices involved. For instance, I have shown how think tanks present themselves in different ways by privileging particular kinds of language in different 'front-stage' and 'back-stage' settings (Extracts 6 and 7). This kind of analysis is crucial when studying policy because it reveals how the language that think tanks use in their communication with others – deliberately or unconsciously – involves 'persuasion and rationalisation' and 'influences the dynamics of policy debates' (Rydin and Ockwell, 2010: 3).

My account of arriving at 'theory' may sound straightforward. However, novice researchers might be reassured that it is one that I can write about only with hindsight. Social scientists often talk about theory and their theoretical approach in a rarefied way: 'as a subject in its own right, coordinate[d] with, but not really related to the way we do research' (Becker, 1998: 3). Good social scientists do not usually have – or work from – a systematic theory in the style of, say, Talcott Parsons or Michel Foucault. However, most do have a theoretically informed way of working. This way of working guides how they see the world – in my case the world of healthcare – and how they design and undertake their research. Theory then is about 'ways of thinking that help researchers faced with concrete research problems make some progress' (Becker, 1998: 4).

Theoretically informed ways of working do not to appear from nowhere. Rather they emerge out of months – if not years – of studying, reading and thinking (see Wildavsky's chapter on 'Reading with a purpose' for an account of this process, in Wildavsky, 2010: 25–38).

─────────────── **Activity 3** ───────────────

Developing a theoretically informed way of working

Consider the main writers and thinkers that you have engaged with since you began studying or working in research. Pick three that have particularly influenced your thinking to-date. To help to crystallise your own theoretically informed way of working, write 200-300 words on how these writers and their thinking have shaped and guided your current research, making notes about the key features of their thinking and considering how you would describe these to someone who has not read the same work as you.

REPRESENTATION AND WRITING UP

We sought to provide a rich account of findings by grounding them in worked analyses and examples. The process of selecting data extracts was informed by the analytic process described above, and by our identifying examples of 'the telling case' (Mitchell, 1984). Following Harper (2003), we sought examples where a particular position or argument was most clearly demonstrated in the shortest space; that could be easily understood without having to refer to the wider context of a particular document or interview; and which gave the most diversity in terms of variations on discursive strategies and contexts. Our intention was to provide readers with an apt illustration of our data and analysis so as to make situations come alive.

A prominent concern throughout this process was about how we could write about each of the think tanks within our sample. Each had agreed that we could reveal their identity, however discussion amongst the research team and with participating sites ultimately led us to anonymise each of the think tanks within the study outputs.

We deliberately selected 'telling cases' and data extracts that were drawn from across each of the four think tanks, and, throughout the writing process, remained conscious of the need to focus on our overarching concern with the role of think tanks in shaping health reforms (rather than focusing on the role of individual organisations).

Given our focus on linguistic ethnography, which encourages authors to ground their writing in worked analysis of data, we were keen to illustrate our analysis by drawing on specific examples. We were careful in our selection of such examples that they reflected analysis across our collective case and not simply one think tank and, where an important analytic point was relevant to only one think tank, we made this explicit. Where appropriate, we shortened extracts to ensure sensitive aspects of think tanks' work (for instance, about the process of influencing specific aspect of policy – Extract 6) that we had been asked not to recount publicly.

We assured confidentiality and anonymity for individuals. The think tank world is a small one, and the number of think tanks specialising in health reform smaller still. We were therefore meticulous in the way in which we presented extracts, ensuring that pronouns (his, her, they, etc.) were used interchangeably, and, where we were in any doubt about the risk to anonymity, used alternative extracts. The result was, in places, a necessarily sketchy account of findings, but one that we feel remains faithful to what we agreed with each of the think tanks in our sample.

Audiences for research

Our motivation for undertaking the study was to address a significant gap in the literature on think tanks working in the field of health policy and planning. As we describe elsewhere, the literature that does exist tends to focus on broad areas of public policy and aim for 'ever-closer definition and categorisation of think tanks' (Shaw, Russell, Greenhalgh et al., 2014: 448) (there are, of course, several notable exceptions that I have cited). From our perspective, this has 'closed down opportunities for understanding and analysing the role of think tanks in healthcare reform' (p. 448). In contrast, our intention has been to open up opportunities for further academic scrutiny of think tanks working in health policy and planning. Our primary audience for the research has therefore always been the academic community. To-date there has been a good level of interest, not only in terms of scrutinising think tanks' work, but also in terms of the theoretical and methodological approach adopted.

We agreed to share copies of academic papers with study participants ahead of publication. To-date there has been constructive feedback that has helped us to fine tune our analysis. Our study has so far reported on the activities of think tanks, but it is the final phase of the research involving interviews with decision-makers (not reported here) that has proved to be of particular interest to think tanks involved in the study, and this is what most have requested feedback on. At the time of writing our final analysis of this aspect of the research has yet to be completed, but, in line with requests from think tanks in our sample, we anticipate circulating a briefing paper to all those involved, along with an offer of a meeting (for example, with senior executives and/or staff) to discuss our findings in more depth.

CONCLUDING COMMENTS

We have been privileged to be able to do this study without formal funding. The opportunity provided by my own experiences of working at Think Tank B, combined with my academic role at Queen Mary University of London, have enabled us to do the research and to address the messy realities of research as it unfolds – what Becker (1998) calls 'thinking about your research while you're doing it'.

I am confident that this study would have been different had we sought formal funding and been required to define the questions, theories, processes, people and resources at the outset. This is an important point: the funding process potentially shapes and guides research in particular ways that may – or may not – be amenable to ethnography and language.

The downside of our not being formally funded was that the work that we needed to do for our study was sometimes overtaken by other priorities. Completing the study has required persistence. Working with people who are committed and enthusiastic about the research has been key. Ensuring good project management and self-organisation has been vital. Readers who similarly wish to organise the flow of their work would do well to follow Wildavsky's advice about 'how to organize time for scholarly activities' (2010: 41–56).

ACKNOWLEDGEMENTS

My thanks go to Jill Russell, Trish Greenhalgh and Wayne Parsons for their contributions to the study, and their relentless enthusiasm and support for the work. To Fiona Copland and Angela Creese for giving me the chance to tell the research story as it unfolded, and for their patience with me in delivering it to them. And to all of those who have participated in the study from each of the four think tanks, without whom the research would not have been possible. The views expressed in this chapter are those of the author and do not necessarily reflect the perspective either of the individuals interviewed or the organisations in the sample.

KEY READINGS

Becker, H.S. (1998) *Tricks of the Trade: How to Think about Your Research While You're Doing It.* Chicago: University of Chicago Press.

Shaw, S.E., Russell, J., Greenhalgh, T. and Korica, M. (2013) 'Thinking about think tanks in healthcare? A call for a new research agenda', *Sociology of Health & Illness*, 36(3): 447–61.

Wildavsky, A. (2010) *Craftways: On the Organizaton of Scholarly Work*, 2nd edn. New Brunswick, NJ: Transaction Publishers.

Yanow, D. (2000) *Conducting Interpretative Policy Analysis*. Thousand Oaks, CA: Sage.

III

Practical Issues in Linguistic Ethnographic Research

SEVEN
Empiricism, Ethics and Impact

INTRODUCTION

This chapter will discuss three areas – empiricism, ethics and impact. These subjects are not intrinsically related but are linked by the fact that they have all become increasingly important in all fields of research. The chapter will provide a response to problematic issues in these areas from a linguistic ethnographic perspective. As ever, our aim is not to give answers but to open up spaces for thinking about and discussing research issues.

EMPIRICISM

Fiona remembers listening to a discussion on education on a highly respected news programme on the BBC in which the interviewer lambasted the eminent education professors for presenting research findings based on qualitative data. The findings were interpretations rather than proofs, was the presenter's argument, therefore how could they be taken seriously? The view that research should be quantitative, experimental, have control groups and present irrefutable findings continues to be held by many, even those who should be well informed, although as Agar (2008) suggests, understandings of approaches such as ethnography are slowly beginning to extend and improve. Even so, researchers in linguistic ethnography are often asked 'how do you know that?' They may also be asked by other academics in particular about linguistic ethnography's paradigmatic warrant. This section will address both these issues.

The 'how do you know that' in the end comes down to empirical evidence. By empirical evidence we mean data that originate in observation. In linguistic ethnography, there are two kinds of overlapping empirical data: linguistic (for example, recordings, transcripts, texts) and ethnographic (for example, recordings, field notes, interviews, images). These sources intersect because in linguistic ethnography linguistic evidence is ethnographically informed and ethnographic evidence can only be understood as constructed in discourse. In other words, linguistic ethnography holds that both data sources are inseparable.

Traditionally, linguistics has been studied as a natural science and used theoretical modelling and predominantly quantitative data. Language is the object of study, with the focus on linguistic description, underlying structures and linguistic comparison. Hypotheses are provable (or not) and research can be repeated and replicated in the scientific tradition. Much linguistic analysis even looks like traditional scientific writing with diagrams, charts and equations common. However, as we argue in Chapter 1, linguistic analysis of this kind, with its focus on code, grammar and system, often seems far removed from the concerns of those who use language. It can seem sterile and lacking purpose.

On the other hand, as Brewer (2000) points out, to proponents of the natural sciences which take a quantitative approach, ethnographic data may not be considered empirical. Data are created by one researcher (generally) and these cannot be verified (for example, the event observed at a research site cannot be repeated for another researcher to watch and create the same data). Furthermore, researchers observing the same phenomenon may produce different data as they will notice different things (Spencer, 2001). These facts, it is argued, mean that ethnography cannot be generalisable, a key tenet of scientific writing. However, according to Erickson (1990), the task for the researcher is particularisability, rather than generalisability. Quoting Jean-Jacques Rousseau, Erickson rather contentiously suggests, that 'general and abstract ideas are the source of the greatest errors of mankind'. For Erickson it is the local and particular which are essential in empiricism because social action is always situated and 'One discovers universals as manifested concretely and specifically, not in abstraction and generality' (p. 130).

Blommaert and Jie (2010) tackle the criticism of lack of generalisation in a different way and in so doing, clearly and concisely explain the ethnographic endeavour. According to them, the result of ethnographic research will not be a body of findings which can claim representativeness for a (segment of the) population, it will not be replicable under *identical* circumstances, it will not claim objectivity on grounds of an outsider's position for the researcher, it will not claim to produce 'uncontaminated' evidence, and so on. It will be interpretive research in a situated, real environment, based on interaction between the researcher and the subject(s), hence, fundamentally *subjective* in nature, aimed at demonstrating complexity, and yielding hypotheses that can be replicated and tested in *similar*, not identical, circumstances. Ethnography produces theoretical statements, not 'facts' nor 'laws' (Blommaert and Jie, 2010: 17).

The aims of ethnography, it is argued, are different from those of the natural sciences: the data generation processes are particular to each approach and should not be compared. Furthermore, empirical data are collected for different reasons. In a positivist tradition, data are collected to prove (or not) a hypothesis; in ethnography, data are collected to develop a theoretical perspective.

Criticisms of ethnographic empiricism (that is subjective and non-verifiable) and of linguistic empiricism (that it is sterile and detached from its contexts of use) can be met to some extent by bringing them together in linguistic ethnography (see case studies for how this can be done in practice). Rampton et al. (2004) call this process 'tying ethnography down' and 'opening linguistics up' (p. 4) so that the strengths of each off-set the weaknesses of the other. Situating language in context and 'impregnat[ing] local description with analytical frameworks drawn from outside' (p. 4) makes the question, 'How do you know that?' easier to answer and goes some way towards formulating a response to sceptical television presenters, amongst others. As linguistic ethnographers our argument is that good ethnography should be as rigorous as any other methodology, whether from linguistics, or the natural and social sciences.

Erickson (1990) speaks of ethnography as following deliberate lines of enquiry, applying systematic processes of data collection and engaging in rigorous and staged analytical procedures, with researchers always cautious and reflexive about their underlying assumptions. This is not to say that ethnography does not have its weaknesses. Erickson describes major types of evidentiary inadequacy from an interpretive perspective. These include the limitations and partialness of arguing from single events in fieldwork rather than from sustained participation and observation in the field and the danger of researchers leaping to conclusions inductively too early in the research. Nevertheless, rigorous ethnography must not depend on the analytical assistance of linguistics to make it more reliable or robust. It must rely on its own robust methods.

Indeed, where linguistics is used alongside ethnography, as in linguistic ethnography, it demands a view of language beyond the level of the code. In an article entitled 'The limits of awareness' Silverstein (1981) presents a theoretical and methodological argument against a linguistics which analyses language too narrowly at the linguistic, syntactic and referential. An alternative suggested by Silverstein is the anthropologist's model and its programme of understanding 'the properties of ideologies ... that seem to guide participants in social systems' (1981: 21), Silverstein is clear that we cannot rely on the linguist's limited interpretation of cultural action without the ethnographer's insight of language in context.

We can see from this discussion that the bringing together of linguistics and ethnography throws up questions of paradigm and methodology. Many of these issues have already been addressed in Chapter 1 (and see too the *Journal of Sociolinguistics* Special Issue on Linguistic Ethnography (Tusting and Maybin, 2007) in which researchers from different research traditions unpack some of the epistemological and ontological problems with 'marrying' (Wetherall, 2007) linguistics and ethnography). Here we would agree with Blommaert and Jie (2010), drawing on Hymes (1964), that language is central to ethnography and that it is ethnography's job to uncover how language is used as a resource and whose interests it serves. Furthermore, language is never context-less (see Chapter 2); indeed, it is 'deeply and inextricably' (Blommaert and Jie, 2010: 7) situated in social life, and both creates and reflects social life and social relations. One of the most important elements for us in linguistic ethnography is that it makes the relationship between language and ethnography explicit and emphatic and in doing so requires the researcher to pay attention to showing how language is used by people to 'perform as social beings' (Blommaert and Jie, 2010: 7). In other words, the warrant for linguistic ethnography exists in ethnography itself, and calling our work linguistic ethnography champions this theoretical position.

ETHICS

You will have become aware whilst reading that linguistic ethnographic research often takes place at research sites with 'vulnerable' people, such as children (research in schools) and offenders (research in delivering rights in custody), in sites where there is a clear power asymmetry between the research participants (research in teacher education), and in sites where confidentiality and anonymity are vital (research on think tanks). Researchers working in linguistic ethnography more widely also engage participants who are patients, elderly, disabled, and who belong to marginalised groups such as refugees. However, it is also true that researchers in linguistic ethnography have become increasingly interested in researching elites, such as surgeons in theatre (see Bezemer, in press) and health policy think tanks (see Chapter 6, this volume). Each research project brings its own ethical challenges. In this section, our aim is to draw on the case study chapters to highlight important ethical issues and explore potential responses. We do not offer simple solutions however (see, too, Agar, 2008). Ethical issues in the end must be resolved locally, drawing on contextual realities and mutual understandings. In the following we distinguish three aspects of conducting ethical research. We start with a brief discussion of central tenets of ethics. We then move on to institutional requirements with regard to ethics. Finally we examine ethical research in a range of different national and cultural settings.

What is ethics?

Ethics has been a subject of academic discussion since Aristotle. As well as remaining a central concern for philosophers (for example, Habermas, 1995, 2003), it is also a subject of great interest to sociologists (for example, Giddens, 1991;

Bauman, 1993) and political and organisational scientists (for example, Scherer and Palazzo, 2008; Scherer et al., 2009). Ethics remains a concern too for the medical profession (Beauchamp and Childness, 2001; Gillon, 2003) and indeed for education (Eisenhart and Howe, 1997; Kubanyiova, 2008). It is beyond the scope of this book to provide a full and comprehensive account of ethics. Instead, what we offer in this section is an overview of how ethics is understood in academic research, with reference to the four case studies.

Many articles and books in social science research give advice about doing research that is ethical. However, definitions of 'ethics' are less prolific; indeed 'what is ethics?' is a question that has taxed philosophers for many years (see, for example, Williams, 2006). At its simplest, research ethics, in our view, is about what is right and wrong in the research process, contingent on the context. This may appear a fairly clear-cut definition but in reality, deciding what is right and wrong can be difficult and is a matter of judgement rather than of following a formula. Ethics is full of grey areas. Furthermore, what seems right in one context can seem wrong in another, either because of the researchers' beliefs, the cultural norms of the research site or changes in knowledge about how research can affect people, as we will show.

In academia in general and the social sciences in particular, principles of ethical research have been drawn from medical sciences and experimental research, and although it has been argued that these principles do not 'fit' ethnographic endeavour (Agar, 2008) they inform the work of most ethics committees and the questions on ethics approval forms. These principles are: respect for *autonomy*, the participant has the right to refuse to take part; *beneficence*, the researcher should ensure the research is in the interest of the participants; *non-maleficence*, the researcher should do no harm; and *justice*, the researcher should ensure that everyone is treated fairly and equally (Murphy and Dingwall, 2001).

So what does this mean in practice? In terms of autonomy, there are two elements: informed consent and the right to withdraw. Informed consent requires that the researcher explains in full to participants the purpose of the research and the participants' role in it. Participants can then choose to take part or not, according to personal preference. Often, participants will be asked to sign a consent form which outlines these parameters, which can be consulted in case of confusion or dispute. If children are involved in the research, then the parents must provide consent (although in some cases this might also be given by a head teacher acting in *loco parentis* – see section on researching interculturally below). In Frances's case study, she explains how she changed the point at which informed consent was elicited from her participants. As you may recall, the participants were in police custody after being arrested and cautioned and Frances wanted to interview them about their rights in custody. Originally, it was suggested that Frances talk to the participants after they had been cautioned and before a decision was delivered about what was to happen next. For the police, the wait represented dead time and those cautioned had nothing to do. Frances decided that although the timing was good, there were ethical problems with interviewing participants while they waited. Most importantly, she felt those arrested might feel obliged to take part in the study in the belief that their cases would be positively evaluated if they did so. Because of this concern, Frances instead opted to ask participants to be interviewed on leaving police custody. This resulted in less uptake but a more defensible position ethically. It could also be argued that the data were more robust because participants had to opt in fully to the research process.

Informed consent also introduces the issue of quantity and quality of information. How much information should informants be given? Researchers are often concerned that if the focus of research is revealed, the participants might act in a different way, perhaps exaggerating the feature in which the researcher is interested. Research would be better carried out covertly than overtly, they argue (see Murphy and Dingwall, 2001, for an in-depth discussion of covert research). There is also the problem of research focus. In some cases the initial focus of research, and the focus for which ethical approval is sought, changes as the project develops, thereby invalidating to some extent the original informed consent (de Laine, 2000; see Gobo, 2008). Another problem is complexity in terms of research design or theoretical underpinnings. Can we expect participants to understand and be interested in these aspects? Murphy and Dingwall (2001: 342), citing Brewster Smith (1979: 14) comment that, 'without sending informants ... to grad school' it is not always easy to give a detailed explanation of the research objective.

In Figure 7.1 we give an example of a consent letter for a small interview-based research study on the problems children and teachers have when transitioning from primary to secondary school. In terms of autonomy, there was little in the study that could be considered problematic. Nevertheless, the letter aims to give as much detail about the study as possible while remaining easy to access.

In some studies where other languages are involved, consent letters will need to be translated, as was the case in Angela's research where the bilingual nature of the investigation meant that consent letters were provided in two languages. In addition to consent letters, research projects may send out a range of correspondences to key participants. In Angela's complementary school research projects, bilingual information letters were sent out in Phase 1 to all children, administrators and teachers attending the schools with information about the project, its start and end dates, the project aims, the nature of data and how it was to be collected, analysed and used. An important piece of information included was the name of the principal investigator with contact information for further information (see too the consent letter below). In Phase 2 consent letters were sent to different participants and adapted according to the different roles participants would play in the research. Because young people were involved, recordings could not happen without the consent of their parents. Moreover, the parents needed to consent to their own and other family members' involvement in the research as recordings also happened at home as well as in the classroom.

Dear Teacher

Thank you for agreeing to take part in this interview.

We are currently working on a project with the British Council on transition from primary school to secondary school.

The overall purpose of this project is to explore how young learners of English around the world are currently assisted to make the transition from the last year of primary to the first year of secondary schooling. The main aims of the project are to:

- Discover how policy/syllabus documents in various countries aim to inform this transition
- Investigate and map the major transition strategies that school and teachers use
- Better understand transition teachers' perceptions of their roles and responsibilities, including the challenges they face
- Identify what local solutions are used
- Make recommendations for principled guidelines for transition and teacher training.

We are particularly interested in how the change affects students in learning English.

We would like to know your opinions on this subject, which will then form part of the research.

Please read the following and tick the statements you agree with:

( ) I agree that the interview can be recorded.

( ) I agree that what I say can be used in the research project.

( ) I agree that what I say can be used in academic publications.

( ) I understand that I can withdraw from the research at any time by contacting a project team member (details given below).

( ) I understand that my name will not be used and my identity will be confidential.

If you have any questions about the interview or the project, please contact the project leader, Dr XXXXX

Best wishes

Dr XXXXXXXXXXXXXXX

Email: XXXXXXXXXXXXX

Figure 7.1 Example of a letter of consent

In addition to information about the project, the letter above also informs the participant of their right to withdraw, the second facet of the first principle of autonomy. As well as formally informing participants of these rights in documents such as these, researchers should also take any opportunity that arises in the research to check with participants that they are still happy to continue. Kubanyiova (2008) describes how a participant in her research who wanted to pull out was given opportunities but did not do so because she felt an obligation to both the researcher and the research. In the end, Kubanyiova had to find a way to exclude the participant so that her wish to withdraw was honoured. In many cases, it is the fear of disappointing rather than a fear of being exposed that prevents participants from making their wishes about withdrawing known. *Autonomy* requires participants to be given the opportunity, indeed multiple opportunities, to withdraw from the research process without fear of discomfort or reprisal. However, in the field it is sometimes difficult to ensure that participants feel able to step back.

A response to issues of informed consent and right to withdraw can be found in post-modern and feminist approaches to ethnography. Gobo (2008) explains that in this perspective, researchers and participants 'jointly define certain aspects of the research design, discuss the findings, and sometimes write the report together' (p. 137), thus eliminating any covert or complex research focus and ensuring that changes in focus are jointly negotiated. This might not be possible in many projects. However, we can apply the ethos of this approach: involve participants if you can; give as much information as you can; and speak to participants throughout the research process about emerging findings, their right to withdraw, changes in focus and ethical issues that you face.

Beneficence, the second principle, can also be difficult to achieve. In truth, there are multiple benefactors of the research process but the researcher generally is top of the list. The researcher might be carrying out the research to get a qualification, to win research money, to write publications, or a combination of these. And it may also be true that the researcher is carrying out the research in order that the participants, or others in a similar position, could benefit from the results. For example, Frances describes in her case study how her work on the written rights notice used in police custody eventually led to her having input into writing a new version, one that is clearer and more accessible to detainees. However, this was an outcome of the research process rather than an intended impact from it (see below) and originally beneficence of this nature was not part of the research design. With funding bodies putting increasing emphasis on impact, it is likely that beneficence will become an even more important feature of research plans in years to come.

Non-maleficence, do no harm, appears at first straightforward. Most research in linguistic ethnography is non-invasive and aims to provide an emic perspective. Nevertheless, in reality non-maleficence is perhaps the most difficult principle as research findings can present participants and institutions in a negative light and potentially cause psychological harm. For example, what does the researcher do with data which simultaneously provide telling examples, for example, of linguistic use or forms, at the same time as showing the language users displaying prejudices or intolerance? Of course, ensuring anonymity of participants and institutions through pseudonyms and other devices such as disguising features on visual images might address the concern to some extent (although, as Walford (2005) persuasively argues, complete anonymity is often not possible in studies of this kind). The researcher may also argue that the academic audience is unlikely to come into contact with the participants and so participants will not be affected. In the end the researcher must weigh up potential 'harm' against the value of the research and its potential for improving the lives of others not immediately involved in the research (see Murphy and Dingwall, 2001) in making a decision. Scheper-Hughes (2000) provides an insightful discussion of such a dilemma in an article which revisits an ethnographic study she conducted in Ireland 25 years previously. In the course of the paper she asks questions about audience and anonymity, amongst other things, which all who worry about non-maleficence must answer:

> What are the proper relationships between an anthropologist and her subjects? To whom does she owe her loyalties and how can these be met in the course of ethnographic field work and writing . . . ? (p. 127)

We will return to this issue below.

Finally we come to the principle of *justice*, that is, that everyone is treated fairly and equally. In linguistic ethnographic research this will mean that particular positions, particularly those of the powerful, are not privileged above others, particularly those of the weak or disenfranchised. However, as Murphy and Dingwall (2001) reason, this does not mean the suspension of moral judgement; rather it demands that 'the researcher remains committed to developing an analysis which displays an equally sophisticated understanding of the behaviour of both villains and heroes – or heroines' (Dingwall, 1992: 346). Although Sara's case study does not feature villains and heroes in this sense, she is clearly committed to understanding and representing her think-tank informants in a fair and even-handed manner, ensuring their positions are both accessible and substantiated (see, too, Shaw and Russell, in press).

A further complicating issue when considering ethics, and beneficence and justice in particular, is the process of working in teams. This is particularly relevant in Angela's case study. First, the principles described above are multiplied many times as teams of researchers negotiate their ethical stance with participants. Consistency and stability are important matters here and need to be managed across the full research team. Second, there are different power relations in teams, including contractual arrangements, role, pay and prior experience. The rights of researchers in large teams therefore also require ethical attention. The development opportunities presented to early-career and doctoral researchers, the new skills they might learn, prospects to represent themselves in a variety of ways, all become salient ethical issues. The management of large teams of researchers requires attention to the ethical process both internally within the team and externally with the participants in the research.

Having briefly outlined the principles of ethical research in linguistic ethnography, we turn now to another important aspect of this area: institutional requirements.

Institutional requirements

Research on humans requires ethical approval from the institution which sanctions the research. Researchers are generally required to complete an ethics approval form, such as the one shown in Figure 7.2, which will ask them to outline the research design, describe participants, identify ethical issues and explain how these issues will be addressed. Depending on the institution, this form will be presented to a supervisor, an ethics officer, or to an ethics committee for approval. Researchers may also be required to present participant consent forms and research tools such as questionnaires or interview questions. Ethical approval must be gained *before* research begins.

Ethical procedures differ from institution to institution. For example at the University of Birmingham, doctoral researchers prepare the information for the forms but faculty have to complete the ethics form on their behalf. Furthermore, staff are held responsible for ethical compliance. At Aston University, on the other hand, the student completes the form. An example of the form completed at Aston by both undergraduate and postgraduate students is given in Figure 7.2.

Student Research Ethics

Approval Form (REC1)

PLEASE NOTE: You MUST gain approval for any research BEFORE any research takes place. Failure to do so could result in a ZERO mark

---

Name:

Student Number:

Module Name:

Module Number:

Please type your answers to the following questions:

1. What are the aim(s) of your research?

2. What research methods to you intend to use?

3. Please give details of the type of informant, the method of access and sampling, and the location(s) of your fieldwork (see guidance notes).

4. Please give full details of all ethical issues which arise from this research.

5. What steps are you taking to address these ethical issues?

6. What issues for the personal safety of the researcher(s) arise from this research?

7. What steps will be taken to minimise the risks of personal safety to the researcher?

Statement by student investigator(s):

I/We consider that the details given constitute a true summary of the project proposed.

I/We have read, understood and will act in line with the LSS Student Research Ethics and Fieldwork Safety Guidance.

Name	Signature	Date

Statement by module convenor or project supervisor

I have read the above project proposal and believe that this project only involves minimum risk. I also believe that the student(s) understand the ethical and safety issues which arise from this project.

Name	Signature	Date

This form must be signed and both staff and students need to keep copies.

Figure 7.2 Example of student ethics approval form

Although institutional ethical requirements seem straightforward, in practice they are rarely so. Often those responsible for granting ethical approval identify ethical issues which have been missed by the researcher when preparing the form. They may ask for changes, which can delay the research process. In the worst cases, ethical approval is withheld and the research cannot take place. If your research is particularly sensitive, it is worthwhile discussing ethical issues with those responsible at the institution before doing any work at all, for example, at the proposal stage.

In many cases, ethics committees will suggest approaches which can ensure participants are protected as much as possible. For example, one of Fiona's PhD students, Jack (pseudonym), wanted to research students he was teaching. Jack was aware that his relationship with the students could mean that they felt obliged to take part in his project even if they did not wish to do so. In his ethics approval form, he said he would address this problem by informing students of the project in the Welcome Pack they receive when first joining the programme, and ask them to complete a consent form included in the pack. The Ethics Committee rejected this approach, suggesting that including information about the project in official university documentation would put pressure on the students to comply. In the end, a compromise was reached whereby Jack spoke to the students in one of their first classes about the project and then was replaced by a different teacher who collected the consent forms, whether students had signed them or not. In this way, distance was put between the institution and the research and students did not need to make it known if they had agreed or not to take part.

This example also illustrates another positive feature of institutional ethics requirements – support with planning the research project. The questions ethics committees pose in their forms and in the dialogues they have with researchers in the approval process can ensure that researchers carefully consider all aspects of the project, confronting areas which may have been forgotten in the initial enthusiasm for getting the project approved or funded.

Ethical clearance can be particularly problematic when doing linguistic ethnographic research as research designs which are open and responsive to the contingency of the context may not be acceptable to institutional ethics boards, which may demand specifics. For example, it is not always possible to say who the key participants will be until a period of detailed observation has taken place. This can mean that producing interview schedules or attaching consent and information letters prior to the research being conducted is difficult. Another issue is the level of expertise on ethical boards. Linguistic ethnography requires specialist knowledge about technology, privacy and surveillance because researchers are usually collecting interactional and discursive data from their key participants through the use of digital audio and video recordings. Issues of who controls these digital sound and video recordings, the safe storage of these digital data files and for how long, and who has access to them for analysis, are all specific ethical issues for linguistic ethnographers working with interactional data of one form or another.

Because of the nature of linguistic ethnographic research, it is often difficult to predict not only who the participants will be or what methods will be adopted, but also what ethical issues will arise as the project progresses. As we have suggested in previous sections, ethics is not just about setting up the project and getting all the necessary permissions, it permeates the whole process and should be a continual concern. It is perfectly acceptable to approach approval boards as data are collected and analysed if you have ethical concerns. Indeed, attending to microethical dimensions (see the discussion in Fiona's case study) should be a guiding principle in research, wherever it is situated.

Many people working in linguistic ethnography work across cultures and in different countries. This reality can create different ethical dilemmas, as we discuss below.

Intercultural ethics

As argued above, current approaches to ethical research in the social sciences have been influenced by medical research. When applied in Western contexts, they can be helpful as well as challenging and tend to be understood as necessary by research participants. However, this is not always the case. In our experience, macroethical processes in particular can cause distrust and confusion when presented to participants in other countries or in different communities. In this section, we will describe ethical conundrums that have recently been presented to us and how they were resolved.

One ethical issue that repeatedly arises is gaining consent from parents when working with children. Many macroethical processes require this consent, but we are often told that gaining such consent would be inappropriate for a number of reasons. One is that parents consider that at school the teachers adopt the role of parent and therefore know what is in the best interests of the children. Another is that the literacy skills of parents might not always be sufficient to read through and sign consent forms. Yet another is that gaining parental consent exaggerates the importance of the research or suggests that there is going to be some kind of difficult or painful intervention. That the parents would suspect their children to be subject to painful intervention if asked for signed consent for observation and recording classes was the reason given by one head teacher for refusing a request for a linguistic ethnographic study in Japan. He explained that children's parents had to sign to give permission for medical interventions such as inoculation. Decisions about education were the concern of the head teacher and parents would not wish to be involved.

Another case we have come across involves signing. In some cultures, the act of signing is a significant act. It is associated in the main with important legal documents and makes a decision binding. A colleague faced this situation recently in East Africa. She had gone to a school to observe the teaching of primary English and had spent some time explaining to the school teacher (who also happened to be the head teacher) what the research was for and what she wanted to do (observe, interview, take some photographs). The teacher listened, asked questions, and agreed to take part. Then the colleague produced the consent form for the teacher to sign and the atmosphere changed. The teacher was reluctant for the reasons given above and spent the next hour eliciting advice from colleagues and others about whether she should sign. She eventually did but the colleague was left feeling that institutional requirements had been ineffective, indeed potentially damaging, in the field.

As cross-cultural research has kept pace with globalisation, there has been growing interest in the field of intercultural ethics. Habermas (1995), for example, suggests that intercultural ethics be addressed by applying a system of what he called 'discourse ethics'; simply put, an approach in which talk between parties forms the basis of ethical decisions. More recently, Schere and Palazzo (2008: 21) have argued that discourse ethics should be supplemented by a culturalist perspective, in which elements such as an openness towards unfamiliar views and an understanding of the mutual relativity of ethics are taken into consideration. Evanoff (2004) also suggests that dialogicism forms the basis of intercultural ethics. He argues for a constructivist ethics in which each ethical issue is resolved locally by critiquing existing standards and arriving at jointly agreed new ethical norms. In these approaches, the macroethical principles of the researcher's institution are not allowed to dominate. Instead, the role of the institution's ethics committees is to ensure that all parties are satisfied that ethics has been given due consideration.

There is no doubt that once in the field, or when working with researchers from different research backgrounds, that time should be made to discuss and develop a situated ethical approach. Researchers should also think about how they can present such an approach in their written applications for ethical approval. Agar (2008) has some interesting ideas about how to do this. His solution is to be honest in the macroethical process. He argues, 'the best you can do is say that when you sit down to do an interview with someone 'officially' you will get written or oral tape-recorded informed consent' (p. 233). This reduces the requirement to ensure formal consent is given from the beginning of the research process and allows the researcher to devote time to explaining to participants his/her role and interests, a strategy that 'fits the general flow of ethnography, and one that has always been used anyway' (p. 232). Linguistic ethnographers who record institutional or private interactions might need to think whether on-the-spot ethical approval will be sufficient for this kind of field work. A further discussion about the ethics of recording can be found under the section on technology in Chapter 9. For a more detailed discussion of the ethical issues we discussed in this section, see Copland and Creese (forthcoming).

Finally in this chapter we examine the growing importance of impact. We first define it and then explain how evidence for impact can be gathered.

IMPACT

Impact is generally understood to mean a *change to* or an *effect on* an aspect of social life, such as the economy, culture, health, policy, professional practice, and so on, that has resulted from academic research. A change to or effect on academic thinking or practice, therefore, is not considered impact. Impact is tangible in that there is a clear link between research findings and the change/effect. Another way of talking about impact is legacy, and for many this is a preferable term as it is less about cause and effect in the short term and more about social engagement and change in the long term. As we explain above, a good example of this link can be seen in Frances's research, which focused on the wording of the notice of rights used in police stations and on how the caution is delivered to suspects. Her findings resulted in an invitation to contribute to rewriting this important document, which is now used by police officers throughout the UK as they work to ensure suspects understand their legal rights.

In recent years, the importance of impact has grown considerably. It is now commonplace for funding bodies to request an impact plan in applications for research funding. Angela remembers writing at least three kinds of impact statements in the same funding application. These included an impact summary, a pathways to impact document and a section in the case for support under the required heading, 'Outcomes, impact and dissemination'. Such documents describe the application of the research and how it can be exploited; how the research will engage with others and be appropriately communicated; the potential for collaboration and co-production of knowledge; and, the capacity for involving others and creating a legacy from the research. Other documents include an impact summary and consideration of academic beneficiaries.

In the current evaluation of research in British Universities (the 2014 REF), impact case studies, which clearly delineate the relationship between research and changes/effects on social life, are a requirement and worth 20 per cent of the overall grade awarded to a unit of assessment, which in turn determines how much money the government will award the department for its research activities. Authors of impact case studies must complete sections on research underpinning the impact, details of the impact, and sources to corroborate the impact, amongst other things. For many, considering impact in this way has required a step-change in their understanding of what and for whom research is conducted.

Of course, the obligation to demonstrate impact is not without its critics. Particularly in the arts, it might be difficult to show how, for example, a study of a nineteenth-century novelist would impact the social lives of anyone other than students (and the effect on students does not generally count as impact). Furthermore, it has been argued that rewarding impact will inevitably shape research, perhaps by encouraging researchers to focus on producing research that is relevant in the short term (Smith and Meer, 2012). Nevertheless, given ever tighter audit procedures and requirements for funding bodies and government to justify funding decisions, it is likely that impact will be a permanent feature of research, in the UK at least.

For many working in linguistic ethnography, a central principle is that research should be focused on real-world issues. Given this, developing impact plans is often naturally part of the research design, although it may not be conceptualised as impact. However, while developing impact plans is relatively straightforward: measuring impact is not. Fiona's research on teacher training talk illustrates this point. Fiona disseminated the findings of her research at a number of professional conferences attended by teacher trainers. The questions and comments about the research suggested that the findings had an effect on trainers' thinking. However, Fiona would never know if this was the case as she did not follow up to find out how the research affected trainers' practice. She could evidence *dissemination* but she could not evidence *impact*.

Fiona learnt from this experience, and with co-researchers in a recent project on teaching English to young learners put a number of tools in place to gather information about impact. These included evaluation questionnaires, and personal correspondence with potential users of the research, as well as ensuring particular documents were available from a website which counted Twitter, Facebook and email feeds. These tools have provided evidence of practitioner engagement, evidence that can be produced to demonstrate impact. For example, materials from the project have been used to train teachers in the UK and abroad, impact evidenced by emails from teacher educators and by the many hundreds of 'shares' on the website link to the materials.

Research can take some time to have impact and this can be problematic, particularly if there is a set time for research to take place. Generally a research project will take around 2–5 years, but impact derived from the research might not be seen until 10 years later, for example. Sara's research on think tanks is innovative in that think tanks are rarely investigated, particularly using a linguistic ethnographic approach. Her findings show the ways in which policy is produced in front-stage and back-stage regions, through processes which until now have not been made explicit. Given the current focus on transparency in politics, back-stage talk is of particular interest and Sara's work could be influential in this regard. However, in order for her work to have impact (perhaps through monitoring back-stage talk) Sara will have to ensure that her findings are disseminated to those who do policy work in think tanks, for example, board members and politicians. Then, she will need to monitor changes to back-stage talk and demonstrate a link between her findings and the changes made, perhaps through interviewing think-tank members. All this takes time and effort, both of which might not be available after the official end date of a research project.

CONCLUDING COMMENTS

This chapter has engaged with current issues in research and examined them from a linguistic ethnographic perspective. We have suggested concepts and approaches that can support researchers in dealing with similar issues when they arise. We believe that considering empiricism, ethics and impact in the planning stages of research is invaluable but that how we continue to respond to these areas as the research progresses is equally important for the success of a project.

KEY READINGS

Blommaert, J. and Jie, D. (2010) *Ethnographic Fieldwork: A Beginner's Guide*. Bristol: Multilingual Matters.

Eisenhart, M. and Howe, K. (1992) 'Validity in educational research', in M. Le Compte, W. Millroy and J. Preissle (eds) *The Handbook of Qualitative Research in Education* (pp. 642–80). San Diego: Academic Press. Copyright.

Guta, A., Nixon, S. and Wilson, M.G. (2013) 'Resisting the seduction of "ethics creep": using Foucault to surface complexity and contradiction in research ethics review', *Social Science & Medicine*, 98: 301–10.

Murphy, E. and Dingwall, R. (2001) 'The ethics of ethnography', in P. Atkinson, A. Coffey, S. Delamont, J. Lofland and L. Lofland (eds) *Handbook of Ethnography*. London: Sage. pp. 339–51.

EIGHT

Transcription, Translation and Technology

INTRODUCTION

Transcription, translation and technology can all prove daunting to researchers no matter what point they have reached in their careers: technology in particular moves on so quickly that often researchers can feel they have missed important developments while doing field work or when working on publications. This chapter will take both a practical and a theoretical look at each of these three areas with a view to providing readers with guidance on a range of issues that emerge when transcribing, translating or using technology. We will draw on the case studies to contextualise the discussion and to show how we have addressed transcription, translation and technology in our own research.

TRANSCRIPTION

All researchers taking a linguistic ethnographic approach will at some point, and probably quite frequently, have to represent talk through transcription. However, how to transcribe talk requires consideration, particularly in terms of transcription conventions and how much detail to include. These considerations are both interpretative and representational (Bucholtz, 2000) as transcription embeds 'indications of purpose, audience, and the position of the transcriber towards the text' (p. 1440). In other words, transcription, like other aspects of ethnographic work, requires the researcher to be reflective and reflexive so that decisions about transcription are consciously made and can be discussed and defended. Transcriptions (and translations, see below) should therefore be foregrounded.

Bucholtz urges researchers to think about themselves in relation to their transcripts as a way forward to making transcription and translation processes visible.

In this section, we will first consider the more technical aspects of transcription in terms of common conventions for representing talk. We then go on to describe levels of delicacy in transcription, demonstrating how the level of detail can be indicative of purpose, audience and the position of the transcriber, and can also be important for analytic claims. Finally, we will discuss the representation of idiolects and the ethical decisions which representing such talk entail.

A very useful updated resource is Mary Bucholtz and John W. Du Bois' website (http://www.linguistics.ucsb.edu/projects/transcription/representing) operating out of the Department of Linguistics, University of California, Santa Barbara. The site is entitled Transcription in Action and 'collects and disseminates information about the transcription of spoken interaction, including methods, theories, tools, and research'. It provides links to a number of resources for the transcription of discourse, including the transcription programs VoiceWalker and SoundWriter, offers guidelines for discourse transcription developed by Du Bois, and a bibliography of publications related to transcription. Another useful resource is EXMARaLDA (Extensible Markup Language for Discourse Annotation). It gives advice about how to transcribe speech and actions and can be accessed at: http://www.exmaralda.org/en_index.html.

Transcription conventions

A good deal of work on transcription conventions has been done by researchers working from a Conversation Analysis (CA) perspective. Very accurate and detailed transcriptions are clearly of particular importance in a discipline where context is only relevant if it is evoked by speakers in talk. Most CA analysts work with the transcription conventions developed by Jefferson, who, with Sacks and Schegloff, contributed so much to CA in its infancy. These conventions are printed in a number of books such as Wooffitt (2001: 62) and in online resources such as at Charles Antaki's homepages at: http://homepages.lboro.ac.uk/~ssca1/transintro1. htm. Researchers do not always require as detailed a transcription as applying these conventions will produce. Many use simpler ones, which they may devise themselves. Keith Richards (2003) has developed the conventions given in Figure 8.1, which have been used successfully by many.

Blommaert and Jie (2010: 72) argue that transcriptions are there to be *looked at* rather than *read*, as it is in this way that textual patterns in text, such as overlaps and long turns, can be seen. They draw on Hymes's ethnopoetics in presenting their transcriptions, a key feature of which is that 'performed oral narratives are organized in terms of lines, and groups of lines (not in terms of sentences and paragraphs)' (Blommaert and Jie, 2010: 73, drawing on Hymes). What is more, the performance features of the oral narrative need to be rendered (Blommaert, 2005: 88) to show

Basic conventions

.	Falling intonation	That was foolish.
,	Continuing contour	I took bread, butter, jam and honey
?	Questioning intonation	Who was that?
!	Exclamatory utterance	Look!
(2.0)	Pause of about 2 seconds	So (2.0) what are we going to do?
(...)	*Pause of about 1 second	In front of (...) the table
(..)	*Pause of about 0.5 second	Then (..) she just (..) left
(.)	micropause	Put it (.) away
[ ]	Overlap	A: He saw it ⌈to ⌉and stopped B: ⌊oh ⌋
[[	Speakers start at same time	⟦A: And the- ⟦B: So she left it behind.
=	Latched utterances	A: We saw her yesterday.= B: =And she looked fine.
___	Emphasis	Put it a<u>way</u>.
-	Cut off	All over the pl- the floor
:	Sound stretching	We waited for a lo:::ng time
(xxx)	Unable to transcribe	We'll just (xxxxxxxxxx) tomorrow
(send)	Unsure transcription	And then he (juggled) it
(( ))	Other details	Leave it alone ((moves book))

Figure 8.1 Richards' (2003) transcription conventions

the orientation of the speaker. This approach strongly influences how text is organised on the page, with new units of what is called *equivalence* (units of meaning) starting on new lines, or, where space is limited, separated by back slashes. You will find many researchers who take a linguistic ethnographic approach using equivalence in their transcriptions (see Extract 1).

Another technique used by researchers working within linguistic ethnography is to include contextual detail in transcripts to support the reader and to enhance the analysis. These contextual details, which are sometimes called 'stage directions' (Rampton, 2006: xviii), often appear in italics, within double brackets (sometimes followed by a colon), and can give information about the speed and level of the speech, intonation, stylisations (such as performing an accent), or the speaker's intention, amongst other things. In Extract 1, Rampton (2006: 157ff.) uses both equivalence (starting each new unit of meaning on a new line) and stage directions (such as ((claps once))) to bring the transcription to life. He also uses Courier font, which has a fixed character width, and so makes alignment of overlapping utterances easier. However, Courier is not as easy a font to read as some others and Bucholtz (2000) points out that as it is commonly used in scientific writing such as computer programs its adoption can provide a 'technical aura' (p. 1453), which may or may not be desired.

Extract 1: Example of transcript using equivalence and stage directions (Rampton, 2006: 157)

```
 1.  Mr N        ((claps once)) (.)
 2.               alright
 3.               (2.0) ((conversations continue in the background))
 4.  John         Sir
 5.               (.)
 6.               (because) first they were in love
 7.               and they wanted to be:
 8.               (.)
 9.  Masud        togevver
10.  John         to:ge:ther:
11.  Masud        cos if they stayed alive
12.               and they/(              )
13.  Mr N         the only way to be together/was in death
14.  Hanif        ((begins a very loud, fast, falsetto rendition
                  of the Bee Gees 'Staying Alive', carrying on
                  until mid-way through line 24))
```

If you are using video recordings, you will also need to find a way to include the visual data in your transcriptions. This can be done in various ways. Lapadat (2000) suggests that what she calls 'context' is written alongside the transcribed talk on the right hand side and 'real-time codes' on the left (p. 212). Deborah Swinglehurst (Swinglehurst et al., 2011; Swinglehurst, in press) follows a similar approach. As her research focus is the electronic patient record (EPR) in nurse/patient consultations, in addition to representing talk, her transcriptions include two columns on the right, one which provides a description of what she calls 'bodily conduct' and the other which shows what section of the EPR is on the screen – see Figure 8.2.

The strength of this approach to transcription is that bodily action is coordinated with talk and technology in clearly defined units, making it very easy to read. One possible problem with ordering the representation in this way is that

Time	D/P	Spoken word	Bodily conduct	EPR Screen
3.30	D	uh well yo:ur l:ow density cholesterol is is quite high um::(.) over seven so::	D-> EPR; P -> D D sits back in chair -> EPR	Consultation screen showing two entries dated 6 days ago: 1) (nurse): Blood sample taken. Biochemical screening test (fasting cholesterol). Text note: will make app in a week to see Dr X
3.36	D	((sniff))	D scratches nose, raises eyebrows	
		(0.8)		
3.37	D	<al:tho:ugh ju:st because> you've got high blood pressure you don't necessarily need anything to lower the cholesterol (.) .hh >even though you've got hypertension<	D->EPR D turns slightly - > P D returns gaze - > EPR	2) (path lab): displays blood test results incl. Cholesterol 10, Serum LDL cholesterol >7 see doc please. QOF alert (remains throughout consultation). Shows P is on "QOF register" for hypertension and has two QOF items outstanding: "notes summarised" and "recent medication review"
3.45	D	I think you'll probably be well advised to have something t- to lower it↑=	D frowns	
3.49	P	=°°yeah°° mean as a child I couldn't take (.) milk and I still don't like milk	P - > forwards; D -> EPR	
3.53	D	no↓		
		(1.0)		
3.54	P	ehm (.) I can take (0.4) >sort of< hot milk in custard (0.4) but someone gave me a glass of hot milk and I would really be ill.		
4.01	P	ha	P -> D; D - > EPR	
4.02	D	right (.) yeah		
4.03		so maybe there was an intolerance right from a baby ha	P smiles	
		(0.2)		
4.07	D	we ↑↓ll		
4.08	P	who kno↑ws °°ha ha°°	P shakes head slightly, smiling	
4.09	D	°°ha°°	D smiles -> EPR and leans forward -> EPR, placing R hand on keys	
		((C)) (1)	Key stroke	Returns to today's consultation screen. "Problem Title" is automatically highlighted

Figure 8.2 Example of Swinglehurst's transcription

the visual information may appear to be less important than the spoken word as it is positioned to the right of the page and of course we begin reading from the left. Ordering, however, is at the researcher's discretion, and there is no reason why bodily action or EPR could not be placed before talk.

There is also the very real issue of representing action in word. Drawing on the work of many established researchers who use video recordings, Bezemer and Mavers (2011) discuss a number of possibilities for 'transducing' visual data to print form, from transcripts such as Swinglehurst's, to freeze frames. These include boxed inserts of spoken text and outline drawings of participants from photographs which disguise identity at the same time as showing gaze and body position. They argue that the choices researchers make in reproducing visuals are influenced by their epistemological and empirical leanings as well as by the focus of their analytic attention. For example, they show a transcript of a series of stills taken with a video camera from Norris (2004). The stills appear inclusive as they capture whatever is in the range of the camera, whether they are salient to the interaction or not. Bezemer and Mavers suggest that because the stills provide information about such things as skin colour, clothing, gesture and proximity, the transcript reader is able to make inferences about, 'identity, social relations, activity, mood, and so on' (Bezemer and Mavers, 2011: 200), without being guided by the researcher.

Whether transcribing talk only or talk and visual data, it is impossible to produce a transcript that is perfect (see Lapadat, 2000, for a discussion of why this is so). Nevertheless, transcriptions need to be fit for purpose. By this we mean that transcriptions should provide the level of detail required for the job they have to do. If you are producing a transcript in order to do a content or corpus analysis, then it should be enough to get down the words that the speakers use. If you want to create a transcription to share with a lay audience or one which is not used to reading transcripts, then it may be best to create a 'clean' transcript, taking out pauses, hesitations, repetitions and so on and inserting appropriate punctuation to make it readable (although as Wooffitt (2000: 36) points out, 'an easily read transcript which uses standard writing conventions' can suggest that what is being presented is a truthful account and a claim for the veracity of the presented interpretation). Hammersley (2010: 556) provides a useful list of the decisions involved in creating transcriptions in a discussion which also asks us to consider the extent to which transcriptions are constructions or reproductions of talk. Whichever we select, it is important to remember that a transcript is never final and that it can only ever be a best effort.

Most of us will want to show how interaction is developed between speakers, and for this we will need a greater level of what is often called 'delicacy'.

The following extracts from Fiona's data, show two transcripts of the same piece of raw data. The first is the rough transcription she produced in order to carry out the genre analysis of feedback conferences. The transcript shows no pauses, repetitions, interruptions or prosodic features such as stress or pitch.

Extract 2

1. Trainer: but let's think about your overall aims for the lesson cos I mean I
2. know however people sort of hear the word aims and shudder but I mean
3. that's the starting point it's what I want my learners to achieve what I
4. want them to get better at what I want them to take away from the lesson
5. so what were you hoping that your learners would get better at?
6. Trainee: Just like I was hoping that they would sort of be able to get
7. together and plan a role play together and use
8. Trainer: Is being able to sorry to interrupt is being able to plan a role play an
9. appropriate aim for a language lesson?
10. Trainee: mmm no

However, through the analytic process described in the case study, the extract became pertinent as it showed how the trainer used her powerful position to present a view of legitimate knowledge around aims in language teaching. In order to show how this was achieved not only in the content of what the trainer said but also in how the talk unfolded, a more delicate transcription was needed. Pauses, back channels, interruptions and prosodic features were all added to allow a fuller and more nuanced analysis to be carried out:

Extract 3

1. Trainer: but let's think about your overall ai:ms for the lesson cos I mean I
2. know however people sort of hear the =
3. Trainee: = mhm =
4. Trainer: = word aims and shudder but I mean that's the starting point it's
5. what I want my learners to achieve what I want them to get better
6. at what I want them to take away from the lesson so what were
7. you hoping that your learners would get better at?
8. Trainee: Just like I was hoping that they would sort of be able to get
9. together and plan a role play together () and use ((inaudible))
10. [
11. Trainer: is being able to pl ((quickly)) sorry to
12. interrupt is being able to plan a ((slowly)) ro:le play () an
13. appropriate aim for a language lesson?
14. Trainee: (..) mmm (....) no

A full analysis of this section is available in Copland (2012). Here, though, we would like to discuss a few features that are particularly relevant. First, there is an interruption at line 10, with the trainer successfully taking the floor. It is important to show this in the transcription as it relevant to the negotiation of power at this point between the interlocutors. As Greatbatch (1992) suggests, interruptions allow participants to show the strength of feeling regarding the issue at hand. Had the trainer waited till the end of the trainee's turn, these feelings would have had less force. Furthermore, the trainer is allowed to interrupt the trainee. The very act demonstrates who the powerful interlocutor is in this discussion.

Second, there are two stage directions – 'quickly' and 'slowly'. The first accompanies the apology made by the trainer to the trainee for the interruption. The fact that she makes the apology quickly suggests that she places little value on it; it is an apology in name only, not intention. The stage direction 'slowly' accompanies 'role play'. This prosodic choice means the phrase is emphasised (the elongated [o] phoneme reinforces this emphasis), bringing the trainee's attention to it and contrasting the trainer's views (that doing a role play is not an appropriate aim for a language lesson, lines 12 and 13) with the trainee's (that planning a role play was an appropriate aim, line 9).

A further addition is the pauses. In line 14, the trainee pauses twice for long periods. The first pause is in response to the trainer's question. Pomerantz (1984) points out that preferred seconds, that is, responses that provide the response that the first part of the adjacency pair seems to require, are typically not marked, that is, there is no pause. The trainee's second, however, is marked with pauses and hesitations, casting doubt on its veracity. Although the trainee says, 'no', she might not mean it. If the pauses were not marked, this interpretation might not be as plausible.

Bezemer and Mavers (2011), suggest that all transcripts are 'artefacts', created for particular audiences and focusing on the concerns of the researcher. The comparison presented here illustrates this reality. The decisions Fiona made when producing both transcriptions reveal her ideological and theoretical assumptions. For example, she decided to show the interruptions in the talk in the second transcript because she was interested in how trainers exert power in feedback conferences and she believes the interruptions demonstrate this. Theoretically, she used an easily readable font so that the transcripts were accessible to professionals as well as academics. She also decided against using equivalence as she felt this created a further level of interpretation. However, she did include stage directions. Other ideological and theoretical decisions may be less apparent; choices are not always made consciously but are down to our 'scholarly disposition[s]' (Bucholtz, 2000: 1446, drawing on Wald, 1995). Sharing transcriptions with others (and with the research participants) might be a way of uncovering these unconscious choices.

Another transcription issue concerns how different idiolects are represented. For example, if a participant uses a dialect or has a speech style, to what extent should this be represented in the transcription? On the one hand, in attempting to reproduce the idiolect faithfully, we may inadvertently produce a cartoon-like text or one that seems to suggest that the speaker is using a substandard English (or whatever language). On the other, representing dialect in standard forms can diminish the speaker's linguistic repertoire and style and fundamentally misrepresent him/her. Rampton (2006) seems to choose a middle way. For example, he consistently represents the phrase 'don't know' as 'dunno' (a nonstandard spelling) in his transcriptions, and often represents a missing phoneme at the end of a word with ' (for example, e.g. 'tellin' me, askin' me'). Rampton's aim, which is shared by many other researchers, seems to be to give a flavour of the local use of English in order to relate the talk to its context. As Rampton shows, decisions such as these need to be articulated otherwise readers may well surmise that 'flavor and color in transcripts are artificial additives' (Bucholtz, 2000: 1457).

For many, transcriptions will require researchers to transcribe more than one language and then to translate other languages (usually) into English. It is to the area of translation then that we now turn.

TRANSLATION

Translation is a common activity in linguistic ethnography and is a regular practice when researching communication in contexts of mobility, diversity and change. Translation is relevant where researchers have an interest in, for example, bilingual and multilingual contexts, multilingual literacies, shifting identities, heritage, youth language, social media and online languages and literacies in the digital age. The contemporary era has seen extensive and far-reaching movements, not only of people, but also of ideas and objects. As these ideas, objects and people move from one context to another they undergo translation and transformation. According to Cronin (2013), we have arrived at the 'translation age' (Cronin, 2013) where ideas, objects and signs meet in social spaces, which is the 'contact zone' (Pratt, 1991).

In its broadest sense, translation can be viewed as a richly formative process offering insights into the process of communication and miscommunication. From a narrower and more technical perspective it is often associated with the mechanics of rendering one language or code into another. Scholars in translation studies point to the dangers of the narrow view. Temple (2008: 361) argues that, 'It is neither epistemologically, methodologically nor ethically sound to assume that interpretation and translation can be treated as mere technical exercises'. This is because surrounding any translation or interpretation activity are factors shaping the transformation of meaning. Wolf (2011: 3) argues for making these 'outdoor' factors more apparent. She argues, 'there is always a context in which the translation takes place, always a history from which a text emerges and into which a text is transposed' (p. 3). According to Wolf, widening the contextual environment in translation practice requires considering the power relations underlying any translation activity; viewing translators as social agents; and conceptualising translation as a process in which various persons and institutions participate. Wolf points out 'Translation not only reflects and transfers existing knowledge, but continuously creates new knowledge, thus revealing its often neglected political and ideological dimension' (2011: 20). There is much in common here with the way the ethnography is portrayed in this book. Wolf's definition of translation is in keeping with our earlier discussion of the Peircean sign in Chapter 1. A sign is always 'in translation' because new meanings are always being made.

To illustrate these quandaries we present below two different examples of translated texts from authors adopting a variety of analytical perspectives. Overall, we argue that retaining an open ethnographic stance is the most appropriate response to conceptualising and doing translation. First, though, we address three important distinctions and dilemmas in translation theory.

Distinctions and dilemmas

Before we move to the two examples, it is important to acknowledge three other core distinctions and dilemmas in translation studies. The first is the difference between translation and interpretation. According to Shäffner (2004), translation and interpretation differ in terms of time and text. With translation, texts are available for the translator to work with over a period of time. This means that errors can be rectified, translations compared and changed and that original documents can be viewed by others with a view to checking the translation for accuracy. Interpretation, on the other hand, is done in real time and it is not always possible for the interpreter to have a copy of what the speaker is going to say before he/she speaks. While these are real concerns and pose a number of challenges particular to the translator and interpreter, for the purposes of this chapter, we will not differentiate between translating and interpreting.

The second is the overlap between translation and transcription. In a sense rendering a spoken text into a written text is both an act of translation and transcription because both involve adaption and interpretation. However, this is not the typical distinction made between translation and transcription. Whereas translation is usually understood as a change from one language to another in order to access an unfamiliar code and replace it with a familiar code, transcription is about the convention of representing one modality in the form of another (e.g. spoken to written). When working multilingually both processes happen simultaneously, often involving a third stage, transliteration. Transliteration is the conversion of a text from one script to another based on phonetic similarity.

Script choice can be both a political and highly charged process as well as a local and idiosyncratic one (Rosowsky, 2010). Bender (2008) argues that attention to processes of script choice and transliteration can shed slight on the social contexts and ideologies underpinning them. A script is associated with language ideology and social categories and contributes to which voices are heard. Bender shows how an analysis of script choice can reveal past and ongoing tensions and dialogues about wider social contexts.

The third dilemma concerns representation. Bucholtz (2007) identifies the significant challenge in the 'unhappy choice between a colloquial translation style, which may imply that the speakers are 'just like us', despite significant cultural and other differences, and a formal translation style, which may position the speakers as 'not like us at all', but rather as foreign, stiff, and old-fashioned.' (p. 801). How we put participants' voices on the page, therefore, has 'significant analytical and political consequences' (p. 786). However, it is futile to seek eradication of variation from transcription practice. Rather, it is necessary to understand the motivations and effects of variation because they are an inevitable part of the translation and transcription process, which Bucholtz points out is true of linguistic representation more generally.

Below we provide one example of presenting multilingual texts and summarise some of the interpretation and representation issues which they evoke.

A multilingual ethnographic approach

Blackledge and Creese start their 2010 book with a 'Note on transcription'. This states, 'In keeping with the theoretical approach to linguistic practice which emerged from this work, we make no distinction between different "languages" in the transcribed data. We use romanised transliteration for all languages other than Cantonese and Mandarin, where we retain Chinese orthography'. Although the authors summarise their approach and highlight the importance of translation and transcription issues at the beginning of the book, the lengthy debates they had as a research team about these issues are not expanded elsewhere in the manuscript. However, Angela remembers the transcripts going through many different presentation formats before the team settled on a simplified presentation style which the team felt was not only most accessible but reflected the theoretical arguments being made about translanguaging and heteroglossia (see Creese and Blackledge (2010) and Blackledge and Creese (2014) for full discussion). Below Angela provides an account of these debates she remembers about translation, transcription and transliteration in the research team.

The representation debate: orthographies and standard varieties

The first issue was to address different participant perspectives and consider these as representation issues. For example, while on the one hand teachers, young people and researchers practised flexible and dynamic bilingualism, on the other hand they argued for languages to be kept separate. Typically, in the community-run schools that we researched, the standard and prestige variety of the national language was taught and accorded status (Creese and Blackledge, 2011). We reached the decision to publish our research reports in standard English as well as in Bengali, Cantonese, Gujarati, Mandarin, Panjabi and Turkish using national alphabets and standard orthographies. This was a lengthy and time-consuming exercise not made easier by using publication processes that were used to working in English only. However, we considered the symbolic and political rationale for the translations of our work to be more important than the practical difficulties.

The second decision we faced regarding translation was about font and position of the bilingual text within the transcript. This sounds rather trivial but in fact came to represent a major theoretical shift for the team. It is common for multilingual data to distinguish between languages using italics, underlining and bold, as in the following example from Martin et al. (2006: 11).

Extract 4

T: OK everybody concentrate on the next line. .. **shu laikhu chhe**? ‹ *what is written?* ›
S: **malam. malam** ‹ *ointment* ›
T: what does it mean **malam ghus**? ‹ *rub ointment* ›
S: ointment. rub ointment
T: copy that on your handwriting sheet. that's fine. copy in your book

If a third language were involved in the interaction above, it would likely be underscored.

We consciously decided not to present the multilingual data in this way which placed us outside usual conventions. We wanted to avoid the potential risk of 'marking' languages as more or less important through the use of 'normal', bold and underlined font. Even more important to us was avoiding an emphasis on the switch of languages. To highlight the code meant focusing on the language rather than the speaker. Our interest was in speaker agency within the constraints of the social context and so we focused on the different signs they made use of in interaction. We argued this reflected the flexible bilingualism typical of participants' daily lives. In other words our transcription and translation conventions were tied very closely to our theoretically driven work on translanguaging (Creese and Blackledge, 2010). An example of a transcript made from an audio recording of the Gujarati classroom is provided below in which the teacher, PB is asking students to discuss their daily routines.

Extract 5

PB: bolwanu
      ‹*speak*›
Ss: shu bolwanu?
      ‹*speak what?*›
PB: je discuss karyu hoi
      ‹*what you discussed*›
Ss: oh... [chat]...etle we discuss it and then decide what we gonna say...miss ame
      ek bijanu kaie ke ek ek...
      ‹*so we discuss it....miss, do we speak about each other or one by one...*›

As Auer (1998) reminds us, what counts as code is not easily answerable, for it must refer to participants' not to linguists' notion of code. In the extract above, the use of linguistic signs from a variety of sources represents the normative way of speaking for these young people and teachers. Our perspective on the social practices we were observing and recording suggested that participants were deploying their languages resourcefully, drawing on their communicative repertoire rather than on one language and then another. This observation required us to find a different way to represent talk, avoiding the well-established code-switching or languages-in-alternation approach to presenting data. Having said this, there are still times when we do choose to use these conventions especially when they assist in clarification and argumentation.

As a team we also discussed at length issues of transliteration. The research team reached the decision to represent the spoken interactions of Gujarati and Panjabi in the roman alphabet (as in Extract 5). We wanted to make the reading of transcripts easy for wider audiences. It also represented the practices of pedagogy in these classrooms as teachers often used the roman alphabet to represent sounds in Gujarati and Panjabi. However, we reached an entirely different transliteration decision for the Chinese case study. Here we decided to maintain the contrast between Traditional and Simplified Chinese scripts because they indexed important political, social and cultural differences in the Cantonese and Mandarin speaking schools which would have been lost if the English alphabet was used. An example from an interview is provided below:

Extract 6

W: 您自己对这样子情形的看法怎么样？您喜欢人家这样用吗？
    ‹ What do you think of that? Do you like people doing that?›
P: 什么？‹ What?›
W: 就是这样汉语、英语、汉语、英语这样用？

    ‹ Just like this, using Chinese, English, Chinese, English?›

In other words, decisions about translation, transcription and transliteration were all contingent on wider factors than technical presentation and because of this they varied. Like Bucholtz (2001), we would rather avoid a prescriptive or standardised transcription system because this mitigates against the contingencies of translating speech into writing.

TECHNOLOGY

As we say above, technology moves fast, and this makes it a difficult subject for discussion in a book. Rather than surveying available technology in this section, therefore, we will focus on three areas which transcend availability issues and which we wish we had considered more thoroughly before beginning our research projects. These are: managing data; researcher anxiety and working with sound and video files.

Managing data

Before data collection even starts, it is worthwhile spending some time thinking about how they will be organised. Even ensuring that your field notes and other written data are easy to access and backed up requires some planning: however, when data also include recorded data, organisation becomes even more important. Knowing where files are and being able to access them efficiently makes life easier during all stages of the research process.

Researching talk in context usually requires that spoken data be recorded. Most researchers will opt for sound recording only, though an increasing number are deciding to make video recordings to capture multi-modal features (see, for example, Lefstein and Snell, 2013). Recording equipment is becoming easy to use and also smaller, and these two realities mean that making recordings is less stressful and also that the technology is less intrusive in the research site.

Most recording devices make files. In many cases, a fresh start means the start of a new file, although pausing on the device allows you to continue to use the same file. It is then important to transfer the files onto a computer or into a virtual bank and then to delete them on the recording device. This has two advantages. You will be able to back up your files (usually on a network hard drive or in a virtual bank) which will mean that your files are safe. Furthermore, you will be protecting the identity of the research participants as small recording devices and mobile phones can be lost or stolen (and frequently are). University ethics committee often require interactional data to be downloaded and protected on a secure server. Research teams can then negotiate with their universities how long and for whom the data will continue to be made available. Due to the sensitive nature of digital language data, a corpus is not usually made available to researchers beyond the project team. The data collected can potentially comprise interactions of a personal nature and so a heightened sensitivity towards the digital data is necessary.

Transferring is usually quite straightforward. In most cases, it requires that the recording device is connected to the computer and that the recording device is switched on. You will then be able to drag and drop. You can then label the file appropriately. Once on the computer, a copy should be made to ensure file safety. Virtual banks, such as 'Icloud', 'Dropbox' and 'Google Docs', have the advantage of being accessible wherever you are. You can also store a large amount of data in them, important when working with audio and visual files which often eat up a lot of memory. Angela has used the 'Microsoft Sharepoint' programme as a way to file data and make it available to others across the research team working from different universities. However, for the filing system to work effectively, prior thought needs to be given to setting up folders so that data can be tagged across data sets.

Despite the seeming simplicity of filing processes, things can go wrong. A build-up of files on the recording device can make it difficult to locate an empty folder or to find enough space for that day's recording. As we argue above, emptying the recording device at the end of the day is the best way to avoid this scenario (there is nothing more frustrating than realising that the great data you thought you had collected that day is not actually on the recording device!). Emptying the device also means that you do not risk recording over previously recorded data with new data and makes labelling a good deal easier.

Researcher anxiety

Neither Angela nor Fiona were particularly technology savvy when they began their research and this led to them becoming anxious at various stages about it. In this section, common triggers of anxiety will be described as will some possible responses.

It should go without saying that learning to work the recording equipment is essential, yet once in the research site, it is easy to forget or to misremember how to do simple things. Having instructions to hand is useful, and so is writing out your own basic instructions so that you can access them easily. Arrive if possible in plenty of time so that you can set up the equipment calmly, and, if possible, store the files digitally on another device before you leave the site so that you reduce concerns about losing the newly recorded data.

Recording is quite greedy in terms of power so charging up the recording devices before going to the research site is recommended. On one occasion, Fiona was observing and recording her research participants when a beeping noise started. This was the recording device indicating it was out of battery. While it was simple to change the batteries, the beeping had interrupted the interaction, drawn attention to the recording device and resulted in a brief hiatus while the batteries were changed and the device repositioned. It also sent Fiona's stress levels soaring. Having to change the batteries was both unnecessary and unprofessional and could have been avoided had Fiona made a basic pre-recording check.

In Angela's research there are many references across researchers' field notes about technology anxiety. For example Jaspreet, one of the other field researchers, makes the following entry in her field notes:

Extract 7

I have spent all week trying to charge and configure the voice recorders and trying to work out how to use them myself so I can successfully show the kids and teachers! I arrive at about 9.45 and feeling really nervous. I know that everyone has agreed to recording but there is a still a level of angst when actually giving them the recorders, just in case they decide that it is not their cup of tea after all! (JT, 12.2)

While Angela records the following anxieties.

Extract 8

I arrive at about 11.50 and immediately wire HL up. However, I can't answer any of her questions about the equipment and my dread of being exposed as a technological dim wit comes true. As the key participant young people come in I take them to the room next door to talk them through the equipment, recording protocol and the diary. All of them are gracious and I am nervous and bumbling. (AC12.2)

Anxiety about the equipment was not only a researcher concern. Angela and team were aware that as they started recordings in the classroom they were being disruptive. The equipment also became an anxiety for the teachers.

Extract 9

The children notice that KS is wearing a voice recorder and they say 'ah K is being recorded so he has to be nice to us now!' As soon as the voice recorders are on, K totally changes. He speaks nearly completely in Panjabi, is very formal and is very wary of the voice recorder – to a point where I start to feel uncomfortable and for the first time genuinely feel as though I am imposing. The kids tease him for it. I think I need to have a word with him next week and reiterate the importance of being natural, but for some reason I doubt it will work. The children notice clearly and tease him. (JT, 12.2)

These field notes point to the well-known observer's paradox discussed in Chapter 2 in collecting interactional data. Speer and Hutchby (2003) suggest that rather than worrying that the data are somehow inauthentic, because the teacher is behaving differently from usual, we should consider the orientation to the recording as analytically relevant. The researcher could ask why is K so nervous and why do the children behave like this? Answers to these questions can be contextually relevant: Angela and team found when recording in families, between friends and in other domestic settings, the recorder became a presence for which the participants performed. This created rich, creative and intimate data which allowed insights into participants' lives. Cynthia Gordon (2012) makes a similar point in her research on families, when she notes how participants manipulated the presence of the recorder to display identities.

Working with files

Once the files have been downloaded on to a computer, they can be played and analysed. However, they may first need to be converted to something readable across different programmes. Transcription will often be involved in this and different pieces of equipment exist to support this process. To play files, computers require the relevant software, and this software will usually allow the speed of the recording to be altered, a helpful feature when trying to work through a difficult section of talk. Researchers will want to edit their sound files, often producing truncated and spliced versions for presentation.

Researchers may also want to annotate their transcripts. For some, the comments box in word will be sufficient for this job. However, if you require detailed annotation, the 'Transcriber SG' software, free to download, is good. Described as a tool for 'segmenting, labeling and transcribing speech', Transcriber SG is particularly useful for creating equivalence in transcription and also for recognising word stress and accurately identifying features such as where interruptions and overlaps start. Although it takes some time to learn how to use this software, many researchers find that Transcriber SG (and other software such as Transana) saves them time in the end.

Using audio and video data in presentations is a common practice and requires a number of steps. First, files may need to be converted from one format to another. Recording devices often create 'WMA' files which need converting into mp3/4 files for manipulation. 'Format Factory' a multifunctional media converter can make these conversions free of charge via access on the internet. Second, for presentation purposes the file will probably need to be cut from a much longer recording. An audio editing software like Audacity (http://audacity. sourceforge.net/) can do this. It is also freely available. Once the file has been cut, it is exported back to 'My Documents' and is ready for embedding into whatever presentation software is being used. For PowerPoint (pptx) this simply requires inserting a sound file on the same slide which shows the transcript and translation to the audience. The inclusion of the sound file alongside the written transcript during the actual presentation provides the audience with a good deal of information not available before the advent of digital technologies. Audience members are in a position to hear intonation, pauses, pronunciation, irony, stylisations, grammar and a range of emotions in the speakers' voices and can make judgements about the accuracy of the transcript while simultaneously listening and reading.

Video files can be treated in much the same way as audio files although it is even more difficult to protect anonymity with video data. Lefstein and Snell (2013) have made use of Sony Movie Studio Platinum 12.0, with a free third part filter developed by NewBlueFx to disguise participants in their research. This software allows the researcher to 'laminate' the video data with a cartoon effect making video appear as a hand-drawn cartoon. While the effect might not be substantial enough to disguise a face from someone who knows it well, it certainly makes face recognition a great deal more difficult.

CONCLUDING COMMENTS

This chapter has examined three important facets of linguistic ethnographic research – transcription, translation and technology. At some point, all researchers working under the linguistic ethnographic umbrella will have to face the challenges afforded by at least one of these features. Our hope is that this chapter has suggested some theoretical and practical responses to these challenges.

In our view, it is important in research reports to foreground dilemmas faced and decisions made about transcription, translation and technology. They are not neutral or unimportant by-products of the research we do but instead reveal methodological and epistemological stances, which are not to be taken lightly. The recommended reading that follows this conclusion will point you in a number of useful directions as you continue to consider how to use and represent transcription, translation and technology in your work.

KEY READINGS

Bezemer, J. and Mavers, D. (2011) 'Multimodal transcription as academic practice: a social semiotic perspective', *International Journal of Social Research Methodology*, 14(3): 191–206.

Bucholtz, M. (2000) 'The politics of transcription', *Journal of Pragmatics*, 32: 1439–65.

Snell, J. and Lefstein, A. (2012) 'Interpretative and representational dilemmas in a linguistic ethnographic analysis: Moving from "interesting data" to a publishable research article', *Working Papers in Urban Language & Literacies*, 90. London: King's College London. Available at: https://www.kcl.ac.uk/sspp/departments/education/research/ldc/publications/workingpapers/the-papers/WP90.pdf (accessed 20 January 2014).

Wolf, M. (2011) 'Mapping the field: Sociological perspectives on translation', *International Journal of Sociology*, 20(7): 1–28.

NINE

Writing Up: Genres, Writer Voice, Audience

INTRODUCTION

As should have been evident throughout the book, representation is an issue which runs throughout the research journey and occurs in data collection, analysis and writing up. The representation of those we research is a methodological and analytical consideration as well as a process of important deliberation for publication. At every stage in linguistic ethnography representation requires being thoughtful about which participants' voices are included and how evidence is presented. Representation is a reflexive activity because who we are shapes what we notice, pursue analytically and write about. We shape the research context and the research context shapes us. This means that as researchers we exercise power in determining which narratives are told and which are not. How we tell people's stories, what we report on during these methodological and analytical journeys and why we choose to engage with some audiences and not others in our final written accounts are all issues of representation. Representation is simultaneously about author, subject and audience. Any written text produces information about all three elements.

As an author of a linguistic ethnography you will develop a number of different authorial voices in your written accounts as you write for various audiences. Outputs might include: doctoral theses and dissertations, research reports, academic journal articles, policy briefings, toolkit resources, conference presentations and posters, abstracts, blogs, and much more. Each can be said to belong to a genre with a particular set of expectations for convention, style and register. For example, a policy briefing will be written and presented in a very different manner from a doctoral thesis; a poster presentation will require a style of engagement very different from the working paper; and, the research article will demand a level of detail different from a press release. This chapter considers some of these different genres of writing and provides examples and advice on how to write academic and professional prose in linguistic ethnography. What this chapter cannot provide is a scholarly account of the literature on academic writing, genre studies or specialised discourses, although a substantial research literature exists in these areas (see, for example, Swales, 1990; Hyland, 2005; Curry and Lillis, 2013). Nor can the chapter provide advice about negotiating academic writing if you are writing in a second language, although we recognise the challenges that this presents. Rather, we write from the perspective of doctoral supervisors of some experience, as editors and reviewers of journals, as writers of academic papers for publication and presentation, and as academics who have engaged with policy stakeholders. We set out to provide examples of different writing styles and genres, offer accounts of questions and quandaries raised, and provide some guidance based on previous experiences.

Rampton defines genre as 'a set of conventionalized expectations that members of a social group or network use to shape and construe the communicative activity that they are engaged in' (Rampton, 2006: 128). The definition emphasises convention and expectation as well as agency. Bakhtin (1981) contrasts genres, describing some as generally more rigid and some as generally more fluid. On the one hand there is 'a well-defined system of rigid generic factors' (p. 8) to which there is strict adherence; while on the other there is a 'genre-in-the-making' (p. 11) in which there is 'an indeterminancy, a certain semantic openendedness, a living contract with unfinished, still evolving contemporary reality' (p. 7). Bakhtin reminds us there is always tractability as genres renew and reinvent themselves.

Linguistic ethnographers like any group of social scientists or linguists, are aware of the role genre plays in being part of a scholarly community. Conventions of writing up, the need to stay within the boundaries of the canon, the expectations of publication protocols, all bind us throughout our academic careers, although there is always same wiggle room. Without the social conventions and expectations of the relevant genre, we would be rather at sea. Indeed, we rely on genres as models of audience expectation and seek their evaluation through peer review. In what follows we provide examples of various genres in order to address questions of representation, voice and audience.

DOCTORAL THESES

One of the rationales for this book is founded on the very questions we faced as students, doctoral researchers (DRs), teachers and supervisors. A particularly intense point of question asking comes at the writing-up stage of the thesis. Such questions may include:

- How should the thesis be structured?
- Is the analytical argument presented as separate from the data or should data and argument be presented together in the same chapter?
- Where do I write about my different roles in the research project?
- Should I describe the conflicts in my different roles?
- How and where do I report on dilemmas faced in the field?
- What about the changes of direction I took, the reworking of my research questions, and where do these accounts go in the overall structure?
- How do data, analysis and the literature review connect?

Many of these questions are generic to all doctoral studies. Indeed, there are numerous other questions which you can probably imagine asking. There are also multiple and varied answers possible to these questions. Thrown into this mix are the different university requirements and wider protocols for structuring and presenting theses. Word length, appendices, referencing formats, headings, sub-headings, numbering, and other style conventions, are all tremendously important in the presentation of a thesis and university guidance must be followed carefully. However, there is one particular issue which we would like to highlight in relation to linguistic ethnography in particular and this is in relation to one section of the methodology chapter which is usually sub-titled something like 'Analysis' or 'Analytical approaches to data'. This section often comes towards the end of a methodology chapter and most often contains a description of how the researcher prepared data for analysis and applied analytical procedures in order to make the arguments in the following data driven analytical chapters. The analysis section in the methodology chapter does not make any analytical arguments connected to the data but rather describes to the reader how analysis was conducted. In terms of the kinds of questions asked by students, it is in the order of:

- How and where can I document the detailed procedures and processes of doing the analysis which I undertook in doing this piece of research?

We take up this particular point here because in our experience it is one of the areas of thesis writing and presentation which gives students most difficulty. It is also the area of ethnography most commonly criticised, that analytical procedures are not made explicit enough. Indeed, in our view, much more can be done to make the processes of analysis in ethnography transparent and the 'analysis' section of the methodology chapter is the place for this. The section should be confident, robust and coherent. Descriptions of analysis should not be hidden in the appendices or assume an overly comfortable 'you know – that's how things are done' approach. Analysis is not an act of faith but a rigorous systematic activity. Like any other kind of empirical research, the process of analysis in linguistic ethnography requires full description. Below we provide examples from recently completed doctoral work in linguistic ethnography to discuss these issues. We are very grateful to our former students for permission to document their work in this regard. We make three specific suggestions in relation to writing the analysis section in the methodology section of a thesis.

The first suggestion is to provide examples of 'data types' to illustrate the methods used. The composition of the data set should be presented. An example of a field note, an interview extract, a field document, a photo, and an audio recorded transcript could be included in the methodology chapter, not for analytical purposes but so that the reader can glean what kind of data you have and what it looks like before it undergoes analysis. Once examiners understand what materials will provide evidence, they will have more confidence in the analytical arguments that follow. In presenting examples of materials or 'raw data', the author can explain the differences and overlaps in the data sets, and this in turn allows for a commentary on the affordances of some approaches and not others. An example of this is provided below in the work of Wei Lu (2013, and http://etheses.bham. ac.uk/4723/1/Lu13PhD.pdf).

Extract 1

Today is a sunny day. It is nice and warm. I came by car and arrived 30 minutes before school started. I saw my student Ying already sitting in the classroom. I started a conversation with her and she provided me with the following information about herself:

Ying is eleven years old. Her mother is Chinese and her father is English. The reason she arrived early was because she had two hours of German language lessons in the morning at the same grammar school. She says that she prefers to stay in the school while waiting for the Chinese class to begin. Apart from Chinese and German, Ying is also learning French and Latin at school. She says that she has been interested in learning languages since she was a little girl. To be honest, Ying's Mandarin pronunciation is even better than mine. This is because her mother came from the northern part of China where the actual dialect is standard Chinese. I, on the other hand, come from the Guang Xi province which is located in the south. As Mandarin is not the local dialect, my pronunciation of the language more or less does come with some accent. (Wei Lu, 2013: 90)

Wei Lu makes several uses of this extract in her thesis. In the analytical chapters which follow the methodology chapter it is put to use in discussions of identity and language learning. However, in the methodology chapter she uses it to look at data types, researcher assumptions and researcher/participant relationships in the field. In particular, Wei Lu argues that field notes and ethnographic interviews are not distinct data sets but overlap, as shown here. This is an important methodological point and the data extract serves to help Wei Lu make it.

The second suggestion is to set about describing the stages of analysis in detail. Describing how data were drafted and redrafted, cut and pasted, moved around and put back together again helps the reader understand the rigour in the analytical process and how arguments were developed. An example of this comes from the work of Amanda Simon (2013). Simon describes the analysis of the field notes as beginning in the field. She describes how after each observational session in which she wrote field notes, she introduced another section entitled 'thoughts'. In this section she recorded her own reflections of what she had observed. After she left the field, Simon was guided by Emerson et al. (1995) in her post-field analysis processes. She describes three stages: preparing the data, core analysis Stage 1, and core analysis Stage 2. In preparing the data Simon describes rearranging the format of her original field notes to achieve maximum accessibility to the data. This involved photocopying her A5 field note book for inclusion into a larger A4 note book. She used the new column for annotation and left a space for the insertion of written memos at the end of each entry. An example is provided in Figure 9.1.

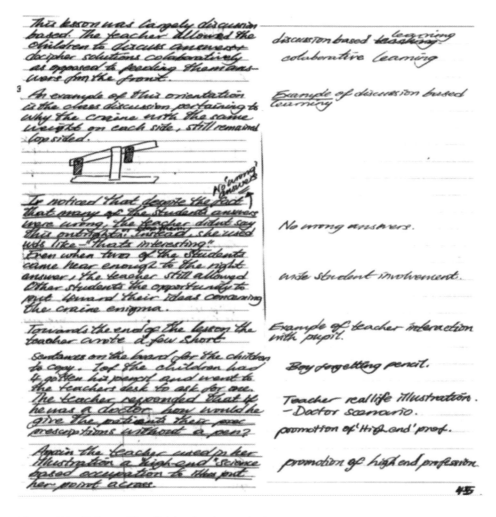

Figure 9.1 Reformatting field notes for analysis

Stage 1 of the analysis involved reading through the field notes as a complete corpus. Simon (2013: 143) observes, 'immersing in the entire field experience (Emerson et al., 1995) in this way enabled me to chart shifts in my perspective and stance'. Simon records how a core assumption she had made initially about the research context changed during this read through of her field notes at Stage 1.

Core analysis Stage 2 involved an inductive examination of the data in a process of 'open coding' (Emerson et al., 1995). This involved going through the field notes again to code for themes. Once this was complete, another reading took place to check existing codes, add to existing codes and where appropriate amalgamate and reduce codes. Reflecting on this stage, Amanda notes: 'I seemed to be searching for elements of distinction that separated the school from mainstream schooling and that distinguished it as an African-Caribbean school. These initial reflections enabled me to contextualize and critically assess what I had written, adding to the overall validity of the data gathered'. A final reading incorporated the writing of 'initial memos' which constituted analytic commentaries. It was here that Simon began drawing together common themes and relating instances within the notes. As Emerson points out, it is through this memoing and coding process that the researcher is able to retreat slightly from the field context in order to 'identify, develop and modify broader analytic themes and arguments (Emerson et al., 1995). After annotating the full corpus of notes Simon went on to produce spray diagrams (see Figure 9.2 for an example) which documented all the themes that were apparent within the field notes, along with corresponding data references.

The transfer of data into a spray diagram allowed Simon to synthesise the data, 'merging codes under more widely encompassing theme labels' (Simon, 2013: 145). Simon felt this made her data more manageable and the 'dynamics more visible' (p. 145).

A third suggestion is to find ways to summarise the methodological procedures, providing an overview of the complexity. Such summaries may culminate in diagrams, tables and vignettes. An example of a diagrammatic summary can be found in the thesis of Elizabeth Chilton (2012, and at http://etheses. bham.ac.uk/3811/) who shows evidence of a weekly cycle of participant observation which brought together a range of different data collection methods. She presents a diagrammatic outline of the weekly observational cycle (Figure 9.3) demonstrating how the data collection methods of writing *field notes*, *audio recording*, keeping a *research diary* and supplementing these with '*head notes*' was integrated into her design.

Chilton (2012) follows this diagram with a description of how she learned to use and apply these methods:

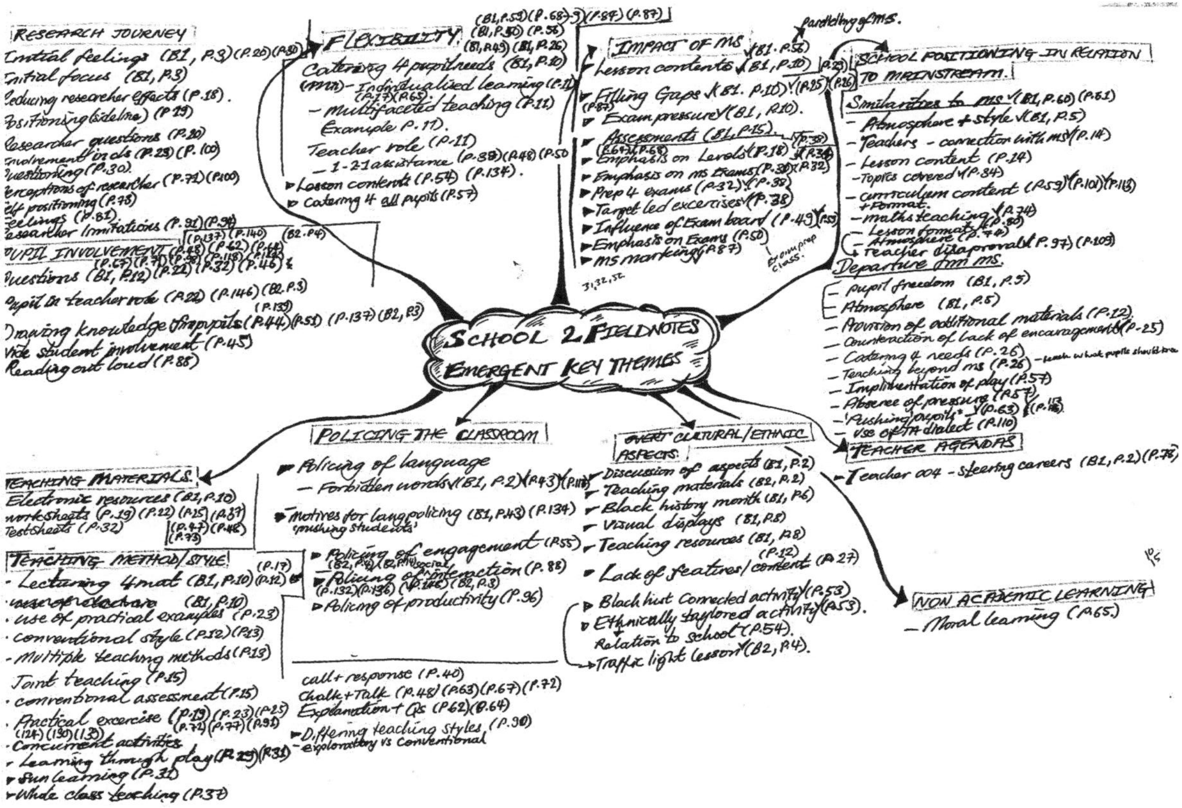

Figure 9.2 Example of a spray diagram

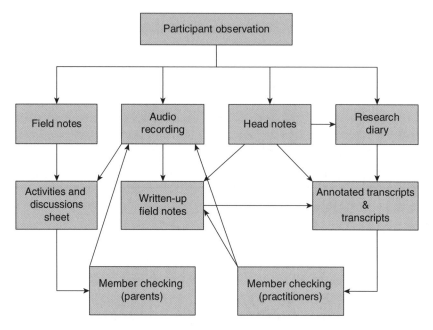

Figure 9.3 Diagrammatic outline of the weekly observational cycle (Chilton, 2012)

Extract 2

The first time that I practised taking fieldnotes I thought that I would not have to take many notes as the audio recorder would be able to provide an accurate record of the situation and my fieldnotes would act to supplement the audio-recording. However, what I realized when I started to write up my notes was that I was not providing enough contextual detail and I was over-relying on the information I thought would be made available through the audio-recording. I then made a conscious decision to try to note down elements of the social situation that I knew would be forgotten if not recorded. (pp. 88–9)

A doctoral thesis is written in a particular genre with a clear set of expectations and requirements. Detailing analysis in the methodology chapter is a convention expected for achieving a doctorate. In the next section, we consider a very different genre, which although distinct from thesis writing, will often emerge from it.

THE RESEARCH ARTICLE

In this section we consider the writing up of linguistic ethnography for publication in a research journal. Many excellent resources are available for would-be authors of academic journals and we cannot summarise them here. Rather we focus specifically on one particular element of writing up linguistic ethnographies in academic journals, that of presenting the thesis for publication as a research article. This requires issues of reduction, reorganisation and content. Theses are very long (usually around 85,000 words) while research articles are fairly short (usually between 7000 and 10,000 words)! Reducing and reorganising content can be a daunting experience, especially as just having completed a beautifully coherent and well-constructed thesis, you are now seeking to summarise, précis and divide it into a number of individual separate standalone articles.

Deciding what to include

Writing for a journal means making decisions about what arguments and themes to take from a complex and contextually rich research project. In your thesis, several themes may run across several chapters, or it may already be organised into thematic chapters. Themes will also already be linked to specific literatures in your thesis. All of this means that with a newly completed doctorate you are almost ready to move forward with writing research articles. You have a rich source of research ready for publication. However, you still face a number of issues.

You will have to make complex decisions about which data examples to use. This can be very painful as some data will inevitably be discarded. Interview extracts and transcriptions of interactions take up space, particularly when the analysis of these data is also given. However, they are crucial in developing arguments and so care must be taken in selecting examples that do this most effectively. A related discussion is the inclusion and exclusion of context which is crucial to the interpretation. Vignettes and field note accounts (and also interviews and transcriptions), where contextual detail is often found, are also very wordy and finding ways to include descriptive data requires the researcher to make difficult decisions. Sometimes the decision will be to introduce fewer but more in-depth examples of data and argumentation.

Another issue you will face is describing your methodology in a format which must retain detail while not being overly complex. Journals always demand methodological rigour and its description, but they are centrally focused on the analytical arguments made through bringing together data and theory, and the greater part of a research article is dedicated to this aspect. Methodology is crucial but it must be explained concisely. This can be frustrating because the reflexive nature of doing ethnographic research usually produces rich methodological accounts and the detail and depth of these can usually not be included. There are of course several journals which publish methodological scholarship, but even here the argument tends to be about methodology as theory rather than the detail of methods/approach used.

Making a decision about what to write into an article does not have to be a singular and lonely decision. Indeed it is often best made in discussion with peers, colleagues, supervisors and even your doctoral examiners. The writing of an article may well emerge from previous opportunities to orally present work at an academic seminar or conference where an engaged audience has already contributed with questions which contribute to fine tuning arguments and clarifying examples. At some universities, academics form reading groups to peer review each other's papers and bids. Other avenues for trying out writing ideas and processes are through working paper series. Such series provide a forum for presenting student and faculty work in progress. They are often organised by particular departments and many respond to their own student communities. They are usually run by staff and students jointly and can be very supportive in providing feedback. Some working papers form networks such as the three individual working papers listed below:

- King's College London: Working Papers in Urban Language and Literacies - http://www.kcl.ac.uk/sspp/departments/education/research/ldc/publications/workingpapers/download.aspx
- Tilburg University: Tilburg Papers in Cultural Studies - http://www.tilburguniversity.edu/research/institutes-and-research-groups/babylon/tpcs/
- University of Pennsylvania: Working Papers in Educational Linguistics - http://www.gse.upenn.edu/wpel/

Selecting a journal

Once you have selected your theme for publication, rehearsed the arguments in a variety of forums, you will need to select a journal. All peer-reviewed journals provide an overview of their aims and scope, along with lists of who is on their editorial board, on their websites. Author guidelines are also provided. It is a good idea to be familiar with all this information before you start to write for any particular journal. Two relevant examples are provided below of the kinds of aims and scope listed:

1 *Anthropology & Education Quarterly* is a peer-reviewed journal that draws on anthropological theories and methods to examine educational processes in and out of schools, in US and international contexts. Articles rely primarily on ethnographic research to address immediate problems of practice as well as broad theoretical questions. http://onlinelibrary.wiley.com/journal/10.1111/(ISSN)1548-1492 [visited January 2014])

2 The *Journal of Linguistic Anthropology* explores the many ways in which language shapes social life. Published in the journal's pages are articles on the anthropological study of language, including analysis of discourse, language in society, language and cognition, and language acquisition and socialisation. The *Journal of Linguistic Anthropology* is published three times per year.

The first journal asks for 'no more than 35 pages' while the second requires 9000 to 10,000 words. These are actually both generous length restrictions and reflect the ethnographic perspectives which both journals expect. Other leading journals set limits below this at between 7000 and 8500 words. Do pay attention to the format which the journal requires. To publish in one journal, Fiona had to learn 'APA' which has very specific rules about organisation as well as presentation, and which took her some time to grasp.

Responding to reviewers' comments

It is rare that an academic paper gets accepted for publication on the first submitted draft. Each journal has a series of recommendations from 'accept' to 'reject' and these usually include something along the lines of minor changes and major changes. If you are lucky, your submitted paper will be returned to you with minor or major changes and review comments from two or three peers (we say lucky as most submissions don't make it this far. The vast majority are rejected without getting to review stage). You may also receive advice from the journal editor about how to revise the paper based on these comments. Although receiving comments can be disheartening (in the pursuit of rigour, some reviewers can appear unkind), usually the comments will help you to write a better paper. On resubmitting within the time frame given, you will have to provide a list of the changes so that reviewers can check if their points have been attended to.

A problem often encountered is the seemingly contradictory suggestions made by different reviewers (who only see other reviews once they have all been submitted). If this happens, contact the editor for advice. When you submit your list of changes, you can explain why you have paid attention to some points at the expense of others. If you really believe that a change should not be made, you can of course resist. Again, be clear in your list of changes why you have made that decision.

Finally, reviewing takes some time. Most journals will tell you how long you should expect to wait to hear a decision and electronic submission has certainly helped editors to keep an eye on this aspect. However, there is no harm in writing politely to the journal editor if you have not had a decision within the time given.

Remember that writing for publication is a process. From first draft to final publication, the paper may go through seemingly endless critiques and revisions. This is completely normal and if you can respond positively to feedback, submit by deadlines and seek advice, you will be successful in getting work published.

One way to become a better writer is to become a reviewer. As a reviewer you can learn a huge amount about the structuring of theory, methodology, argumentation and implication in journal article writing. The criteria for acceptance into journals requires originality, significance, rigour and contribution, and it helps to understand these terms by undertaking reviews yourself. There are several ways to start reviewing. If a more senior colleague, doctoral supervisor or tutor oversees a journal, you might volunteer to be part of an internal review process. Often articles are reviewed internally before they are sent out for external review. Another approach might be to review books. Journals often seek reviewers and requests may come through your tutor or through online fora/mailing lists. Writing a book review can be particularly satisfying if it is done under the tutelage of somebody more experienced.

WRITING A PRESENTATION

Presentation papers are usually 20 or 30 minutes in length with time at the end for questions. Papers can either be 'read' or 'presented'. Some scholars prefer to read out a paper as they can ensure that their timing is accurate. Another advantage of this approach is that the discussion can be carefully crafted, structurally and linguistically. However, in front of an audience, it can be challenging to make such papers come to life as there tends to be little interaction between the presenter and audience, with the presenter constantly looking at the script. Furthermore, if the argument is dense, it can be difficult for the audience to follow. Therefore, it is more usual these days to deliver a presentation without a script; instead, presenters use slides and notes to support their discussion.

Of course, this approach brings its own challenges. First, it is essential that the presenter who uses slides goes through a similar process to the presenter who uses text in terms of ensuring the presentation is clear, logical, effective and to time. A presentation is a snapshot of research not the whole of it and the audience does not need to hear every detail of method and every theoretical concept that have influenced the findings (although it may be helpful to devote some time to explaining linguistic ethnography if presenting to a non-specialist audience). Only points that develop the argument should be included in the talk. Ruthlessness is required in terms of discarding information and data which do not support the central argument. In particular, try not to get lost in the detail of describing the background to the study.

Second, a decision must be made about what to put on the slides. The general rule here is that less is more. Fiona remembers watching a plenary presentation by an eminent scholar who was using PowerPoint for the first time. The slides were dense with text and the presenter did not always read the text on the slides but covered other ground. By the end of the talk, Fiona was exhausted. The lesson she learnt is that it is difficult for the audience to listen and to read at the same time: slides should support the talk rather than compete with it. For this reason, it is generally valuable to reserve slides for visuals, quotations, and sound and video files. Slides can also effectively structure the talk as they help to keep the presenter on track and provide useful signals to the audience. For example, there is often a slide at the beginning which outlines the presentation's contents, slides which summarise the information or argument, and slides which present the findings. Again, less is more: a large font (20+) is essential; bullet points are more effective than prose; and one or two points per slide is ample.

Third, presentations are an opportunity to communicate with interested colleagues about research. It is, of course, perfectly acceptable to have notes to refer to during the talk. However, much of the time should be spent talking to the audience and for this eye contact is essential. Engaging in this way also helps to gauge if the audience understands the talk so that adjustments can be made in real time.

While practice is unlikely to make perfect, it will develop confidence, particularly if you are delivering in a language other than your own. The TED talks (www.TED.com) are worth watching in terms of structuring, slide design, and presenting with skill and confidence.

Finally, questions can be intimidating but they can also be useful in that they support articulation of thinking, highlight features in the research that might require more consideration, and open up new avenues of investigation. Successful question and answer sections usually require the presenter to be open to different interpretations or even critiques of their work. While the researcher is the person who has the epistemological high ground in terms the research, there is a fine line to tread between defending findings and appearing defensive. As we know, research is never a finished product and answering questions is an opportunity to take stock and engage in discussion of the work to this point.

WRITING A POSTER

In Chapter 8 we considered how issues of transcription shape the presentation of data. We looked at two of Fiona's transcripts to consider how they differed according to the analytical focus. We showed how transcription differed in detail and delicacy depending on the analytical focus on hesitation and interruption. In this section we extend this point. However, rather than considering how different representations of a transcript are used to make analytical points, we consider instead how transcripts are presented in different ways to make them are accessible. We look at the publication of posters to illustrate this. Posters have become a popular format for presenting work to others. Many universities run training sessions in their design and there are numerous online resources which give advice. This advice includes making them eye-catching and easy to read; prioritising information, and making the structure easy to follow. Usually visuals are combined with text.

Two transcripts are presented below from the work of Elizabeth Chilton (2012). These come from a longer document which included seven versions of the same transcript formatted for different audiences. The audiences include herself, her research participants, a software program and an academic audience. Chilton explains how each transcript went through a series of recontextualisations each time it was translated from an audio file for a different audience. Below only two of these are illustrated. The first transcript was the version she presented to the research participants. Chilton did this regularly. Member checking of this kind is usual in ethnography but in Chilton's case it became of analytical interest as she considered researcher/researched relationships and dynamics in more detail. The second format of the transcript was included in the poster she presented at BAAL's annual conference in 2010. The poster illustrates Chilton's growing interest in researcher positioning during the research.

Extract 3

Transcript 1 – for participants

Tutor1	Ok?
Researcher	My next point ...
Tutor1	*(laughs)*
Tutor2	Do you feel like this is an inquisition ... T1?
Tutor1	Yes.
Tutor2	Do you?
Tutor1	*(laughs)* I've never had to think about it all so much
Tutor2	I think ...
Tutor1	-the freebies
Tutor2	{I feel it's}
Tutor1	{I have to get them} and it's a big drain on my time
Tutor2	Yes.
Tutor1	And thinking what to get and how to get it.
Tutor2	Yes.
Tutor1	I haven't got any resources ...
Tutor2	I agree
Tutor1	I can just dip into. So it is quite a big thing to do, to organise. And to be questioned about it as well *(laughs)*. I don't mind.
Researcher	No but ...
Tutor1	Next one. Come on now, I'm all excited. Can I get this one right? *(laughs)*
Researcher	It's not a right or a wrong!
Tutor1	I know! *(laughs)*
Researcher	No 'cause I do feel that sometimes I know that it's like I'm asking stuff and you think 'oh'
Tutor1	Oh no.
Tutor2	I haven't heard from OW you know.

This transcript is unelaborated, with few conventions for showing features of discourse. It is written for people with knowledge of the research design and uses words such as 'tutor' and 'researcher' and reference to a third party (such as 'OW') without any explanation beyond the transcript. It is easy to read and allows participants to check for accuracy.

Extract 4

Transcript 2 – version for poster

The poster in which this representation of the transcript appeared won the 2010 British Association of Applied Linguistics Poster Prize. The use of visuals and a mock-up of the interview are devices which bring the written transcript to life. Chilton used the poster to show researcher positioning and the power dynamics created by the

Figure 9.4 Transcript 2 – version for poster

interview. Her use of comic strip serves to give drama to the interaction as well as provide an accessible way into it. Posters must compete for attention and creating a strong visual like this draws in the audience who is then curious to read the other information on the poster, or to listen to what the poster presenter has to say.

WRITING POLICY AND BRIEFING PAPERS

In Chapter 7 we discussed the growing importance of impact in the social sciences and argued that linguistic ethnography's central concern with real-world issues lends itself well to responding to this agenda. In this section we consider the writing up of ethnographic evidence to make it accessible to local and national policy-makers. We consider the creation and distribution of the 'policy brief' in linguistic ethnography. We draw heavily on the ideas in an excellent article by Jennifer Keys Adair (2011) who walks the reader through the production of a policy brief entitled, 'Ethnographic Knowledge for Early Childhood' which focused on making the case for ethnography as evidence within US early childhood federal policy.

In her article, Adair argues for ethnography to counter the risks of high-stakes testing environments which fail to address issues of inequity. Her short article describes the process of synthesising a large body of scholarship into a format which can be used to brief policymakers. She also describes the challenges. These included:

- understanding that policy moves quickly while ethnography is rather slow;
- translating academic language into the language of policy brief, which requires synthesising large, complicated research studies into direct, assertive sentences, and this can be difficult for ethnographers.

We have summarised the stages Adair went through in producing the document and the advice she gives:

1   *Use existing networks to collect and document research.* Adair used the Council on Anthropology and Education (CAE) and the American Association of Anthropology (AAA) to engage with and contact scholars. This produced over fifty submissions for potential inclusion in the policy brief. She solicited submissions rather than writing a review which 'was a conscious effort to connect a broad range of studies and scholars' (p. 424).

2   *Determine the audience.* Adair describes how she located the most appropriate federal office amongst many to engage with. She describes how choosing a specific federal office helped define the scope of the policy brief and allowed the brief 'to travel quickly through many staff members concerned with the education of young children' (2011: 423).

3   *Be prepared to engage in a process of translation* as ethnographic scholarship becomes reshaped from in-depth description and analysis to direct and accessible language for a large audience. Check these revisions with the original authors to make sure they are satisfied with how their research is represented.

4   *Retain the common elements of ethnography,* which Adair describes as 'emphasis on context, multiple perspectives, and the everyday effects of particular pedagogical approaches and cultural practices' (2011: 427). Know what is specific and original about ethnographic research and play to these strengths.

5   *Produce a series of recommendations.* In Adair's case, these were:

    (a) Utilise ethnographic evidence that is based on the intentions, goals, and contexts meaningful to parents, children and teachers;
    (b) Integrate research-based assessments that include ethnographic data as much as statistics and developmental milestones;
    (c) Include the expertise of anthropologists who are informed by the perspectives of teachers, children and families involved in early learning when developing policy guidance, designing program evaluation requirements, and conducting needs-based assessments;
    (d) Encourage state-based programmes and research units to include ethnographic data as part of programme design and evaluations so that local policymakers can better understand what is important and motivating to children, teachers and parents.
    (e) Make the document visually appealing and do not over cite. Follow up and track the policy brief after it has been distributed.

The important point here in terms of writing up is that ethnographic studies are presented in a positive, clear and engaging manner for the audience the paper is aimed at. Adair's final policy brief can be found at: http://www.aaanet.org/sections/cae/wp-content/uploads/2011/10/Ethnography__ECE_Brief_Final_Adair2.pdf

The impact agenda has become fully embedded in academic scholarship and we need to carefully consider the way we write for non-academic audiences. Although we may be well practised in writing reports for professionals such as teachers, and funding agencies, we need to consider how best our scholarship can be made accessible to those that directly shape European, national and local government and policy as well as those in positions which shape what is funded in future calls for research. Using our existing scholarly forums (e.g. LEF, BAAL), professional links (e.g. teacher organisations and unions) and interdisciplinary engagement with non-academic partners (e.g. third sector organisations, local city councils) allows us to extend conversations beyond academia and into important policy and media debates.

CONCLUDING COMMENTS

This chapter has considered the different opportunities which postgraduate and early career researchers have to present their work. The different genres of the doctoral thesis, the research article, the research poster and the policy brief have been explored. We have suggested that writing for publication is a process that can be both arduous and lengthy. We have also suggested that writing for different audiences requires the researcher to consider how representations of the work, the audience and the researcher are made. For many researchers, writing is the most difficult part of the research process. Seeking advice and support from those who understand the writing genres you aspire to produce is a practical and rewarding way of developing success in writing for different audiences.

KEY READINGS

Adair, J.K. (2011) 'Advocating for ethnographic work in early childhood federal policy: Problems and possibilities', *Anthropology and Education Quarterly*, 42(4): 422–33. See also CAE's website: http://www.aaanet.org/sections/cae/

Curry, M.J. and Lillis, T. (2013) *A Scholar's Guide to Getting Published in English: Critical Choices and Practical Strategies*. Bristol: Multilingual Matters.

Hudley, A.H.C. (2013) 'Sociolinguistic engagement in schools: Collecting and sharing data', in C. Mallinson, B. Childs and G. Van Herk (eds) *Data Collection in Sociolinguistics: Methods and Applications*. London: Routledge. pp. 269–80.

Malinson, C. (2013) 'Sharing data and findings', in C. Mallinson, B. Childs and G. Van Herk (eds) *Data Collection in Sociolinguistics: Methods and Applications*. London: Routledge.

TEN

Ways Forward

INTRODUCTION

The discussions in this book have touched on a whole range of issues pertinent to linguistic ethnography as it develops as an approach to investigating real-world problems. In this final section, we pick up some of the main themes from the book and suggest how we might move forward as a group of linguistic ethnographers. We end with two final vignettes from Angela and Fiona which reflect on the process of writing the book and on how their understandings of linguistic ethnography have developed as a result.

INTERDISCIPLINARITY

One theme that has emerged is interdisciplinarity. In Chapter 1 we describe two approaches to interdisciplinary research drawing on Rampton et al. (in press). The first approach brings different academic disciplines together to work on a problem while the second brings academics and non-academics together. The case studies provide examples of each mode. Angela describes her work in teams with educational researchers; Frances explains how she worked with professional writers and a police officer on the wording of the caution. It is our belief that both types of interdisciplinarity will increase in popularity and importance and that linguistic ethnography, which combines an openness to method with methodological rigour, is well placed to support this kind of work. Indeed, a new volume of work by linguistic ethnographic researchers which focuses on interdisciplinarity is currently in press (Snell et al., in press). The papers include reports of interdisciplinary work between a researcher and surgeons (Bezemer) and between researchers from health and linguistics (Collins).

THE STATUS OF DATA

A second theme, linked to interdisciplinarity and central to this book, is the status of data. Different kinds of data were collected, analysed and presented by case study writers. All engage with field notes and interviews. Given the focus on *ethnography*, this is to be expected. However, other researchers working in the area have argued that it is interactional data that is central to the *linguistic* ethnographic endeavour (see Lefstein and Isreal, in press) with field notes and other data supporting their analysis. However, there are two problems inherent in this approach from our perspective. First, how can colleagues who do not collect interactional data be accommodated? Is it not possible to do linguistic ethnographic work without interactional data? Second, in our view, one of the strengths of linguistic ethnography is the way in which data sets are brought together in analysis, in an almost iterative process. We have illustrated how this can be achieved in the case study chapters and in Chapter 9. Given this, how can one data set have a higher status than another? All should combine to create an analysis that is detailed and nuanced.

We expect the debate about data and status to continue in the linguistic ethnographic community, particularly as the field moves forward and its (permeable) parameters are sketched out. However, we also expect that competing views will continue to co-exist as linguistic ethnography is as much about community as it is about method.

BREADTH AND DEPTH IN LINGUISTIC ETHNOGRAPHY

This brings us to another theme of the book – the range of work that takes a linguistic ethnographic perspective. Although applied linguistics in general has become dominated by work in education and particularly in language learning (see the list of presentations at the BAAL conference and papers in the journal *Applied Linguistics* to get a sense of this), linguistic ethnography's constituency, in contrast, comprises researchers working, for example, in health, journalism, crime, multilingualism, migration and employment, as well as education. The result of this is a healthy cross-fertilisation of ideas, approaches and theoretical perspectives. The Linguistic Ethnography Forum (www.lingethnog.org), a special interest group of BAAL (www.baal.org.uk), provides a supportive meeting place where these different disciplines can mingle. It also sponsors e-seminar discussions from a range of disciplines (migration, health, education are recent themes) and a biennial conference. Likewise, training programmes such as those offered at King's College London on ethnography, language and communication, and at the University of Birmingham on researching multilingualism, provide the opportunity for researchers from different backgrounds to meet and develop their research skills. If you have found the approaches presented in this book of interest, you might consider joining the forum or attending the training courses or conferences. These organisations are an outward sign of the strength of interest in linguistic ethnography.

LINGUISTIC ETHNOGRAPHY AND LINGUISTIC ANTHROPOLOGY

A theme touched on in the book but one that may deserve more attention is the relationship between linguistic ethnography, which we have argued has a largely European constituency and outlook, and linguistic anthropology, which is generally centred on work in North America. While scholars from linguistic anthropology have visited universities in Europe to discuss their work and, in some cases, the development of linguistic ethnography (and vice versa), the relationship between the two movements might benefit from more sustained and focused engagement. We believe that there is much to be gained on each side from such interaction in terms of developing methodological approaches and theoretical perspectives.

FINAL COMMENTS

The final theme in this section is the status and definition of linguistic ethnography itself. There has been an understandable reluctance from linguistic ethnographic scholars to promote linguistic ethnography except in circumspect ways. Discussions of linguistic ethnography by Rampton et al. (2004), Creese (2008) and Tusting and Maybin (2011), for example, have tended to a critical perspective. However, the publication of this book and of *Linguistic Ethnography: Interdisciplinary Explorations* (Palgrave Macmillan) suggests that the movement is now reaching a level of maturity which may support a more celebratory discourse. As the writers of this book (and contributors to the other) we are not in a position to start the fanfare. It is our hope that the work we have presented convinces you, the reader, that linguistic ethnography can make an important contribution.

We end the book with vignettes from Angela and Fiona which they wrote in response to a suggestion from a reviewer that the book should end as it had started. The vignettes provide an insight into our experiences of writing the book and what we have learnt from it.

CONCLUDING VIGNETTES

Angela

Writing a book about the processes of doing research is a salutary experience at whatever point you are in your career. Questions that I ask of my students – how do you know that; how did you find that; what did you do to analyse that – are tough questions to answer even if you have worked on a number of different linguistic ethnographic projects as I have. These questions never go away, nor should they. And I think facing up to them is what we have tried to do in this book. However, revealing the mechanics and processes of the methodological journey is not the most glamorous aspect of doing research. Methodological accounts don't usually make it onto the red carpet alongside their more elegant and alluring cousins, 'the research findings'. Because they are grubbier they tend to attract less prominence in the field of academia, and take up their place behind the scenes. Walking the reader through the detail of the research, warts and all, showing the scribbled 'workings out' of data collection and analysis; describing the technicalities of data reduction and problem solving may be crucial in any research process but it rarely makes it on to the front page of our research outputs. Certainly in writing this book there was not much glamour in reassembling old data sets and remembering procedures long put to rest. This was at times frustrating as I tried and sometimes failed to put my hands on stuff which I knew was somewhere if only I could remember where. However, I persevered because although many linguistic ethnographies are hugely rich, innovative and theoretically ground-breaking, the detail of how authors reach their findings is too often missing from their stories and we wanted to redress this.

In writing this book with Fiona, Frances and Sara I have learned a huge amount. Firstly, it has reminded me that those questions I ask my students, which may trip easily off the tongue in a supervisory meeting, are not only for novices but for veterans too. Second, this book has confirmed for me that collaborating with others, writing together, critiquing our work side-by-side and undertaking rigorous peer-review is one of the most pleasurable and most informative ways to learn.

Fiona

As we get ready to submit the book for publication, I am aware that I have gained a great deal from the process of co-authoring. Although not discussed or agreed in advance, each of us naturally took on different roles: Angela was fantastic about keeping us on course, interpreting feedback, making sensible plans and knowing when something we have written just hadn't worked. For my part, I ensured that we kept the reader firmly kept in mind, that we addressed current issues emerging from discussions among linguistic ethnographers, and that Jai at Sage, and Frances and Sara, our case study writers, were kept informed of progress.

I was surprised at how engaging, motivating and satisfying sustained collaborative writing was. That is not to say we have always agreed. Sometimes we had heated discussions about the importance of a theoretical or analytical point or whether a particular topic should be emphasised. Ultimately, I think the disagreements have made the book stronger, forcing us to defend our territory or to concede in the interests of clarity and balance. In this way, writing this book has mirrored the research process: both are enriched through the discussion and disagreement that different perspectives offer.

I have also learnt a great deal about linguistic ethnography through the process of writing about it. Some of my assumptions have been confirmed while others have been challenged. Frances's and Sara's contributions have been central to the development of these understandings and incorporating their case studies has ensured that we have integrated different perspectives into the chapters that sandwich them. I have also found it particularly helpful to read how co-writers have interpreted linguistic ethnography practically: details of interviewing approaches and text analysis put meat on the bones of abstract methodologies and provide us with a lens through which to view research practices. These descriptions have caused me to consider how I approach my own research. The interview as go-along and corpus analytic approaches to text analysis have struck me as particularly pertinent to my own research interests.

I hope those who read the book find it useful and informative. It is the book that I wish I had had when I started out as a researcher and one that I will keep close at hand when planning my own research projects or advising research students. The fact that it uses real research projects to illustrate how research can be done is in the end what makes it, I think, of value.

References

Adair, J.K. (2011) 'Advocating for ethnographic work in early childhood federal policy: problems and possibilities', *Anthropology and Education Quarterly*, 42(4): 422–33.

Agar, M. (2005) 'Local discourse and global research: the role of local knowledge', *Language in Society*, 34(1): 1–22.

Agar, M. (2008) *The Professional Stranger*, 2nd edn. Bingley: Emerald Group Publishing.

Agha, A. (2003) 'The social life of cultural value', *Language and Communication*, 23(3/4): 231–73.

Agha, A. (2005) 'Voice, footing, enregisterment', *Journal of Linguistic Anthropology*, 15(1): 38–59.

Agha, A. (2007) *Language and Social Relations*. Cambridge: Cambridge University Press.

Alexander, R. (2005) 'Culture, dialogue and learning: notes on an emerging pedagogy', keynote presentation given at the 10th International Conference of the International Association for Cognitive Education and Psychology, Durham.

Anderson, L. (2006) 'Analytic autoethnography', *Journal of Contemporary Ethnography*, 35(4): 373–95.

Anthony, L. (2005) 'AntConc: Design and Development of a Freeware Corpus Analysis Toolkit for the Technical Writing Classroom'. *IEEE International Professional Communication Conference Proceedings*, 10–13 July 2005. Available at: http://ieeexplore.ieee.org/xpl/mostRecentIssue.jsp?punumber=10002

Arnesen, A.L. (2003) 'Constructions of an "outsider": contradictions and ambiguities in institutional practices', in D. Beach, T. Gordon and E. Lahelma (eds) *Democratic Education: Ethnographic Challenges*. London: Tufnell Press. pp. 52–65.

Arundale, R. (2006) 'Face as relational and interactional: a communication framework for research on face, facework and politeness', *Journal of Politeness Research*, 2(2): 193–216.

Arundale, R. (2010) 'Constituting face in conversation: face, facework, and interactional achievement', *Journal of Pragmatics*, 42(8): 2078–105.

Atkin, A. (2013) 'Peirce's theory of signs', in E.N. Zalta (ed.) *The Stanford Encyclopedia of Philosophy*, http://plato.stanford.edu/archives/sum2013/entries/peirce-semiotics/

Atkinson, P. and Silverman, D. (1997) 'Kundera's immortality: the interview society and the invention of the self', *Qualitative Inquiry*, 3(3): 304–25.

Auer, P. (1996) 'From context to contextualisation', *Links and Letters*, 3: 11–28, http://ddd.uab.cat/pub/lal/11337397n3p11.pdf (accessed 31 May 2013).

Auer, P. (ed.) (1998) *Code-Switching in Conversation: Language, Interaction and Identity*. London: Routledge.

Austin, J.A. (1962) *How to Do Things with Words*. Cambridge, MA: Harvard University Press.

British Association for Applied Linguistics (BAAL) (2000) *Recommendations for Good Practice in Applied Linguistics Student Projects*. Available at: http://www.baal.org.uk/dox/goodpractice_stud.pdf (accessed 31 January 2014).

Bailey, B. (2008) 'Interactional sociolinguistics', in W. Donsbach (ed.) *The International Encyclopaedia of Communication*. Oxford: Blackwell Publishing. pp. 2314–18.

Bacchi, C.L. (2000) 'Policy as discourse: What does it mean? Where does it get us?', *Discourse Studies in the Cultural Politics of Education*, 21(1): 45–57.

Baker, C.D. (2002) 'Ethnomethodological analysis of interviews', in J.F. Gubrium and J.A. Holstein (eds) *Handbook of Interview Research: Context and Method*. London: Sage. pp. 777–95.

Bakhtin, M.M. (1981) *The Dialogic Imagination: Four Essays*. Edited by M. Holquist, translated by C. Emerson and M. Holquist. Austin: University of Texas Press.

Bamber, G. and Sappey, J. (2007) 'Unintended consequences of human research ethics committees: au revoir workplace studies?', *Monash Bioethics Review*, 26(3): 26–36.

Barton, D. and Hamilton, M. (1998) *Local Literacies: Reading and Writing in One Community*. London: Routledge.

Barton, D., Hamilton, M. and Ivanič, R. (eds) (2000) *Situated Literacies*. London: Routledge.

Bauman, Z. (1993) *Post-Modern Ethics*. Oxford: Blackwell Publishing.

Baxter, J. (2002) 'Is PDA really an alternative? A reply to West', *Discourse & Society*, 13(6): 853–9.

Baxter, P. and Jack, S. (2008) 'Qualitative case study methodology: study design and implementation for novice researchers', *The Qualitative Report*, 13(4): 544–59. Available at: http://www.nova.edu/ssss/QR/QR13-4/baxter.pdf (accessed 25 April 2013).

Baynham, M. (1995) *Literacy Practices: Investigating Literacy in Social Contexts*. New York: Longman.

Beaumont, T.L. and Childness, J.F. (2001) *The Principles of Biomedical Ethics*, 5th edn. New York: Oxford University Press.

Becker, H.S. (1998) *Tricks of the Trade: How to Think about Your Research While You're Doing It*. Chicago: University of Chicago Press.

Bender, M. (2008) 'Indexicality, voice, and context in the distribution of Cherokee scripts', *International Journal of Sociology of Language*, 192: 91–103.

Berg, B.L. (1998) *Qualitative Research Methods for the Social Sciences*. Boston, MA: Allyn and Bacon.

Bevir, M. and Rhodes, R.A.W. (2004) 'Interpreting British governance', *British Journal of Politics and International Relations*, 6(2): 130–6.

Bezemer, J. (in press) 'Linguistic ethnography in health care: challenges and potentials', in J. Snell, S. Shaw and F. Copland (eds) *Linguistic Ethnography: Interdisciplinary Explorations*. Basingstoke: Palgrave Macmillan.

Bezemer, J. and Mavers, D. (2011) 'Multimodal Baker transcription as academic practice: a social semiotic perspective', *International Journal of Social Research Methodology*, 14(3): 191–206.

Billig, M. (1988) 'Methodology and scholarship in understanding ideological explanation', in C. Antaki (ed.) *Analysing Everyday Explanation*. Beverley Hills, CA: Sage. pp. 199–215.

Bilmes, J. (1988) 'The concept of preference in conversation analysis', *Language in Society*, 17(2): 161–81.

Blackledge, A. and Creese, A. (2010) *Multilingualism: A Critical Perspective*. London: Continuum.

Blackledge, A. and Creese, A. (2014) 'Heteroglossia as practice and pedagogy', in A. Blackledge and A. Creese (eds) *Heteroglossia as Practice and Pedagogy*. New York: Springer. pp. 1–20.

Blackledge, A., Creese, A. and Takhi, J.K. (2013) 'Beyond multilingualism: heteroglossia in practice', in Stephen May (ed.) *The Multilingual Turn: Implications for SLA, TESOL and Bilingual Education*. London and New York: Routledge. pp. 191–215.

Blackledge, A., Creese, A. and Takhi, J.K. (2014) 'Discourses of aspiration and distinction in the local school economy', in J.W. Unger, M. Krzyzanowski and R. Wodak (eds) *Multilingual Encounters in Europe's Institutional Spaces*. London: Routledge.

Blackledge, A., Creese, A. and Takhi, J.K. (in press) 'Emblems of identities in four European urban settings', in J. Nortier and B.A. Svendsen (eds) *Multilingual Urban Sites: Structure, Activity, Ideology*. Cambridge: Cambridge University Press.

Blommaert, J. (2005) *Discourse: A Critical Introduction*. Cambridge: Cambridge University Press.

Blommaert, J. (2006) *Ethnographic Fieldwork: A Beginner's Guide*. Available at: https://www.jyu.fi/hum/laitokset/kielet/tutkimus/hankkeet/paattyneet-hankkeet/fidipro/en/courses/fieldwork-text (accessed 16 September 2014).

Blommaert, J. (2007a) 'On scope and depth in linguistic ethnography', *Journal of Sociolinguistics*, 11(5): 682–8.

Blommaert, J. (2007b) 'Sociolinguistic scales', *Intercultural Pragmatics*, 4(1): 1–19.

Blommaert, J. (2007c) 'Genre', paper presented at the ESRC Research Methods Course, Ethnography, Language and Communication, London University Institute of Education.

Blommaert, J. (2010) 'Policy, policing and the ecology of social norms: ethnographic monitoring revisited', *Working Papers in Urban Language & Literacies*, 63.

Blommaert, J. and Jie, D. (2010) *Ethnographic Fieldwork: A Beginner's Guide*. Bristol: Multilingual Matters.

Blommaert, J. and Rampton, B. (2011) 'Language and superdiversity', *Diversities*, 13(2): 1–22.

Bloomaert, J., Leppänen, S. and Spotti, M. (2012) 'Endangering multlingualism', in J. Blommaert, S. Leppänen, P. Pahat and T. Räisänen (eds) *Dangerous

Multilingualism: Northern Perspectives on Order, Purity and Normality. Basingstoke: Palgrave Macmillan.

Blumer, H. (1954) 'What is wrong with social theory?', *American Sociological Review*, 18: 3–10.

Bourdieu, P. (2000) *Pascalian Meditations*. Cambridge: Polity Press.

Bourgois, P. (1995) *In Search of Respect: Selling Crack in El Barrio*. Cambridge: Cambridge University Press.

Brandt, C. (2006) 'Allowing for practice: a critical issue in TESOL teacher preparation', *ELT Journal*, 60(4): 335–64.

Brewer, J. (2000) *Ethnography*. Buckingham: Open University Press.

Brewster Smith, M. (1979) 'Some perspectives on ethical/political issues in social science research', in M. Wax, and J. Cassell (eds) *Federal Regulations: Ethical Issues and Social Research*. Boulder, CO: Westview Press. pp. 11–22.

Briggs, C. (1986) *Learning How to Ask: A Sociolinguistic Appraisal of the Role of the Interview in Social Science Research*. Cambridge: Cambridge University Press.

Brown, P. and Levinson, S. (1987) *Politeness: Some Universals in Language Use*. Cambridge: Cambridge University Press.

Bryman, A. (1988) *Quantity and Quality in Social Research*. London: Unwin Hyman.

Bucholtz, M. (1995) 'Language in evidence: the pragmatics of translation and the judicial process', in M. Morris (ed.) *Translation in the Law*. Amsterdam and Philadelphia: John Benjamins. pp. 115–29.

Bucholtz, M. (2000) 'The politics of transcription', *Journal of Pragmatics*, 32(10): 1439–65.

Bucholtz, M. (2003) 'Theories of discourse as theories of gender: discourse analysis in language and gender studies', in J. Holmes and M. Meyerhoff (eds) *The Handbook of Language and Gender*. Malden, MA: Blackwell. pp. 43–68.

Bucholtz, M. (2007) 'Variation in transcription', *Discourse Studies*, 9(6): 784–808.

Bucholtz, M. and Hall, K. (2008) 'All of the above: New coalitions in sociocultural linguistics', *Journal of Sociolinguistics*, 12(4): 401–31.

Caldeira, T.P.R. (2002) 'The paradox of police violence in democratic Brazil', *Ethnography*, 3(3): 235–63.

Cameron, D. (2000) 'Styling the worker: gender and the commodification of language in the globalized service economy', *Journal of Sociolinguistics*, 4(3): 323–47.

Chilton, E.H. (2012) 'The discursive construction of a Family Literacy, Language and Numeracy programme: an exploration of practitioners' narratives-in-interaction', unpublished PhD dissertation, University of Birmingham.

Cicourel, A. (1974 [1968]) 'Police practices and official records', in R. Turner (ed.) *Ethnomethodology: Selected Readings*. Harmondsworth: Penguin Books. pp. 85–95.

Clare, I. and Gudjonsson, G. (1992) *Devising and Piloting an Experimental Version of the 'Notice to Detained Persons'*, Royal Commission on Criminal Justice, Research Study No. 7. London: HMSO.

Clare, I., Gudjonsson, G. and Harari, P. (1998) 'Understanding the current police caution (England and Wales)', *Journal of Community and Applied Psychology*, 8(5): 323–9.

Coffey, A. (1999) *The Ethnographic Self*. London: Sage.

Cook, G. (2011) 'Discourse analysis', in J. Simpson (ed.) *The Routledge Handbook of Applied Linguistics*. London: Routledge. pp. 431–44.

Copland, F. (2008) 'Deconstructing the discourse: understanding the feedback event', in S. Garton and K. Richards (eds) *Professional Encounters in TESOL*. London: Palgrave. pp. 5–23

Copland, F. (2010) 'Causes of tension in feedback: an alternative view', *Teaching and Teacher Education*, 26(3): 466–72.

Copland, F. (2011) 'Negotiating face in the feedback conference: a linguistic ethnographic approach', *Journal of Pragmatics*, 43(15): 3832–43.

Copland, F. (2012) 'Legitimate talk in feedback conferences', *Applied Linguistics*, 33(1): 1–20.

Copland, F. and Creese, A. (forthcoming) 'Ethical issues in linguistic ethnography: Balancing the micro and the macro', in P. I. De Costa (ed.) *Ethics in Applied Linguistics Research: Language Researcher Narratives*. New York: Routledge.

Copland, F. and Garton, S. (2011) '"I felt that I do live in the UK now": international students' self-reports of their English language speaking experiences on a pre-sessional programme', *Language and Education*, 25(3): 241–55.

Cotterill, J. (2000) 'Reading the rights: a cautionary tale of comprehension and comprehensibility', *Forensic Linguistics*, 7(1): 4–25.

Creese, A. (2003) 'Language, ethnicity and the mediation of allegations of racism: negotiating diversity and sameness in multilingual school discourses', *International Journal of Bilingual Education and Bilingualism*, 6(3–4): 221–36.

Creese, A. (2005) *Teacher Collaboration and Talk in Multilingual Classrooms*. Clevedon: Multilingual Matters.

Creese, A. (2008) 'Linguistic ethnography', in K.A. King and N.H. Hornberger (eds) *Encyclopaedia of Language and Education*, 2nd edn. New York: Springer Science+Business Media LLC. pp. 229–41.

Creese, A. (2010a) 'Educational linguistics in multilingual classrooms', in F. Hult (ed.) *Directions and Prospects in Educational Linguistics: Theoretical and Methodological Issues*. Dordrecht: Springer. pp. 33–48.

Creese, A. (2010b) 'Linguistic ethnography', in E. Litosseliti (ed.) *Research Methods in Linguistics*. London: Continuum. pp. 138–54.

Creese, A. (2011) 'Making local practices globally relevant in researching multilingual education', in F.M. Hult and K.A. King (eds) *Educational Linguistics in Practice*. Bristol: Multilingual Matters. pp. 41–55.

Creese, A. and Blackledge, A. (2011) 'A flexible and separate bilingualism in complementary schools', *Journal of Pragmatics*, 43, 1196–208.

Creese, A. and Blackledge, A. (2012) 'Voice and meaning-making in team ethnography', *Anthropology & Education Quarterly*, 43(3): 306–24.

Creese, A. and Blackledge, A. (in press) *Negotiating Authenticity and Legitimacy in the Community Language Classroom.*

Creese, A. and Martin, P. (eds) (2003) *Multilingual Classroom Ecologies.* Clevedon: Multilingual Matters.

Creese, A., Bhatt, A., Bhojani, N. and Martin, P. (2006) 'Multicultural, heritage and learner identities in complementary schools', *Language and Education,* 20(1): 23–43.

Creese, A., Bhatt, A., Bhojani, N. and Martin, P. (2008) 'Fieldnotes in team ethnography: researching complementary schools', *Qualitative Research,* 8(2): 223–42.

Creese, A., Bhatt, A. and Martin, P. (2009) 'Multilingual researcher identities: interpreting linguistically and culturally diverse classrooms', in J. Miller, M. Gearon and A. Kostogriz (eds) *Linguistically and Culturally Diverse Classrooms: New Dilemmas for Teachers.* Clevedon: Multilingual Matters. pp. 215–33.

Creese, A. and Blackledge, B., with Bhatt, A., Jonsson, C., Juffermans, K., Li, J., Martin P., Muhonen, A. and Takhi, J.K. (in press) 'Researching bilingual and multilingual education multilingually: a linguistic ethnography', in W.E. Wright, S. Boun and O. Garcia (eds) *Handbook of Bilingual & Multilingual Education.* Malden, MA, and Oxford: Wiley/Blackwell.

Cronin, M. (2013) *Translation in the Digital Age.* London: Routledge.

Crystal, D. (1997) *The Cambridge Encyclopedia of Language,* 2nd edn. Cambridge: Cambridge University Press.

Curry, M.J and Lillis, T. (2013) *A Scholar's Guide to Getting Published in English: Critical Choices and Practical Strategies.* Bristol: Multilingual Matters.

Czarniawska, B. (2007) *Shadowing and Other Techniques for Doing Fieldwork in Modern Societies.* Malmö: Liber.

D'Arcy, A. and Young, T.M. (2012) 'Ethics and social media: implications for sociolinguistics in the networked public', *Journal of Sociolinguistics,* 16(4): 532–46.

de Laine, M. (2000) *Fieldwork, Participation and Practice: Ethics and Dilemmas in Qualitative Research.* London: Sage.

Degeling, P. (1996) 'Health planning as context-dependent language play', *International Journal of Health Planning and Management,* 11(2): 101–17.

Delamont, S. (2002) *Fieldwork in Educational Settings: Methods, Pitfalls and Procedures,* 2nd edn. London: Falmer.

Department of Health (DH) (2010) *Equity and Excellence: Liberating the NHS.* Cm 7801. London: The Stationery Office.

Dingwall, R. (1992) '"Don't mind him – he's from Barcelona": qualitative methods in health studies', in J. Daly, I. McDonald and E. Ellis (eds) *Researching Health Care.* London: Routledge. pp. 161–75.

Donnell Johnson, J. (2004) 'God's gypsy and God's enforcer: the educational significance of constructions of motherhood and mother–daughter relationships', in G. Troman, B. Jeffrey and G. Walford (eds) *Identity, Agency and Social Institutions in Educational Ethnography.* Oxford: Elsevier. pp. 43–69.

Drew, P. and Heritage, J. (1992) *Talk at Work: Interaction in Institutional Settings.* Cambridge: Cambridge University Press.

Drew, P. and Sorjonen, M. (1997) 'Institutional dialogue', in T. Van Dijk (ed.) *Discourse Studies: A Multidisciplinary Introduction. Vol. 2: Discourse as Social Interaction*. London: Sage Publications. pp. 92–118.

Eckert, P. and McConnell-Ginet, S. (1992) 'Think practically and look locally: language and gender as community based practice', *Annual Review of Anthropology*, 21: 461–90.

Edwards, P. and Bélanger, E. (2008) 'Generalizing from workplace ethnographies: from induction to theory', *Journal of Contemporary Ethnography*, 37(3): 291–313.

Eisenhart, M. and Howe, K. (1992) 'Validity in educational research', in M. Le Compte, W. Millroy and J. Preissle (eds) *The Handbook of Qualitative Research in Education*. San Diego: Academic Press. pp. 643–80.

Ellis, C. and Bochner, A. (2000) 'Autoethnography, personal narrative, reflexivity: researcher as subject', in N. Denzin and Y. Lincoln (eds) *Sage Handbook of Qualitative Research*, 2nd edn. Thousand Oaks, CA: Sage. pp. 733–68.

Ellis, C., Adams, T.E. and Bochner, A.P. (2010) 'Autoethnography: an overview', *Forum Qualitative Sozialforschung / Forum: Qualitative Social Research*, 12(1). Available at: http://nbn-resolving.de/urn:nbn:de:0114-fqs1101108 (accessed 25 April 2013).

Emerson, R.M., Fretz, R.I. and Shaw, L.L. (1995) *Writing Ethnographic Fieldnotes*. Chicago: University of Chicago Press.

Erickson, F. (1990) 'Qualitative methods', in R.L. Linn and F. Erickson (eds) *Research in Teaching and Learning: Volume Two*. New York: Macmillan. pp. 77–194.

Erickson, F. (1992) 'Ethnographic micoanalysis of interaction', in M.D. LeCompte, L. Millroy and J. Preissle (eds) *The Handbook of Qualitative Research in Education*. London: Academic Press. pp. 201–26.

Erickson, F. (1996) 'Ethnographic microanalysis', in S.L. McKay and N.H. Hornberger (eds) *Sociolinguistics and Language Teaching*. New York: Cambridge University Press. pp. 283–306.

Erickson, F. (2004a) 'Demystifying data construction and analysis', *Anthropology and Education Quarterly*, 35(4): 486–93.

Erickson, F. (2004b) *Talk and Social Theory: Ecologies of Speaking and Listening in Everyday Life*. Malden: Polity Press.

Erickson, K. and Stull, D. (1998) *Doing Team Ethnography: Warnings and Advice*. London: Sage.

Evanoff, R.J. (2004) 'Universalist, relativist, and constructivist approaches to intercultural ethics', *International Journal of Intercultural Relations*, 28(5): 439–58.

Fairclough, N. (2001) *Language and Power*. Harlow: Longman.

Fairclough, N. (2010) *Critical Discourse Analysis: The Critical Study of Language*. London: Routledge.

Farr, F. (2006) 'Reflecting on reflection: the spoken word as a professional development tool in language teacher education', in R. Hughes (ed.) *Spoken English, TESOL and Applied Linguistics: Challenges for Theory and Practice*. Palgrave Macmillan. pp. 182–215.

Fine, M. (1994) 'Working the hyphens: reinventing self and other in qualitative research', in N.K. Denzin and Y.S. Lincoln (eds) *Handbook of Qualitative Research*. Thousand Oaks, CA: Sage.

Fischer, F. (2003) *Reframing Public Policy: Discursive Politics and Deliberative Practices*. Oxford: Oxford University Press.

Fischer, F. and Forrester, J. (eds) (1993) *The Argumentative Turn in Policy Analysis and Planning*. London: Duke University Press/UCL Press.

Flynn, P., van Praet, E. and Jacobs, G. (2010) 'Emerging linguistic ethnographic perspectives on institutional discourses', *Text & Talk*, 30(2): 97–103.

Gains, F. (2011) 'Elite ethnographies: potential, pitfalls and prospects for getting "up close and personal"', *Public Administration*, 89(1): 156–66.

García, O. (2009) *Bilingual Education in the 21st Century*. Oxford: Wiley Blackwell.

Garton, S. and Copland, F. (2010) '"I like this interview; I get cakes and cats!": The effect of prior relationships on interview talk', *Qualitative Research*, 10(5): 533–51.

Gee, J. (2005) *Discourse Analysis: Theory and Method*, 2nd edn. London: Routledge.

Gee, J.P. and Handford, M. (2012) *The Routledge Handbook of Discourse Analysis*. London: Routledge.

Geertz, C. (1988) *Works and Lives: The Anthropologist as Author*. Cambridge: Polity Press.

Giddens, A. (1991) *The Consequences of Modernity*. Oxford: Blackwell Publishing.

Gillon, R. (2003) 'Ethics needs principles – four can encompass the rest – and respect for autonomy should be "first among equals"', *Journal of Medical Ethics*, 29(5): 307–12.

Gobo, G. (2008) *Doing Ethnography*. London: Sage.

Goffman, E. (1959) *Presentation of Self in Everyday Life*. New York: Anchor.

Goffman, E. (1967) *Interactional Ritual*. New York: Basic Books.

Goffman, E. (1969 [1959]) *The Presentation of Self in Everyday Life*. London: Penguin.

Goffman, E. (1971 [1959]) *The Presentation of Self in Everyday Life*. Harmondsworth: Penguin Books.

Goffman, E. (1975) *Frame Analysis: An Essay on the Organization of Experience*. Cambridge, MA: Harvard University Press.

Goffman, E. (1981) *Forms of Talk*. Philadelphia: University of Pennsylvania Press.

Goldring, J.E. (2010) 'Between partisan and fake, walking the path of the insider: empowerment and voice in ethnography', in J. Scott Jones and S. Watt (eds) *Ethnography in Social Practice*. London: Routledge. pp. 126–40.

Goodenough, W.H. (1994) 'Toward a working theory of culture', in R. Borosky (ed.) *Assessing Cultural Anthropology*. New York: McGraw Hill. pp. 262–73.

Goodwin, D., Pope, C., Mort, M. and Smith, A. (2003) 'Ethics and ethnography: an experiential account', *Qualitative Health Research*, 13(4): 567–77.

Gordon, C. (2012) 'Beyond the observer's paradox: the audio-recorder as a resource for the display of identity', *Qualitative Research*, 13(3): 299–317.

Graddol, D. (2006) *English First*. London: British Council.

Grahame, P. (1998) 'Ethnography, institutions, and the problematic of the everyday world', *Human Studies*, 21(4): 347–60.

Greatbatch, D. (1992) 'On the management of disagreement between news inter-viewees', in P. Drew and P. Heritage (eds) *Talk at Work: Interaction in Institutional Settings*. Cambridge: Cambridge University Press. pp. 268–301.

Green, J., Franquiz, M., Dixon, C. and Green, J. (1997) 'The myth of the objective transcript: transcribing as a situated act', *TESOL Quarterly*, 31(1): 172–76.

Grindsted, A. (2005) 'Interactive resources used in semi-structured research inter-viewing', *Journal of Pragmatics*, 37(7) 1015–35.

Guillemin, M. and Gillam, L. (2004) 'Ethics, reflexivity and "ethically important moments" in research', *Qualitative Inquiry*, 10(2): 261–80.

Gumperz, J. (1982) *Discourse Strategies*. Cambridge and New York: Cambridge University Press.

Gumperz, J.J. (1999) 'On interactional sociolinguistic method', in S. Sarangi and C. Roberts (eds) *Talk, Work and Institutional Order*. Berlin: Mouton de Gruyter. pp. 451–71.

Gumperz, J. (2003) 'Interactional sociolinguistics: a personal perspective', in D. Schiffrin, D. Tannen and H. Hamilton (eds) *The Handbook of Discourse Analysis*. Oxford: Blackwell. pp. 215–28.

Gumperz, J.J., Jupp, T.C. and Roberts, C. (1979) *Cross-talk: The Wider Perspective*. Southall: National Centre for Industrial Language Training.

Gusterson, H. (1997) 'Studying up revisited', *Political and Legal Anthropology Review*, 20(1): 114–19.

Guta, A., Nixon, S. and Wilson, M.G. (2013) 'Resisting the seduction of "ethics creep": using Foucault to surface complexity and contradiction in research ethics review', *Social Science & Medicine*, 98: 301–10.

Habermas, J. (1995) *Justification and Application: Remarks on Discourse Ethics*. Cambridge, MA: MIT Press.

Habermas, J. (2003) 'Rightness versus truth: on the sense of normative validity in moral judgements and norms', in J. Habermas (ed.) *Truth and Justification*. Cambridge, MA: MIT Press.

Hajer, M. (2005) 'Setting the stage: a dramaturgy of policy deliberation', *Administration & Society*, 36(6): 624–47.

Hajer, M. and Wagenaar, H. (2003) *Deliberative Policy Analysis: Understanding Governance in the Network Society*. Cambridge: Cambridge University Press.

Halliday, M. and Hasan, R. (1976) *Cohesion in English*. London: Longman.

Hammersley, M. (2003) 'Conversation analysis and discourse analysis: Methods or paradigms?', *Discourse and Society*, 14(6): 751–81.

Hammersley, M. (2006) 'Ethnography: problems and prospects', *Ethnography and Education* 1(1): 3–14.

Hammersley, M. (2007) 'Reflections on linguistic ethnography', *Journal of Sociolinguistics*, 11(5): 689–95.

Hammersley, M. (2010) 'Reproducing or constructing? Some questions about tran-scription in social research', *Qualitative Research*, 1(5): 553–69.

Hammersley, M. and Atkinson, P. (1983) *Ethnography Principles in Practice*. London: Routledge.

Harper, D. (2003) 'Developing a critically reflexive position using discourse analysis', in L. Finlay and B. Gough (eds) *Reflexivity: A Practical Guide for Qualitative Researchers in Health and Social Science*. Oxford: Blackwell. pp. 78–92.

Hart, P. and Vromen, A. (2008) 'A new era for think tanks in public policy? International trends, Australian realities', *Australian Journal of Public Administration*, 67(2): 135–48.

Haugh, M. and Bargiela-Chiappini, F. (2010) 'Face in interaction', *Journal of Pragmatics*, 42(8): 2073–7.

Haverkamp, B.E. (2005). 'Ethical perspectives on qualitative research in applied psychology', *Journal of Counseling Psychology*, 52: 146–55.

Heller, M. (1984) 'Sociolinguistic theory', *Annual Review of Applied Linguistics*, 5: 47–58.

Heller, M. (2008) 'Doing ethnography', in L. Wei and M.G. Moyer (eds) *The Blackwell Guide to Research Methods in Bilingualism and Multilingualism*. Malden, MA: Blackwell. pp. 249–62.

Heller, M. (2011) *Paths to Post-Nationalism: A Critical Ethnography of Language and Identity*. New York: Oxford University Press.

Heritage, J. and Sefi, S. (1992) 'Dilemmas of advice: aspects of the delivery and reception of advice in interactions between health visitors and first-time mothers', in P. Drew and J. Heritage (eds) *Talk at Work: Interaction in Institutional Settings*. Cambridge: Cambridge University Press. pp. 359–417.

Hertz, R. (ed.) (1997) *Reflexivity and Voice*. Thousand Oaks, CA: Sage.

Hey, V. (2002) '"Not as nice as she was supposed to be": schoolgirls' friendships', in S. Taylor (ed.) *Ethnographic Research: A Reader*. London: Sage.

Hindmarsh, J. and Heath, C. (2000) 'Sharing the tools of the trade: the interactional constitution of workplace objects', *Journal of Contemporary Ethnography*, 29(5): 523–62.

Holman Jones, S. (2005) 'Autoethnography: making the personal political', in N.K. Denzin and Y.S. Lincoln (eds) *The Sage Handbook of Qualitative Research*. London: Sage. pp 763–92.

Holmes, J. (2006) *Gendered Talk at Work*. Oxford: Wiley-Blackwell.

Holmes, J. and Stubbe, M. (2003) *Power and Politeness in the Workplace: A Sociolinguistic Analysis of Talk at Work*. London: Pearson.

Holmes, J., Stubbe, M. and Vine, B. (1999) 'Constructing professional identity: "Doing power" in policy units', in C. Roberts and S. Sarangi (eds) *Talk, Work and Institutional Order*. Berlin: Mouton de Gruyter. pp. 351–85.

Holstein, J.A. and Gubrium, J.F. (2004) 'The active interview', in D. Silverman (ed.) *Qualitative Research: Theory, Method and Practice*. Thousand Oaks, CA: Sage. pp. 140–61.

Home Office (2013a) *PACE Code C*. Available at: https://www.gov.uk/government/publications/pace-code-c-2013 (accessed 30 January 2014).

Home Office (2013b) *Police Workforce, England and Wales, 31 March 2013*. London: Home Office.

Home Office (2014) *Notice of Rights and Entitlements*. Available at: https://www.gov.uk/government/publications/notice-of-rights-and-entitlements-english (accessed 28 January 2014).

Hornberger, N. (1995) 'Ethnography in linguistic perspective: understanding school processes', *Language and Education*, 9(4): 233–48.

Hornberger, N.H. (2002) 'Multilingual language policies and the continua of biliteracy: an ecological approach', *Language Policy*, 1(1): 27–51.

House, J. (2003) 'Misunderstanding in intercultural university encounters', in J. House, G. Kasper and S. Ross (eds) *Misunderstanding in Social Life: Discourse Approaches to Problematic Talk*. Longman: London. pp. 22–56.

House of Commons (2012) *Health and Social Care Act 2012*. London: HMSO.

Hudley, A.H.C. (2013) 'Sociolinguistic engagement in schools: Collecting and sharing data', in C. Mallinson, B. Childs and G. Van Herk (eds) *Data Collection in Sociolinguistics: Methods and Applications*. London: Routledge. pp. 269–80.

Hutchby, J. and Wooffitt, R. (1998) *Conversation Analysis*. Oxford: Polity Press.

Hyland, K. (2005) 'Stance and engagement: a model of interaction in academic discourse', *Discourse Studies*, 7(2): 173–92.

Hymes, D. (1964) *Language in Culture and Society: A Reader in Linguistics and Anthropology*. New York: Harper and Row.

Hymes, D. (1968) 'The ethnography of speaking', in J. Fishman (ed.) *Readings in the Sociology of Language*. The Hague: Moulton. pp. 99–138.

Hymes, D. (1972) 'On communicative competence', in J.B. Pride and J. Holmes (eds) *Sociolinguistics*. Harmondsworth: Penguin. pp. 269–93.

Hymes, D. (1974) *Foundations in Sociolinguistics: An Ethnographic Approach*. Philadelphia: University of Pennsylvania Press.

Hymes, D. (1980) 'Language in education: forward to fundamentals', *Language in Education: Ethnolinguistic Essays*. Washington, DC: Center for Applied Linguistics.

Institute of Advanced Studies University of Birmingham, Available at: http://www.birmingham.ac.uk/research/activity/ias/index.aspx (accessed 16 September 2014).

Jackson, J.E. (1990) '"I am a fieldnote": fieldnotes as a symbol of professional identity', in R. Sanjeck (ed.) *Fieldnotes: The Makings of Anthropology*. Itahaca, NY: Cornel University Press. pp. 3–33.

Jacobs, G. and Slembrouck, S. (2010) 'Notes on linguistic ethnography as a liminal activity', *Text & Talk*, 30(2): 235–44.

Jakobson, R. (1960) 'Linguistics and poetics', from *Selected Writings II*. The Hague: Mouton.

Jewitt, C. (2008) *Technology, Literacy and Learning: A Multimodal Approach*. London: Routledge.

Katz, J. (2002) 'From how to why: on luminous description and causal inference in ethnography (Part 2)', *Ethnography*, 3(1): 63–90.

Kelle, U. (2004) 'Computer-assisted qualitative data analysis', in C. Seale, G. Gobo, J.F. Gubrium and D. Silverman (eds) *Qualitative Research Practice*. London: Sage. pp. 443–60.

Kerekes, J. and West, B. (2006) 'Winning an interviewer's trust in a gatekeeping encounter', *Language in Society*, 35(1): 27–57.

Korica, M. (2011) 'Performing governance and accountability in the public sphere: an ethnography of situated orderings'. DPhil dissertation, Green Templeton College, Oxford University.

Kramsch, C. (2009) 'Ron Scollon: a master of the axe handle', *Journal of Applied Linguistics*, 6(3): 261–66.

Kubanyiova, M. (2008) 'Rethinking research ethics in contemporary applied linguistics: the tension between macroethical and microethical perspectives in situated research', *Modern Language Journal*, 92(4): 503–18.

Kusenbach, M. (2003) 'Street phenomenology: the go-along as ethnographic research tool', *Ethnography*, 4(3): 455–85.

Kvale, S. (1996) *InterViews: An Introduction to Qualitative Research Interviewing*. London: Sage.

Lapadat, J.C. (2000) 'Problematising transcription: purpose, paradigm and quality', *International Journal of Social Research and Methodology*, 3(3): 203–19.

Latuca, L. (2001) *Creating Interdisciplinarity: Interdisciplinary Research and Teaching among College and University Faculty*. Nashville, TN: Vanderbilt University Press.

LeBaron, C. (2008) 'Microethnography', in W. Donsbach (ed.) *The International Encyclopedia of Communication*. Oxford: Blackwell. pp. 763–72.

Lefstein, A. and Israel, M. (in press) 'Applying linguistic ethnography to educational practice – notes on the interaction of academic research and professional sensibilities', in J. Snell, S. Shaw and F. Copland (eds) *Linguistic Ethnography: Interdisciplinary Explorations*. London: Palgrave Macmillan.

Lefstein, A. and Snell, J. (2011) 'Professional vision and the politics of teacher learning', *Teaching and Teacher Education*, 27(3): 505–14.

Lefstein, A. and Snell, J. (2013) *Better Than Best Practice: Developing Learning and Teaching through Dialogue*. London: Routledge.

Lemert, C. (1997) 'Goffman', in C. Lemert, and A. Branaman (eds) *The Goffman Reader*. Oxford: Blackwell. pp. ix–xlv.

Leonard-Barton, D. (1990) 'A dual methodology for case studies: synergistic use of a longitudinal single site with replicated multiple sites', *Organization Science*, 1(3): 248–66.

Liddicoat, A.J. (2011) *An Introduction to Conversation Analysis*. London: Continuum.

Lilford, R., Richardson, A., Stevens, A., Fitzpatrick, R., Edwards, S., Rock, F. and Hutton, J. (2001) 'Issues in methodological research: perspectives from researchers and commissioners', *Health Technology Assessment Monograph*, 5(8).

Lillis, T. (2008) 'Closing the gap between text and context in academic writing: Ethnography as method, methodology, and "deep theorizing"', *Written Communication*, 25: 353.

Lillis, T. and Curry, M. (2006) 'Professional academic writing by multilingual scholars: interactions with literacy brokers in the production of English medium texts', *Written Communication*, 23(1): 3–35.

Louw, W.E. (1993) 'Irony in the text or insincerity in the writer? The diagnostic potential of semantic prosodies', *Text and Technology: In Honour of John Sinclair*. Amsterdam: John Benjamins. pp. 157–76.

Malinson, C. (2013) 'Sharing data and findings', in C. Mallinson, B. Childs and G. Van Herk (eds) *Data Collection in Sociolinguistics: Methods and Applications*. London: Routledge.

Mann, S. (2011) 'A critical review of qualitative interviews in applied linguistics', *Applied Linguistics*, 32(1): 6–24.

Markee, N. (2005) 'Conversation analysis for second language acquisition', in E. Hinkel (ed.) *Handbook of Research in Second Language Learning and Teaching*. New York: Routledge. pp. 355–74.

Martin, P., Bhatt, A., Bhojani, N. and Creese, A. (2006) 'Managing bilingual interaction in a Gujarati complementary school in Leicester', *Language and Education*, 20(1): 5–22.

Maschler, Y. (1994) 'Metalanguaging and discourse markers in bilingual communication', *Language in Society*, 23(3): 325–66.

Maybin, J. (2006) *Children's Voices: Talk, Knowledge and Identity*. Basingstoke: Palgrave Macmillan.

Maybin, J. and Tusting, K. (2011) 'Linguistic ethnography', in J. Simpson (ed.) *Routledge Handbook of Applied Linguistics*. Abingdon: Routledge. pp. 515–28.

McConnell-Ginet, S. (2011) *Gender, Sexuality, and Meaning: Linguistic Practice and Politics*. Oxford: Oxford University Press.

McDermott, R.P. (1976) 'Kids make sense: An ethnographic account of the interactional management of success and failure in one first grade classroom'. Unpublished PhD dissertation, Standord University, CA.

McElhinney, B. (1995) 'Challenging hegemonic masculinities: female and male police officers handling domestic violence', in K. Hall and M. Bucholtz (eds) *Gender Articulated*. London: Routledge. pp. 217–44.

McElhinny, B., Hols, M., Holtzkener, J., Unger, S. and Hicks, C. (2003) 'Gender, publication and citation in sociolinguistics and linguistic anthropology', *Language in Society*, 32(3): 299–328.

McGann, J. (2013) *2012 Global Go To Think Tanks Report and Policy Advice*. Philadelphia: University of Pennsylvania Press.

McKinney, K.D., Marvasti, A.B, Holstein, J.A. and Gubrium, J.F. (eds) (2012) *The SAGE Handbook of Interview Research: The Complexity of the Craft*. London: Sage.

Medvetz, T. (2008) *Think Tanks as an Emergent Field*. New York: Social Science Research Council.

Medvetz, T. (2010) 'Think Tanks', in G. Ritzer (ed.) *Blackwell Encyclopedia of Sociology*. Blackwell Reference Online: http://www.sociologyencyclopedia.co

Miles, M.B. and Huberman, A.M. (1994) *Qualitative Data Analysis*, 2nd edn. London: Sage.

Mills, S. (2003) *Gender and Politeness*. Cambridge: Cambridge University Press.

Mishler, E.G. (1986) *Research Interviewing: Context and Narrative*. London: Harvard University Press.

Mishler, E. (1991) 'Representing discourse: the rhetoric of transcription', *Journal of Narrative and Life History*, 1(4): 255–80.

Mitchell, J. (1984) 'Producing data: case studies', in R. Ellen (ed.) *Ethnographic Research: A Guide to General Conduct*. London: Academic Press. pp. 237–41.

Mitteness, L.S. and Barker, J.C. (2004) 'Collaborative and team research', in C. Seale, G. Gobo, J. Gubrium and D. Silverman (eds) *Qualitative Research Practice*. London: Sage Publications. pp. 276–94.

Moerman, M. (1988) *Talking Culture: Ethnography and Conversation Analysis*. Philadelphia: University of Pennsylvania Press.

Muller, J.H. (1992) 'Narrative approaches to qualitative research in primary care', in B.F. Crabtree and W.L. Miller (eds) *Doing Qualitative Research in Primary Care: Multiple Strategies*. London: Sage. pp. 221–38.

Murphy, E. and Dingwall, R. (2001) 'The ethics of ethnography', in P. Atkinson, A. Coffey, S. Delamont, J. Lofland and L. Lofland (eds) *Handbook of Ethnography*. London: Sage. pp. 339–51.

Myers, G. and Lampropoulou, S. (2012) 'Impersonal you and stance-taking in social research interviews', *Journal of Pragmatics* 44(10): 1206–18.

Nader, L. (1972) 'Up the anthropologist: perspectives gained from studying up', in D. Hymes (ed.) *Reinventing Anthropology*. New York: Pantheon Books. pp. 284–311.

Nicolini, D. (2009) 'Zooming in and out: studying practices by switching theoretical lenses and trailing connections', *Organization Studies*, 30(12): 1391–1418.

Norris, S. (2004) *Analyzing Multimodal Interaction*. London: RoutledgeFalmer

Ockwell, D.G. and Rydin, Y. (2010) 'Analysing dominant policy perspectives: the role of discourse analysis' in J.C. Lovett and D.G. Ockwell (eds) *A Handbook of Environmental Management*. Northampton, MA: Edward Elgar. pp. 168–97.

Odendahl, T. and Shaw, A.M. (2001) 'Interviewing elites', in J.F. Gubrium and J.A. Holstein (eds) *Handbook of Interview Research*. London: Sage. pp. 299–316.

O'Keefe, A. and Walsh, S. (2012) 'Applying corpus linguistics and conversations analysis in the investigation of small group teaching in higher education', *Corpus Linguistics and Linguistic Theory*, 8(1): 159–81.

Palomares, M. and Poveda, D. (2010) 'Linguistic ethnography and the study of welfare institutions as a flow of social practices: the case of residential child care institutions as paradoxical institutions', *Text & Talk*, 30(2): 193–212.

Paltridge, B. (2012) *Discourse Analysis*, 2nd edn. London: Bloomsbury.

Paperman, P. (2003) 'The uniform as an interaction device', *Ethnography*, 4(3): 397–419.

Parsons, W. (1995) *Public Policy: An Introduction to the Theory and Practice of Policy Analysis*. Cheltenham: Edward Elgar.

Parsons, W. (2004) 'Not just steering but weaving: Relevant knowledge and the craft of building policy capacity and coherence', *Australian Journal of Public Administration*, 63(1): 43–57.

Peirce, C. (1955) *Collected Papers II. Philosophical Writings of Peirce*. Edited by J. Buchler. New York: Dover.

Player, S. and Leys, C. (2011) *The Plot Against the NHS*. London: Merlin Press.

Pomerantz, A. (1984) 'Agreeing and disagreeing with assessments: some features of preferred/dispreferred turn shapes', in J.M. Atkinson and J. Heritage (eds) *Structures of Social Action*. Cambridge: Cambridge University Press. pp. 57–101.

Pratt, M.L. (1991) 'Arts of the contact zone', *Profession*, 91: 33–40.

Psathas, G. (1995) *Conversation Analysis: The Study of Talk in Interaction*. London: Sage.

Ragin, C. (1992) 'Introduction: Cases of "What is a case?"', in C. Ragin and H. Becker (eds) *What is a Case? Exploring the Foundations of Sociology*. Cambridge: Cambridge University Press. pp. 1–18.

Rai, L. and Lillis, T. (2013) '"Getting it write" in social work: exploring the value of writing in academia to writing for professional practice', *Teaching in Higher Education*, 18(4): 1–13.

Rampton, B. (2006) *Language in Late Modernity: Interaction in an Urban School*. London: Cambridge University Press.

Rampton, B. (2007a) 'Neo-Hymesian linguistic ethnography in the United Kingdom', *Journal of Sociolinguistics*, 11(5): 584–607.

Rampton, B. (2007b) 'The micro-analysis of interactional discourse in linguistic ethnography: an illustration focused on the job interview', paper prepared for the ESRC Researcher Development Initiative, *Ethnography, Language and Communication*, Oxford.

Rampton, B. (2011) 'Language, social categories and interaction', *Working Papers in Urban Language & Literacies*, Paper 75. Available at: http://www.kcl.ac.uk/sspp/departments/education/research/ldc/publications/workingpapers/75.pdf (accessed 25 April 2013).

Rampton, B., Maybin, J. and Roberts, C. (forthcoming) 'Introduction: explorations and encounters in linguistic ethnography', in J. Snell, S. Shaw and F. Copland (eds) *Linguistic Ethnography: Interdisciplinary Explorations*. Palgrave Macmillan.

Rampton, B., Tusting, K., Maybin, J., Barwell, R., Creese, A. and Lytra, V. (2004) 'UK linguistic ethnography: A discussion paper'. Available at: www.ling-ethnog.org.uk (accessed 25 April 2013).

Rapley, T. (2001) 'The art(fulness) of open-ended interviewing: some considerations on analysing interviews', *Qualitative Research*, 1(3): 303–23.

Reform (2011) *Annual Review 2011*. London: Reform. Available at: http://www.reform.co.uk/resources/0000/0413/Website_PDF.pdf (accessed 4 February 2014).

Richards, K. (2003) *Qualitative Inquiry in TESOL*. Basingstoke: Palgrave Macmillan.

Richards, K. (2006) *Language and Professional Identity: Aspects of Collaborative Interaction*. Basingstoke: Palgrave Macmillan.

Richardson, L. (2000) 'Writing: a method of inquiry', in N. Denzin and Y. Lincoln (eds) *The Handbook of Qualitative Research*, 2nd edn. Thousand Oaks, CA: Sage. pp. 923–48.

Roberts, C. (2012) 'Translating global experience into global models of competency: Linguistic inequalities in the job interview', *Diversities*, 14(2): 49–72.

Roberts, C. and Sarangi, S. (1999) 'Hybridity in gatekeeping discourse: Issues of practical relevance for the researcher', in C. Roberts and S. Sarangi (eds) *Talk, Work and Institutional Order Discourse in Medical, Mediation and Management Settings*. Berlin: Mouton de Gruyter. pp. 473–504.

Roberts, C. and Sarangi, S. (2001) '"Like you're living two lives in one go": negotiating different social conditions for classroom learning in a further education context in England', in M. Heller and M. Martin-Jones (eds) *Voices of Authority: Education and Linguistic Difference*. Westport, CT: Ablex. pp. 171–92.

Rock, F. (2001) 'Policy and practice in the anonymisation of linguistic data', *International Journal of Corpus Linguistics*, 6(1): 1–26 ISSN 1384–6655.

Rock, F. (2005) '"Sometimes you pinch stuff": communities of practice in an institutional setting', in D. Barton and K. Tusting (eds) *Beyond Communities of Practice*. Cambridge: Cambridge University Press. pp. 77–104.

Rock, F. (2007) *Communicating Rights: The Language of Arrest and Detention*. Basingstoke: Palgrave.

Rock, F. (2012) 'The caution in England and Wales', in L. Solan and P. Tiersma (eds) *The Oxford Handbook of Language and Law*. Oxford: Oxford University Press. pp. 312–25.

Rock, F. (2014) FuzzyLaw. Available at: www.fuzzylaw.cardiff.ac.uk (accessed 20 January 2014).

Rosowsky, A. (2010) 'Writing it in English: Script choices among young multilingual Muslims in the UK', *Journal of Multilingual and Multicultural Development*, 31(2): 163–79.

Roulston, K. (2006) 'Close encounters of the CA kind: A review of literature analysing talk in research interviews', *Qualitative Research*, 6(4): 515–34.

Ruane, S. (2005) 'The future of health care in the UK: think-tanks and their policy prescriptions', in M. Powell, K. Clarke and L. Bauld (eds) *Social Policy Review 17*. Bristol: Policy Press. pp. 147–66.

Russell, J., Greenhalgh, T., Byrne, E. and McDonnell, J. (2008) 'Recognising rhetoric in healthcare policy analysis', *Journal of Health Services Research and Policy*, 13(1): 40–6.

Russell, S. (2000) '"Let me put it simply": the case for a standard translation of the police caution and its explanation', *Forensic Linguistics*, 7(1): 26–48.

Rydin, Y. and Ockwell, D. (2010) 'Analysing dominant policy perspectives: the role of discourse analysis', in J.C. Lovett and D. Ockwell (eds) *A Handbook of Environmental Management*. Cheltenham: Edward Elgar. pp. 168–97.

Sacks, H. (1984) 'Notes on methodology', in J. Atkinson, and J. Heritage (eds) *Structures of Social Action: Studies in Conversation Analysis*. Cambridge: Cambridge University Press. pp. 21–7.

Salzman, P.C. (1989) 'The lone stranger and the solitary quest', *Anthropology Newsletter*, 30(5): 16–44.

Sanjeck, R. (ed.) (1990) *Fieldnotes: The Makings of Anthropology*. Ithaca, NY: Cornel University Press.

Sapir, E. (1921) *Language: an Introduction to the Study of Speech*. London: Hart-Davies.

Scheflen, A.E. (1973) *Communicational Structure: Analysis of a Psychotherapy Transaction*. Bloomingdale, IN: Indiana University Press.

Schegloff, E. and Sacks, H. (1973) 'Opening up closings', *Semiotica* 8(4): 289–327.

Scheper-Hughes, N. (2000) 'Ire in Ireland', *Ethnography*, 1(1): 117–40.

Scherer, A.G. and Palazzo, G. (eds) (2008) *Handbook of Research on Global Corporate Citizenship*. Cheltenham: Edward Elgar.

Scherer, A.G., Palazzo, G. (eds) and Matten, D. (Guest Editors) (2009) Special Issue on 'The Changing Role of Business in Global Society: New Challenges and Responsibilities', *Business Ethics Quarterly*, 19(3).

Scollon, R. and Scollon, S.W. (2007) 'Nexus analysis: Refocusing ethnography on action', *Journal of Sociolinguistics*, 11(5): 608–25.

Seale, C. (1998) 'Qualitative interviewing', in C. Seale (ed.) *Researching Society and Culture*. London: Sage. pp. 202–16.

Sealey, A. (2007) 'Linguistic ethnography in realist perspective', *Journal of Sociolinguistics*, 11(5): 641–60.

Searle, J.R. (1969) *Speech Acts*. London: Cambridge University Press.

Shäffner, C. (ed.) (2004) *Translation Research and Interpreting Research: Traditions, Gaps and Synergies*. London: Multilingual Matters.

Shaw, S.E. (2006) 'Out of Utopia: The (re)production of primary care research policy', unpublished PhD dissertation, University of London.

Shaw, S.E. (2010) 'Reaching the parts that other theories and methods can't reach? How and why a policy-as-discourse approach can inform health-related policy', *Health*, 14(2): 196–212.

Shaw, S.E. and Russell, J. (In press) 'Researching health policy and planning: The influence of linguistic ethnography', in J. Snell, S.E. Shaw and F. Copland (eds) *Linguistic Ethnography: Interdisciplinary Explorations*. London: Palgrave Macmillan.

Shaw, S.E., Russell, J., Greenhalgh, T. and Korica, M. (2014) 'Thinking about think tanks in healthcare; a call for a new research agenda', *Sociology of Health & Illness*, 36(3): 447–461.

Shaw, S.E., Russell, J., Parsons, W. and Greenhalgh, T. (2014) 'The view from nowhere? How think tanks work to shape health policy and planning', *Critical Studies*.

Sherman Heyl, B. (2001) 'Ethnographic interviewing', in P. Atkinson, A. Coffey, S. Delamont, J. Lofland and L. Lofland (eds) *Handbook of Ethnography*. London: Sage. pp. 369–83.

Silverman, D. (2001) *Interpreting Qualitative Data*, 2nd edn. London: Sage Publications.

Silverstein, M. (1976) 'Shifters, linguistic categories, and cultural description', in K. Basso and H. Selby (eds) *Meaning in Anthropology*. Albuquerque: University of New Mexico Press. pp. 11–55.

Silverstein, M. (1981) *The Limits of Awareness*. Sociolinguistic Working Paper Number 84.

Silverstein, M. (1985) 'Language and the culture of gender', in E. Mertz and R. Parmentier (eds) *Semiotic Mediation*. New York: Academic Press. pp. 219–59.

Silverstein, M. (2003) 'Indexical order and the dialectics of sociolinguistic life', *Language and Communication*, 23: 193–229.

Simon, A.R. (2013) 'The social positioning of supplementary schooling', unpublished PhD dissertation, University of Birmingham.

Simons, H. (2009) *Case Study Research in Practice*. London: Sage Publications.

Sinclair, J. (1991) *Corpus, Concordance, Collocation*. Oxford: Oxford University Press.

Sinclair, J. and Coulthard, M. (1975) *Towards an Analysis of Discourse*. Oxford: Oxford University Press.

Smith, D. (2005) *Institutional Ethnography: A Sociology for People*. Lanham, MD: AltaMira Press.

Smith, D. (2005) *Institutional Ethnography: A Sociology for People*. Lanham: AltaMira Press.

Smith, K.E. (2013) 'Institutional filters: the translation and re-circulation of ideas about health inequalities within policy', *Policy & Politics*, 41(1): 81–100.

Smith, K. and Meer, N. (2012) 'REF's effort to make knowledge visible may have cloudy results', *Times Higher Education*. Available at: http://www.timeshigher-education.co.uk/419128.article (accessed 30 March 2013).

Snell, J. and Lefstein, A. (2012) 'Interpretative and representational dilemmas in a linguistic ethnographic analysis: moving from "interesting data" to a publishable research article', *Working Papers in Urban Language & Literacies*, 90. London: King's College London. Available at: http://www.kcl.ac.uk/innovation/groups/ldc/publications/workingpapers/the-papers/WP90.pdf (accessed 20 January 2014).

Snell, J. and Lefstein, A. (in press) 'Moving from "interesting data" to publishable research article – some interpretive and representational dilemmas in a linguistic ethnographic analysis', in P. Smeyers, D. Bridges, N. Burbules and M. Griffiths (eds) *International Handbook of Interpretation in Educational Research Methods*. Dordrecht: Springer.

Snell, J., Shaw, S. and Copland, F. (eds) (forthcoming) *Linguistic Ethnography: Interdisciplinary Explorations*. London: Palgrave Macmillan

Solomon, N. (1996) 'Plain English: from a perspective of language in society', in R. Hasan and G. Williams (eds) *Literacy in Society*. London: Longman. pp. 279–307.

Spradley, J.P. (1979) *The Ethnographic Interview*. Belmont, CA: Wadsworth Publishing Company.

Speer, S.A. and Hutchby, I. (2003) 'Presence and relevance of recording devices from ethics to analytics: aspects of participants' orientations to the presence and relevance of recording devices', *Sociology*, 37(2): 315–33.

Speer, S. and Stokoe, E. (2014) 'Ethics in action: consent-gaining interactions and implications for research practice', *British Journal of Social Psychology*, 53(1): 54–73.

Spencer, J. (2001) 'Ethnography after post-modernism', in P. Atkinson, A. Coffey, S. Delamont, J. Lofland and L. Lofland (eds) *Handbook of Ethnography*. London: Sage.

Spradley, J.P. (1979) *The Ethnographic Interview*. Belmont, CA: Wadsworth Publishing Company.

Stake, R.E. (1995) *The Art of Case Study Research*. Thousand Oaks, CA: Sage.

Stokoe, E. (2013) 'The (in)authenticity of simulated talk: comparing role-played and actual conversation and the implications for communication training', *Research on Language and Social Interaction*, 46(2): 1–21.

Stone, D. (1996) *Capturing the Political Imagination: Think Tanks and the Policy Process*. Abingdon: Frank Cass.

Stone, D. (2000) 'Non-governmental policy transfer: the strategies of independent policy institutes', *Governance: An International Journal of Policy and Administration*, 13(1): 45–62.

Stross, B. (1974) 'Speaking of speaking: Tenejapa Tzeltal metalinguistics', in R. Bauman and J. Sherzer (eds) *Explorations in the Ethnography of Speaking*. Cambridge: Cambridge University Press. pp. 213–39.

Stubbs, M. (1983) *Discourse Analysis*. Oxford: Blackwell.

Sunderland, J. (2010) 'Research questions in linguistics', in L. Litosseliti (ed.) *Research Methods in Linguistics*. London: Continuum. pp. 9–28.

Swales, J. (1990) *Genre Analysis: English in Academic and Research Settings*. Cambridge: Cambridge University Press.

Swinglehurst, D. (In press) 'How linguistic ethnography may enhance our understanding of electronic patient records in healthcare settings', in J. Snell, S. Shaw and F. Copland (eds) *Linguistic Ethnography: Interdisciplinary Explorations*. London: Palgrave Macmillan.

Swinglehurst, D., Roberts, C. and Greenhalgh, T. (2011) 'Opening up the "black box" of the electronic patient record: a linguistic ethnographic study in general practice', *Communication and Medicine*, 8(1): 3–15.

Takhi, J.K. (2012) 'Researcher vignette', unpublished document.

Tallerico, M. (1991) 'Applications of qualitative analysis software: a view from the field', *Qualitative Sociology*, 14(3): 275–85.

Talmy, S. and Richards, K. (2011) 'Theorising qualitative research interviews in applied linguistics', *Applied Linguistics*, 32(1): 1–5.

Taylor, S. (2002) *Ethnographic Research: A Reader*. London: Sage.

Temple, B. (2008) 'Narrative analysis of written texts: reflexivity in cross language research', *Qualitative Research*, 8(3): 355–65.

ten Have, P. (2007) *Doing Conversation Analysis: A Practical Guide*, 2nd edn. London: Sage.

Thorpe, H. (2012) 'The ethnographic (i)nterview in the sports field: towards a postmodern sensibility', in K. Young and M. Atkinson (eds) *Qualitative Research on Sport and Physical Culture*. Bingley: Emerald Group Publishing. pp. 51–78.

Tierney, W. (2002) 'Get real: representing reality', *Qualitative Studies in Education*, 15(15): 385–98.

Timmins, N. (2012) *Never Again? The Story of the Health and Social Care Act 2012*. London: Kings Fund/Institute for Government.

Tracy, K. (2008) '"Reasonable hostility": situation-appropriate face attack', *Journal of Politeness Research*, 4: 169–91.

Triggle, N. (2010) 'NHS "to undergo radical overhaul"', BBC News (Health), 12 July. Available at: http://www.bbc.co.uk/news/10557996 (accessed 25 April 2013).

Tsitsipis, L.D. (2007) 'Relationality in sociolinguistics: a dialogue with linguistic ethnography', *Journal of Sociolinguistics*, 11(5): 626–40.

Tusting, K. (2010) 'Eruptions of interruptions: managing tensions between writing and other tasks in a textualised childcare workplace', in D. Barton and U. Papen (eds) *The Anthropology of Writing: Understanding Textually Mediated Worlds*. London and New York: Continuum. pp. 67–89.

Tusting, K. (forthcoming) 'Workplace literacies and the audit society', in J. Snell, S. Shaw and F. Copland (eds) *Linguistic Ethnography: Interdisciplinary Explorations*. London: Palgrave Macmillan.

Tusting, K. and Maybin, J. (2007) 'Linguistic ethnography and interdisciplinarity: opening the discussion', *Journal of Sociolinguistics*, 11(5): 575–83.

VanderStaay, S. (2003) 'Believing Clayboy', *Qualitative Inquiry*, 9(3): 374–94.

Venkatesh, S. (2002) 'Doin' the Hustle', *Ethnography*, 3(1): 91–111. Excerpts from references – I have included here only the pages I've commented on:

Vásquez, C. (2004) '"Very carefully managed": advice and suggestions in post-observation meetings', *Linguistics and Education*, 15(1): 33–58.

Wacquant, L. (2004) 'Following Pierre Bourdieu into the field', *Ethnography*, 5(4): 387–414.

Wagenaar, H. (2011) *Meaning in Action: Interpretation and Dialogue in Policy Analysis*. NewYork: M.E. Sharpe.

Wagenaar, H. and Cook, N. (2003) 'Understanding policy practices: action, dialogue, dialectic and deliberation in policy analysis', in M. Hajer and H. Wagenaar (eds) *Deliberative Policy Analysis*. Cambridge: Cambridge University Press. pp. 139–71.

Waite, D. (1995) *Rethinking Instructional Supervision: Notes on its Language and Culture*. London: Falmer Press.

Wajnryb, R. (1998) 'Telling it like it isn't – exploring an instance of pragmatic ambivalence in supervisory discourse', *Journal of Pragmatics*, 29(5): 531–44.

Wald, B. (1995) 'The problem of scholarly disposition' (Review article), *Language in Society*, 24(2): 245–57.

Walford, G. (2005) 'Research ethical guidelines and anonymity', *International Journal of Research & Method in Education*, 28(1): 83–95.

Wall, S. (2008) 'Easier said than done: writing an autoethnograph', *International Journal of Qualitative Methods*, 7(1): 38–53.

Walsh, S. (2011) *Exploring Classroom Discourse: Language in Action*. Abingdon: Routledge.

Warriner, D.S. (2013) 'Literacy', in J. Simpson (ed.) *The Routledge Handbook of Applied Linguistics*. London: Routledge. pp. 529–28.

Wei Lu (2013) 'An ethnographic study of teaching Chinese as a heritage language and foreign language in three educational contexts in the United Kingdom', unpublished PhD dissertation, University of Birmingham.

Wetherell, M. (2007) 'A step too far: Discursive psychology, linguistic ethnography and questions of identity', *Journal of Sociolinguistics*, 11(5): 662–81.

Wildavsky, A. (1979) *Speaking Truth to Power: The Art and Craft of Policy Analysis*. Boston: Little, Brown and Co.

Wildavsky, A. (2010) *Craftways: On the Organizaton of Scholarly Work*, 2nd edn. New Brunswick, NJ: Transaction Publishers.

Wilkinson, S. (2004) 'Focus group research', in P. Atkinson, A. Coffey, S. Delamont, J. Lofland and L. Lofland (eds) *Handbook of Ethnography*. London: Sage.

Williams, B. (2006) *Ethics and the Limits of Philosophy*. London: Routledge.

Wolf, M. (2011) 'Mapping the field: Sociological perspectives on translation', *International Journal of the Sociology of Language*, 207: 1–28.

Wooffitt, R. (2001) 'Researching psychic practitioners: Conversation analysis', in M. Wetherell, S. Taylor and S.J. Yates (eds) *Discourse as Data: A Guide for Analysis*. London: Sage. pp. 49–92.

Wortham, S. (2003) 'Linguistic anthropology of education: An introduction', in S. Wortham and B.R. Rymes (eds) *Linguistic Anthropology of Education*. Westport, CT: Praeger Press. pp. 1–30.

Wortham, S. (2008) 'Linguistic anthropology of education', *Annual Review of Anthropology*, 37: 37–51.

Yanow, D. (2000) *Conducting Interpretative Policy Analysis*. Thousand Oaks, CA: Sage.

Index